The problem of

Abortion Second Edition

The problem of

Abortion Second Edition

edited by
Joel Feinberg
The University of Arizona

Wadsworth Publishing Company
Belmont, California
A Division of Wadsworth, Inc.

Philosophy Editor: Kenneth King
Production Editor: Toni Haskell
Managing Designer: Paula Shuhert
Interior Design by Patricia Girvin Dunbar
Cover Design by Paula Shuhert
Copy Editor: William Reynolds

Printed in the United States of America
6 7 8 9 10 — 96 95 94 93 92 91 90

Library of Congress Cataloging in Publication Data
Main entry under title:

The Problem of Abortion.

    Bibliography: p.
    1. Abortion—United States—Addresses, essays,
lectures. I. Feinberg, Joel, 1926–
HQ767.5.U5P76   1984   179'.76   83-6813

ISBN 0-534-02890-X

CONTENTS

Introduction

Abortion raises subtle problems for private conscience, public policy, and constitutional law. Most of these problems are essentially philosophical, requiring a degree of clarity about basic concepts that is seldom achieved in legislative debates and letters to newspapers. Most of the philosophical essays in this collection deal primarily with questions concerning the moral justifiability of abortion, and only indirectly with questions of a legal or constitutional nature. The former questions can be divided into two groups: those concerned with problems about the moral status of the unborn and those concerned with the resolution of conflicting claims—in particular, the claims of the mother and those of the fetus. Questions of public policy receive sketchier treatment here, but they also fall into two categories: One type considers the legitimacy, in a pluralistic society, of state enforcement of a set of moral convictions held by some persons, yet strongly contested by others; the other raises issues about the conceptual or moral coherence of ascribing legal rights to "unborn persons," including both the right to be born and, in some extreme circumstances, the right *not* to be born.[1]

Whether or not we hold abortion, at a given stage of fetal life, to be morally justifiable will naturally depend on how we conceive of the unborn being at that stage of its development—on what characteristics we take it to possess and on the moral significance we ascribe to those characteristics. Thus if we hold, as many Roman Catholics do, that "every unborn child must be regarded as a human person with all the rights of a human person, from the moment of conception,"[2] then we will find it at least plausible that the direct and deliberate killing of an unborn child is an act of murder, never to be permitted. On the other hand, if we

---

[1] See in this connection Joel Feinberg, "Is There a Right to Be Born?" in *Understanding Moral Philosophy,* ed. by James Rachels (Belmont, Calif.: Wadsworth, 1976).

[2] *Ethical and Religious Directives for Catholic Hospitals* (St. Louis: The Catholic Hospital Association of the United States and Canada, 1965), p. 4, as quoted in Daniel Callahan, *Abortion: Law, Choice and Morality* (London: Collier-Macmillan, Ltd., 1970), p. 419.

agree with Thomas Szasz that abortion during the "first two or three months of gestation" is similar in all morally relevant respects to "the removal of a piece of tissue from the woman's body,"[3] then we may well regard the killing of an embryo under normal circumstances as being no more reprehensible than an appendectomy or a voluntary sterilization. And of course a range of middle positions is possible; for example, we may consider a fetus an independent being whose claims, while valid, may be outweighed by those of full-fledged persons. In that case, we will be inclined to the view that these "potential persons" (like certain higher species of animals who are regarded as "almost human") are not to be wantonly or frivolously destroyed, but only in special circumstances and for serious and overriding moral reasons.

The issue of abortion, as Roger Wertheimer states it, is "a double-barreled question: At what stage of fetal development, if any, and for what reasons, if any, is abortion justifiable?"[4] The philosopher is thus faced not only with the task of providing *moral principles*—of offering coherent guidelines for determining what sorts of behavior toward a fetus are proper under a given set of circumstances. There is also the problem of deriving *status principles* for distinguishing such concepts as "human" and "nonhuman," "person" and "nonperson" in determining the "status" of the fetus.

The generalized use of the term "fetus" to denote any stage of prenatal development can be misleading. An unborn entity changes and grows continuously, assuming new and dramatically different characteristics along the way, some of which could have moral significance. For this reason it is wiser to adopt the careful terminology of the embryologists and speak of the status of the "ovum," the "zygote," the "conceptus," the "embryo," the "fetus," or the "neonate," rather than adopting one of these terms to do the work of all.

A brief explanation of this usage is in order. Once the female germ cell, the *ovum,* is fertilized by the male germ cell, the *spermatozoon,* it becomes a single cell with a full complement of twenty-three pairs of chromosomes, one in each pair from each parent. At that stage, the unborn is called a *single-cell zygote.* Within twenty-four hours of conception the zygote divides into two cells, then continues the process of cellular cleavage from two cells to four, to eight, and so on, reaching sixteen by the third day. The *multicell zygote* continues to grow and take form as it moves through the Fallopian tube into the uterus. During this stage, and even during its first week of gradual implantation in the uterine wall, it is commonly called a *conceptus.* By the end of the second week, it consists of both an inner cell mass and an outer layer of cells, firmly embedded in the wall of the uterus. From this point until the eighth week, it is called an *embryo.* During the fourth and fifth week the cellular basis for the later development of its organ systems is formed;

---

[3] Thomas S. Szasz, "The Ethics of Abortion," in *Humanist,* vol. XXVI (1966), p. 148.

[4] Roger Wertheimer, "Understanding the Abortion Argument," included in this volume, p. 43.

it begins to acquire a face and limb buds, and will soon become "visibly human." From the eighth week (when brain waves can be monitored) until birth at nine months, it is called a *fetus*.

At present, pregnancy cannot be diagnosed for at least ten days after the delay of onset of menstruation, but abortion of the zygote or conceptus can be accomplished by means of a "morning-after pill" (preventing implantation) or by "menstrual extraction" (sucking out the uterine contents with a special instrument on the chance they may contain a zygote) even before pregnancy can be diagnosed; the latter technique can be used up to the fifth week of pregnancy. From this point on, abortion must be performed by surgical or aspirative methods; these are normally conducted between the fifth and twelfth weeks but, in special circumstances, may be delayed up to the twenty-fourth week or even later.

What is unusual about the issue of abortion, and what is responsible for its peculiar intractability, is that disagreements typically persist even after agreement has been reached about both the relevant scientific facts and the governing moral principles. Whether a fetal organism at a given stage is a person with a right to life is *not* a scientific question, calling for the discovery of some deeply hidden though essentially biological fact. Facts, of course, are highly relevant to how we decide the issue, but human personhood is not itself a state that can be observed under a microscope or discovered by scientific experiment.

Again, the moral problem of abortion is difficult not simply because we may be uncertain which of various rival moral principles apply. We may agree in our moral principles, as well as in our scientific beliefs, and still disagree about the permissibility of abortion. We may agree, for example, that it is wrong to kill a certain kind of being in a certain set of circumstances *if* that being is a person, but we may disagree whether it is a person, or be quite bewildered as to how to go about deciding whether it is a person. This is the problem which the philosopher, in proposing a set of status principles, seeks to solve.

As might be expected, however, the philosophers represented in this volume also disagree strongly with one another when they are debating status principles. Their debate can be useful to the student, though, by demonstrating how a hitherto dark and mysterious problem (neither scientific nor moral) can be made accessible to rational argumentation, and just what the pivotal issues are.

Following conventional usage, we can distinguish three substantive positions (or families of positions) on the problem of the status of the fetus. The *conservative* position is that human personhood begins at the moment of conception. Alternatively, this can be called "the extreme conservative position," thus allowing other positions that approximate it (such as one that draws the line at implantation) to also be called (relatively) "conservative." At the other end of the spectrum is the *liberal* position that the human person does not emerge until after birth, so that even the killing of newborn infants is not, morally speaking, homicide. Alternatively, this can be called "the extreme liberal position," to distinguish it from views that approximate it (such as the relatively liberal positions that personhood begins at birth, or at "viability"). A *moderate* position is any that falls between the conservative and liberal extremes. Thus some moderates will be closer to the liberals and some closer to the conservatives.

What helps to generate the disagreement over status principles is a triad of commonsense propositions which seem to be mutually inconsistent. These can be put roughly as follows:

(i)   "A newborn infant is a human person," or "Babies are people."

(ii)   "A one-celled zygote is not a human person," or "Fertilized eggs are not people."

(iii)   "It is impossible to draw a nonarbitrary line anywhere between conception and infancy such that no beings before that line are human persons and all beings after that line are human persons."

Proposition (i) denies what the extreme liberal position affirms. Proposition (ii) denies what the extreme conservative view maintains. Proposition (iii) denies what the moderate (any moderate) believes. Yet all three propositions seem to have considerable support in common sense. It would seem, then, that any adequate solution to the problem of status will have to be achieved at the expense of at least one commonsense belief.

Proposition (i) can be called a "commonsense belief" at least in the sense that almost everyone accepts it uncritically as a datum for philosophizing, although not as a conclusion of any prior reasoning. But it can be argued that no mere conclusion of philosophical argument is likely to seem, to almost all of us, as certain as this proposition. Hence, some writers use it as a test for philosophical theories, holding that any hypothesis that implies its falsity is thereby reduced to absurdity and may be dismissed.

At first sight, proposition (ii) may not seem quite so self-evident, but a moment's thought will show that its denial is every bit as contrary to normal belief as the denial of (i). After all, a conceptus is a mere "amorphous speck of apparently coagulated protoplasm"[5] with no parts—no face, no limbs, no organs, no brain, no nervous system, no consciousness, no rationality, no concepts—nothing at all that we would recognize as belonging to an actual person, even though it is undeniably a potential person.

Proposition (iii) derives its appeal to common sense from the failure of various attempts to find a point in the continuum of development between conception and infancy where personhood can be said to begin. For wherever one draws the line one must be prepared, as Michael Tooley puts it, "to point to a *morally relevant* difference" between the stage ("personhood") during which killing is no longer permissible and the earlier stages ("prepersonhood") where killing cannot be seriously wrong. Those who have attempted to draw this line at some point during

---

[5] Michael Tooley, "Abortion and Infanticide," in *Philosophy & Public Affairs,* vol. 2 (1972), p. 38.

pregnancy (such as implantation, brain waves, quickening, viability) have notoriously had difficulty explaining why *that* point has moral significance while its predecessor does not. Even birth is not a line which escapes this objection, for it is difficult to point to a morally relevant difference between the fetus one hour before birth and the infant one hour after birth that would justify its destruction in the one case but not in the other. The only very obvious difference is that it has changed its location from inside to outside the mother, but this distinction does not seem to call a serviceable general principle into play.

The apparent truth of proposition (iii) leads both the conservative and the liberal to refuse to compromise with each other by adopting a more moderate position. In fact each is likely to be tempted to use a "slippery slope" argument against the other. (The emergent image for the bystander is of a double slippery slope, consisting of a slippery board attached like a see-saw on a fulcrum, tipping first one way then the other). If the one-celled zygote is not a person, the conservative might argue, then there can be no reason (given the continuity of development) to think of a two-celled zygote as a person, and if a two-celled zygote is not a person, neither can a four-celled zygote be one, and so on all the way until birth and beyond. If the liberal stays off the slippery slope right from the beginning, he or she will eventually be trapped into acknowledging that newborn infants are not persons either, and that infanticide, therefore, is not murder nor even homicide. The liberal can reply that, given proposition (iii), the slide can just as easily be reversed, leading to the equally absurd conclusion that microscopic specks are people. The conservative may not find this conclusion quite so uncomfortable, however, as it carries no danger of justifying the murder of innocent babies, thus adhering to the principle of choosing the lesser moral risk in uncertainty (see Noonan).

The typical conservative, then, accepts commonsense propositions (i) and (iii) but is forced to dismiss proposition (ii). This he or she does by arguing against the liberal that it is more certain that the newly born infant *is* a person than that the zygote is *not* (see Devine and also Lomasky). The typical liberal, on the other hand, accepts commonsense propositions (ii) and (iii) but rejects (i), embracing the opposite view that it is more certain that a one-celled zygote is *not* a person than that a newborn *is*. The liberal will either find grounds other than the personhood of the infant for prohibiting what others call "infanticide" or justify infant destruction in special circumstances (see Warren and Tooley). The moderate accepts propositions (i) and (ii) but breaks with both the liberal and the conservative in rejecting (iii). He or she justifies this partly on the ground that it is less offensive to common sense than denying either (i) or (ii), but primarily by positive arguments: that the slope is not as slippery as the liberal and conservative claim it is, or that a broad line can be drawn between nonadjacent stages in the developmental continuum, with an unavoidable no-man's-land for the uncertain area in between (see VanDeVeer, Sumner, Gillespie).

The conservative position on the status of the fetus problem is represented in this collection by Noonan, Devine, and, to some degree, Wertheimer. The moderate position is implied or defended in the essays by VanDeVeer, Sumner, and Gillespie. The (extreme) liberal position is defended by Warren and Tooley, and in less extreme form (not excluding infants from personhood) by Zaitchik.

The problem of the conflict of claims is addressed in the famous article by Judith Thomson. She approaches the problem of moral decision from a direction opposite that of the status theorists. Instead of focusing her attention on the nature of the reasons that might be advanced in support of the unborn entity's continued existence, she considers reasons that might be advanced on the other side—in support of abortion. She deliberately assumes, for the sake of the argument, that a fetus is a human being with the same stringent claim to continued existence as any other human being. Then she raises the question whether nonetheless there might still be reasons, in certain circumstances, that could justify abortion: in particular, whether the claims of the mother to *her* life, or to "decide what happens in and to her body," might outweigh the claims suppositively ascribed to the fetus. Even if abortion is homicide, she concludes, it is normally justifiable homicide. Thomson's argument is the stimulus to more extensive discussions of the model of self-defense applied to abortion (in English's article) and of the relevance of the woman's responsibility for her pregnancy to the justification of abortion (in Bok's article).

Other writers in this collection, each in his or her own way, downgrade the importance of the status question and emphasize the problem of justifying any type of abortion. S. I. Benn points out that considerations other than rights or claims are involved in making moral decisions and suggests that some of these might support the condemnation of infanticide and late abortion even on the assumption that infants and older fetuses are rightless nonpersons. Jane English sounds the same theme, but points out that the argument cuts both ways: Even if a fetus at a given stage is not a person, killing it in some cases may be wrong; but even if a fetus at a given stage is a person with a right to life, killing it at that stage in some cases may be justified. Thus, "the concept of a person cannot bear the weight usually thrust upon it." Loren Lomasky goes even further in debunking the importance of personhood. It is not because the newborn is a person that it acquires a powerful claim on us, he argues, but because—preperson though it may be—it now plays a responsive social role in that complex web of social interactions that constitute a human community. Lomasky is thus able to vindicate the process of birth as the significant moral boundary, and because it is not personhood that "matters," he can consistently condemn infanticide.

Even if rights and personhood are not always the decisive considerations in resolving moral dilemmas, they naturally play the decisive role in legal deliberations, at least in our constitutional system. In 1973, when the United States Supreme Court finally issued an authoritative opinion about abortion, there were four possible views it might have endorsed about the constitutionality of statutes that prohibit or narrowly restrict abortions. First, it might have held that the constitution implies nothing one way or the other about a woman's right to have an abortion, and also that the constitution does not recognize fetuses as legal persons. In that case there is no constitutional issue of abortion, and legislatures are free to prohibit or permit abortions as they see fit. Second, it might have held that the constitution is silent on the woman's right to an abortion but does recognize fetuses as persons, in which case fetal life is protected by various constitutional provisions applying to legal persons (especially the Fourteenth Amendment), and state statutes prohibiting abortion are valid, if somewhat redundant. Third, it might have turned the second position on its head and held that fetuses are *not* persons in the eyes of the constitution, but that pregnant women *do* have a right to decide whether or not to bear their children, derived from a more general constitutional "right to privacy" implicitly conferred by "the First Amendment . . . the Fourth and Fifth Amendments . . . the penumbras of the Bill of Rights . . . the Ninth Amendment . . . or in the concept of liberty guaranteed by the first section of the Fourteenth Amendment." Finally, it might have held that fetuses *are* full persons within the meaning of the Fourteenth Amendment, and *also* that women have a constitutional right to privacy that permits them to determine as they please what is to be done to their bodies. In that case there is a *prima facie* conflict between constitutional rights which courts must somehow resolve by limiting the scope of one or both of them. (If fetuses are really *full* legal persons, however, one would expect their rights to life to be as "absolute" as any adult's, so that the woman's right to privacy would stop short of the right to abort.)

In the case of *Roe* v. *Wade,* excerpted in this volume, the Supreme Court opted for the third of the positions listed above. The majority opinion held that fetuses are not "full legal persons" and that there is a woman's right to an abortion derived from a more general constitutional right to privacy, but that the latter right is not absolute, being limited by the state's right to regulate medical practice to protect maternal health in the second and third trimester of pregnancy, and the state's "interest in the potentiality of human life" in the final trimester only. In our system, of course, the Supreme Court's decisions are final, and thus a number of hitherto controversial questions of law and policy can now be considered settled, unless or until the Constitution is amended. As this collection of articles indicates, however, the moral and philosophical issues that underlie the abortion controversy even in its constitutional dimension, despite their clarification, remain unsettled. The Supreme Court, whatever its intentions, did not so much avoid these issues as effectively demonstrate their peculiar persistence.

*   *   *

Four articles in this book come from a remarkable journal, *Philosophy & Public Affairs,* which in the decade it has existed has elevated discussion of this and other public issues to a new level. Three of these articles appear in the journal's own reader, *Rights and Wrongs of Abortion,* edited by Marshall Cohen, Thomas Nagel, and Thomas Scanlon (Princeton: Princeton University Press, 1974)—an anthology that is indispensable for all serious students of the abortion debate. I appreciate the cooperation of the editors of *Philosophy & Public Affairs* and its publisher, the Princeton University Press.

Joel Feinberg

An Almost Absolute Value in History

John T. Noonan, Jr.

T he most fundamental question involved in the long history of thought on
abortion is: How do you determine the humanity of a being? To phrase
the question that way is to put in comprehensive humanistic terms what
the theologians either dealt with as an explicitly theological question under
the heading of "ensoulment" or dealt with implicitly in their treatment of abortion.
The Christian position as it originated did not depend on a narrow theological or
philosophical concept. It had no relation to theories of infant baptism.[1] It appealed
to no special theory of instantaneous ensoulment. It took the world's view on
ensoulment as that view changed from Aristotle to Zacchia. There was, indeed,
theological influence affecting the theory of ensoulment finally adopted, and, of
course, ensoulment itself was a theological concept, so that the position was
always explained in theological terms. But the theological notion of ensoulment
could easily be translated into humanistic language by substituting "human" for
"rational soul"; the problem of knowing when a man is a man is common to
theology and humanism.

If one steps outside the specific categories used by the theologians, the answer
they gave can be analyzed as a refusal to discriminate among human beings on the
basis of their varying potentialities. Once conceived, the being was recognized as
man because he had man's potential. The criterion for humanity, thus, was simple
and all-embracing: if you are conceived by human parents, you are human.

Reprinted by permission of the publishers from John T. Noonan, Jr., editor, *The Morality
of Abortion: Legal and Historical Perspectives* (Cambridge, Mass.: Harvard University Press.
Copyright © 1970 by the President and Fellows of Harvard College), pp. 51–59.

[1] According to Glanville Williams (*The Sanctity of Human Life supra* n. 169, at 193), "The
historical reason for the Catholic objection to abortion is the same as for the Christian
Church's historical opposition to infanticide: the horror of bringing about the death of an
unbaptized child." This statement is made without any citation of evidence. As has been
seen, desire to administer baptism could, in the Middle Ages, even be urged as a reason for
procuring an abortion. It is highly regrettable that the American Law Institute was apparently misled by Williams' account and repeated after him the same baseless statement. See
American Law Institute, *Model Penal Code: Tentative Draft No. 9* (1959), p. 148, n. 12.

The strength of this position may be tested by a review of some of the other distinctions offered in the contemporary controversy over legalizing abortion. Perhaps the most popular distinction is in terms of viability. Before an age of so many months, the fetus is not viable, that is, it cannot be removed from the mother's womb and live apart from her. To that extent, the life of the fetus is absolutely dependent on the life of the mother. This dependence is made the basis of denying recognition to its humanity.

There are difficulties with this distinction. One is that the perfection of artificial incubation may make the fetus viable at any time: it may be removed and artificially sustained. Experiments with animals already show that such a procedure is possible. This hypothetical extreme case relates to an actual difficulty: there is considerable elasticity to the idea of viability. Mere length of life is not an exact measure. The viability of the fetus depends on the extent of its anatomical and functional development. The weight and length of the fetus are better guides to the state of its development than age, but weight and length vary. Moreover, different racial groups have different ages at which their fetuses are viable. Some evidence, for example, suggests that Negro fetuses mature more quickly than white fetuses. If viability is the norm, the standard would vary with race and with many individual circumstances.

The most important objection to this approach is that dependence is not ended by viability. The fetus is still absolutely dependent on someone's care in order to continue existence; indeed a child of one or three or even five years of age is absolutely dependent on another's care for existence; uncared for, the older fetus or the younger child will die as surely as the early fetus detached from the mother. The unsubstantial lessening in dependence at viability does not seem to signify any special acquisition of humanity.

A second distinction has been attempted in terms of experience. A being who has had experience, has lived and suffered, who possesses memories, is more human than one who has not. Humanity depends on formation by experience. The fetus is thus "unformed" in the most basic human sense.

This distinction is not serviceable for the embryo which is already experiencing and reacting. The embryo is responsive to touch after eight weeks and at least at that point is experiencing. At an earlier stage the zygote is certainly alive and responding to its environment. The distinction may also be challenged by the rare case where aphasia has erased adult memory: has it erased humanity? More fundamentally, this distinction leaves even the older fetus or the younger child to be treated as an unformed inhuman thing. Finally, it is not clear why experience as such confers humanity. It could be argued that certain central experiences such as loving or learning are necessary to make a man human. But then human beings who have failed to love or to learn might be excluded from the class called man.

A third distinction is made by appeal to the sentiments of adults. If a fetus dies, the grief of the parents is not the grief they would have for a living child. The fetus is an unnamed "it" till birth, and is not perceived as personality until at least the fourth month of existence when movements in the womb manifest a vigorous presence demanding joyful recognition by the parents.

Yet feeling is notoriously an unsure guide to the humanity of others. Many groups of humans have had difficulty in feeling that persons of another tongue, color, religion, sex, are as human as they. Apart from reactions to alien groups, we mourn the loss of a ten-year-old boy more than the loss of his one-day-old brother or his 90-year-old grandfather. The difference felt and the grief expressed vary with the potentialities extinguished, or the experience wiped out; they do not seem to point to any substantial difference in the humanity of baby, boy, or grandfather.

Distinctions are also made in terms of sensation by the parents. The embryo is felt within the womb only after about the fourth month. The embryo is seen only at birth. What can be neither seen nor felt is different from what is tangible. If the fetus cannot be seen or touched at all, it cannot be perceived as man.

Yet experience shows that sight is even more untrustworthy than feeling in determining humanity. By sight, color became an appropriate index for saying who was a man, and the evil of racial discrimination was given foundation. Nor can touch provide the test; a being confined by sickness, "out of touch" with others, does not thereby seem to lose his humanity. To the extent that touch still has appeal as a criterion, it appears to be a survival of the old English idea of "quickening"—a possible mistranslation of the Latin *animatus* used in the canon law. To that extent touch as a criterion seems to be dependent on the Aristotelian notion of ensoulment, and to fall when this notion is discarded.

Finally, a distinction is sought in social visibility. The fetus is not socially perceived as human. It cannot communicate with others. Thus, both subjectively and objectively, it is not a member of society. As moral rules are rules for the behavior of members of society to each other, they cannot be made for behavior toward what is not yet a member. Excluded from the society of men, the fetus is excluded from the humanity of men.[2]

By force of the argument from the consequences, this distinction is to be rejected. It is more subtle than that founded on an appeal to physical sensation, but it is equally dangerous in its implications. If humanity depends on social recognition, individuals or whole groups may be dehumanized by being denied any status in their society. Such a fate is fictionally portrayed in *1984* and has actually been the lot of many men in many societies. In the Roman empire, for example, condemnation to slavery meant the practical denial of most human rights; in the Chinese Communist world, landlords have been classified as enemies of the people and so treated as nonpersons by the state. Humanity does not depend on social recognition, though often the failure of society to recognize the

---

[2] . . . Thomas Aquinas gave an analogous reason against baptizing a fetus in the womb: "As long as it exists in the womb of the mother, it cannot be subject to the operation of the ministers of the Church as it is not known to men" (*In sententias Petri Lombardi* 4.6 1.1.2).

prisoner, the alien, the heterodox as human has led to the destruction of human beings. Anyone conceived by a man and a woman is human. Recognition of this condition by society follows a real event in the objective order, however imperfect and halting the recognition. Any attempt to limit humanity to exclude some group runs the risk of furnishing authority and precedent for excluding other groups in the name of the consciousness or perception of the controlling group in the society.

A philosopher may reject the appeal to the humanity of the fetus because he views "humanity" as a secular view of the soul and because he doubts the existence of anything real and objective which can be identified as humanity. One answer to such a philosopher is to ask how he reasons about moral questions without supposing that there is a sense in which he and the others of whom he speaks are human. Whatever group is taken as the society which determines who may be killed is thereby taken as human. A second answer is to ask if he does not believe that there is a right and wrong way of deciding moral questions. If there is such a difference, experience may be appealed to: to decide who is human on the basis of the sentiment of a given society has led to consequences which rational men would characterize as monstrous.

The rejection of the attempted distinctions based on viability and visibility, experience and feeling, may be buttressed by the following considerations: Moral judgments often rest on distinctions, but if the distinctions are not to appear arbitrary *fiat,* they should relate to some real difference in probabilities. There is a kind of continuity in all life, but the earlier stages of the elements of human life possess tiny probabilities of development. Consider, for example, the spermatozoa in any normal ejaculate: There are about 200,000,000 in any single ejaculate, of which one has a chance of developing into a zygote. Consider the oocytes which may become ova: there are 100,000 to 1,000,000 oocytes in a female infant, of which a maximum of 390 are ovulated. But once spermatozoon and ovum meet and the conceptus is formed, such studies as have been made show that roughly in only 20 percent of the cases will spontaneous abortion occur. In other words, the chances are about 4 out of 5 that this new being will develop. At this stage in the life of the being there is a sharp shift in probabilities, an immense jump in potentialities. To make a distinction between the rights of spermatozoa and the rights of the fertilized ovum is to respond to an enormous shift in possibilities. For about twenty days after conception the egg may split to form twins or combine with another egg to form a chimera, but the probability of either event happening is very small.

It may be asked, What does a change in biological probabilities have to do with establishing humanity? The argument from probabilities is not aimed at establishing humanity but at establishing an objective discontinuity which may be taken into account in moral discourse. As life itself is a matter of probabilities, as most moral reasoning is an estimate of probabilities, so it seems in accord with the structure of reality and the nature of moral thought to found a moral judgment on the change in probabilities at conception. The appeal to probabilities is the most commonsensical of arguments; to a greater or smaller degree all of us base our actions on probabilities, and in morals, as in law, prudence and negligence are often measured by the account one has taken of the probabilities. If the chance is 200,000,000 to 1 that the movement in the bushes into which you shoot is a man's, I doubt if many persons would hold you careless in shooting; but if the chances are 4 out of 5 that the movement is a human being's, few would acquit you of blame. Would the argument be different if only one out of ten children conceived came to term? Of course this argument would be different. This argument is an appeal to probabilities that actually exist, not to any and all states of affairs which may be imagined.

The probabilities as they do exist do not show the humanity of the embryo in the sense of a demonstration in logic any more than the probabilities of the movement in the bush being a man demonstrate beyond all doubt that the being is a man. The appeal is a "buttressing" consideration, showing the plausibility of the standard adopted. The argument focuses on the decisional factor in any moral judgment and assumes that part of the business of a moralist is drawing lines. One evidence of the nonarbitrary character of the line drawn is the difference of probabilities on either side of it. If a spermatozoon is destroyed, one destroys a being which had a chance of far less than 1 in 200 million of developing into a reasoning being, possessed of the genetic code, a heart and other organs, and capable of pain. If a fetus is destroyed, one destroys a being already possessed of the genetic code, organs, and sensitivity to pain, and one which had an 80 percent chance of developing further into a baby outside the womb who, in time, would reason.

The positive argument for conception as the decisive moment of humanization is that at conception the new being receives the genetic code. It is this genetic information which determines his characteristics, which is the biological carrier of the possibility of human wisdom, which makes him a self-evolving being. A being with a human genetic code is man.

This review of current controversy over the humanity of the fetus emphasizes what a fundamental question the theologians resolved in asserting the inviolability of the fetus. To regard the fetus as possessed of equal rights with other humans was not, however, to decide every case where abortion might be employed. It did decide the case where the argument was that the fetus should be aborted for its own good. To say a being was human was to say it had a destiny to decide for itself which could not be taken from it by another man's decision. But human beings with equal rights often come in conflict with each other, and some decision must be made as to whose claims are to prevail. Cases of conflict involving the fetus are different only in two respects: the total inability of the fetus to speak for itself and the fact that the right of the fetus regularly at stake is the right to life itself.

The approach taken by the theologians to these conflicts was articulated in terms of "direct" and "indirect." Again, to look at what they were doing from outside their categories, they may be said to have been drawing lines or "balancing values." "Direct" and "indirect" are spatial metaphors; "line-drawing" is another. "To weigh" or "to balance" values is a metaphor of a more complicated mathematical sort hinting at the process which goes on in moral judgments. All the metaphors suggest that, in the moral judgments made, comparisons were necessary, that no value completely controlled. The principle of double effect was no doctrine fallen from heaven, but a method of analysis appropriate where two relative values were being compared. In Catholic moral theology, as it developed, life even of the innocent was not taken as an absolute. Judgments on acts affecting life issued from a process of weighing. In the weighing, the fetus was always given a value greater than zero, always a value separate and independent from its parents. This valuation was crucial and fundamental in all Christian thought on the subject and marked it off from any approach which considered that only the parents' interests needed to be considered.

Even with the fetus weighed as human, one interest could be weighed as equal or superior: that of the mother in her own life. The casuists between 1450 and 1895 were willing to weigh this interest as superior. Since 1895, that interest was given decisive weight only in the two special cases of the cancerous uterus and the ectopic pregnancy. In both of these cases the fetus itself had little chance of survival even if the abortion were not performed. As the balance was once struck in favor of the mother whenever her life was endangered, it could be so struck again. The balance reached between 1895 and 1930 attempted prudentially and pastorally to forestall a multitude of exceptions for interests less than life.

The perception of the humanity of the fetus and the weighing of fetal rights against other human rights constituted the work of the moral analysts. But what spirit animated their abstract judgments? For the Christian community it was the injunction of Scripture to love your neighbor as yourself. The fetus as human was a neighbor; his life had parity with one's own. The commandment gave life to what otherwise would have been only rational calculation.

The commandment could be put in humanistic as well as theological terms: Do not injure your fellow man without reason. In these terms, once the humanity of the fetus is perceived, abortion is never right except in self-defense. When life must be taken to save life, reason alone cannot say that a mother must prefer a child's life to her own. With this exception, now of great rarity, abortion violates the rational humanist tenet of the equality of human lives.

For Christians the commandment to love had received a special imprint in that the exemplar proposed of love was the love of the Lord for his disciples. In the light given by this example, self-sacrifice carried to the point of death seemed in the extreme situations not without meaning. In the less extreme cases, preference for one's own interests to the life of another seemed to express cruelty or selfishness irreconcilable with the demands of love.

A Liberal Catholic's View

Joseph F. Donceel, S. J.

moral issues —

I fully agree with the basic Catholic principle that we are never allowed to kill an innocent human being. Therefore, if there is a real human being from the moment of conception, abortion would have to be considered immoral at any stage of pregnancy. The majority Catholic opinion holds nowadays that there is indeed a real human being from the first moment of conception, or, at least, that we cannot be certain that such is not the case. But there is also a minority Catholic opinion, which has good standing in the church, which was the opinion of her greatest theologian, Thomas Aquinas,[1] and which is now slowly regaining favor among Catholic thinkers. This minority opinion holds that there is certainly no human being during the early stages of pregnancy. I would like to show you briefly why Thomas held this position, how it was given up by his successors on account of erroneous scientific theories, and how, even after these theories had been given up, the Catholic church did not return to her traditional view because of a philosophy which was at variance with her official doctrine of the nature of man.

Traditional Catholic philosophy holds that what makes an organism a human being is the spiritual soul and that this soul starts to exist at the moment of its "infusion" into the body. When is the human soul infused into the body? Nowadays the majority of Catholic thinkers would not hesitate to answer: at the moment of conception. This is known as the *theory of immediate animation.* However, during long centuries Catholic philosophy and theology held that the human soul was infused into the body only when the latter began to show a human shape or outline and possessed the basic human organs. Before this time, the embryo is alive, but in the way in which a plant or an animal is alive. It possesses, as the traditional terminology puts it, a vegetative or an animal soul, not yet a human

---

From *Abortion in a Changing World,* vol. 1, ed. by Robert E. Hall (New York: Columbia University Press, 1970), pp. 39–45. Reprinted by permission of Robert E. Hall.

---

[1] See *Summa contra Gentiles,* II, 88–89; *De Potentia,* Q. 3, Art. 9–12; *Summa Theologica,* I, Q. 118, Art. 1–3.

soul. In more modern terms we might say that it has reached the physiological or the psychological, not yet the spiritual level of existence. It is not yet a human person; it is evolving, within the womb, toward hominization. This is the *theory of mediate or delayed animation.*

Why did Thomas and the great medieval thinkers favor this theory? Because they held the doctrine of hylomorphism, according to which the human soul is the substantial form of man, while the human body is the result of the union of this soul with materiality, with undetermined cosmic stuff, with what was then known as prime matter. Hylomorphism holds that the human soul is to the body somewhat as the shape of a statue is to the actual statue. The shape of a statue cannot exist before the statue exists. It is not something which the sculptor first makes and subsequently introduces into a block of marble. It can exist only in the completed statue. Hylomorphism holds that, in the same way, the human soul can exist only in a real human body.

Although Thomas knew nothing about chromosomes, genes, DNA, or the code of life, he knew that whatever was growing in the mother's womb was not yet, early in pregnancy, a real human body. Therefore he held that it could not be animated by a human soul, any more than a square block of marble can possess a human shape. The medieval thinkers knew very well that this growing organism would develop into a human body, that virtually, potentially, it was a human body. But they did not admit that an actual human soul could exist in a virtual human body. The Catholic church, which had officially adopted the hylomorphic conception of human nature at the Council of Vienne, in 1312, was so strongly convinced of this position that, for centuries, her law forbade the faithful to baptize any premature birth which did not show at least some human shape or outline.

Under the influence of erroneous scientific reports, however, Catholic thinkers gave up this traditional doctrine. In the early seventeenth century, as a result of a combination of poor microscopes and lively imaginations, some physicians saw in embryos which were only a few days old a tiny human being, a homunculus, with microscopic head, legs, and arms.[2] This view of the fetus implied the *preformation theory,* which held that organic development simply consists of the gradual increase in size of organs and structures which are fully present from the very start. If there really were from the beginning a human body, be it ever so small, there might also from the start exist a human soul. Even a microscopic statue must have a shape. Granted the preformation theory, immediate animation was compatible with the hylomorphic conception of man.

The theory of preformation was eventually replaced by the *theory of epigenesis,* which maintains that the organism, far from being microscopically preformed from the start, develops its organs through a complex process of growth, cleavage, differentiation, and organization.

---

[2] See H. de Dorlodot, "A Vindication of the Mediate Animation Theory," in E. C. Messenger (ed.), *Theology and Evolution,* pp. 273–83, London, 1949.

Why did the Christian thinkers not return to the delayed animation theory, which seems to be demanded by their hylomorphic theory of man? The main reason seems to have been the influence of Cartesian dualism. For Descartes, both man's soul and his body are each a complete substance. The soul is a thinking substance, the body an extended substance. This is no longer hylomorphism. To express it in nontechnical language, this is no longer a "shape in the statue" conception, but rather a "ghost in the machine" conception of the human soul. A full-fledged ghost can manage very well with a microscopic machine. If the soul is no longer the formal cause, the constitutive idea of the body, it might well become its efficient cause, that which produces the ovum's development from the start. Instead of being the idea incarnated in the body, it has turned into the architect and the builder of the body. Just as the architect exists before the first stone of the building is laid, so there can be a real human soul from the first moment of conception, before the emergence of a real human body.[3]

This way of explaining embryogeny is not absurd. The Cartesian outlook, although quite unfashionable nowadays, has been held by many great thinkers. This kind of philosophy calls for immediate animation, which is clearly in conflict with the hylomorphic doctrine of man, solemnly endorsed by the Catholic church at the Council of Vienne.

There have been other influences which explain the shift in Catholic opinion. One of them may have been the long-standing opposition of the church to the idea of evolution. Thomas admitted some kind of evolution of the embryo and the fetus in the mother's womb. How could the church admit this evolution in the womb and reject it in the race? Since the Catholic church has finally come around to admitting the evolution of the human body, it might also be willing to return to Thomas's idea of evolution in the womb.[4]

Moreover, once we give up the idea of immediate animation, we can no longer say when the human soul is infused, when the embryo or the fetus becomes a human person. That is why those who want to play it absolutely safe claim that the human soul is present from the moment of conception. They seem to take it for granted that, since we do not know when the human soul is present, we neither

---

[3]The anonymous author of an article in Latin, "De Animatione Foetus" (*Nouvelle Revue Théologique*, 11:163–86, 268–89 [1879]), quotes a certain Michael Alberti Germaniae Medicus, who wrote in 1725 "quod a primis conceptionis initiis anima rationalis in foetu adsit, eo quod sine anima illa conceptio fieri nequeat, quae tanquam artifex et architecta sui corporis praesto est; a qua deinde actus formationis dependet" (that the rational soul is present in the fetus from the first beginnings of conception, because the conception cannot take place without this soul, which is there *like the maker and the architect of its body;* hence the act of formation depends on it) (my italics). This sounds like pure Cartesianism.

[4]"For the evolutionistic way of thinking, it is more probable that hominization occurs not at the moment of conception, but at a later time of embryonic development," writes J. Feiner in the most recent comprehensive treatise of dogmatic theology, *Mysterium Fidei,* edited by J. Feiner and M. Löhrer, vol. II, p. 581, Einsiedeln, 1967.

can know for sure when it is not yet present. This assumption is false. Let us consider another case, where we do not know when a certain factor is present, while knowing very well when it is not yet present. Nobody can tell with certitude when a child is capable of performing his first free moral choice, but all of us are quite certain that, during the first months or years of his life, a human baby is not yet a free moral agent. Likewise, I do not know when the human soul is infused, when the embryo becomes human. But I feel certain that there is no human soul, hence no human person, during the first few weeks of pregnancy, as long as the embryo remains in the vegetative stage of its development.

Some people make much of the following objection to my position. They say that from the very first the fertilized ovum possesses forty-six human chromosomes, all the human genes, its code of life—that it is a human embryo. This is undeniable. But it does not make it a human person. When a heart is transplanted, it is kept alive, for a short while, outside of the donor. It is a living being, a human heart, with the human chromosomes and genes. But it is not a human being; it is not a person.

The objection may be pressed. Not only does the fertilized human ovum possess the human chromosomes; unlike the heart, it will, if circumstances are normal, develop into a human being. It is virtually a human being. I admit this, but it does not affect my position. The fertilized human ovum, the early embryo, is virtually a human body, not actually. Correctly understood, the hylomorphic conception of human nature, the official Catholic doctrine, cannot admit the presence of an actual human soul in a virtual human body. Let me use a comparison again. A deflated rubber ball is virtually round; when inflated, it can assume no other shape than the spherical shape. Yet it does not actually possess any roundness or sphericity. In the same way, the early embryo does not actually possess a human soul; it is not a human person.

Experimental embryology tells us that every single cell of the early embryo, of the morula, is virtually a human body. It does not follow that each of these cells possesses a human soul. When embryologists carefully separate the cells of a morula in lower organisms, each one of these cells may develop into a complete organism. Starting with the pioneering attempts of Hans Driesch, such an experiment has been performed on many animal species. We do not see why it might not eventually succeed with the human embryo. As a matter of fact, nature frequently performs it on human ova. Identical twins derive from one ovum fertilized by one spermatozoon. This ovum splits into two at an early stage of pregnancy and gives rise to two human beings. In this case the defenders of immediate animation must admit that one person may be divided into two persons. This is a metaphysical impossibility.

Throughout my exposition I have taken for granted the hylomorphic conception of human nature. This is in line with the purpose of my essay, which is not only to present a liberal Catholic's view of fetal animation, but also to show that this view seems to be the only one which agrees with the official Catholic conception of human nature. In other words, I submit that Catholics should give up the immediate animation theory, because it implies a Cartesian, dualistic conception of man, which conflicts with the doctrine endorsed by the Council of Vienne.

In conclusion I would like to say a few words about the standing of hylomorphism among contemporary philosophers. Very few non-Catholic philosophers hold the doctrine of hylomorphism today. Even among Catholics it has fallen into disrepute, although personally I cannot see how one may avoid dualism without this theory or some theory which resembles it. Hylomorphism is radically opposed to dualism, to the doctrine which considers both the soul and the body as complete substances. Contemporary philosophy, as a rule, is also strongly opposed to this kind of dualism. In this sense, negatively, the doctrine I have defended continues to live; it is stronger than ever, although it may be known by other names.

Both linguistic analysis, the leading philosophy in the English-speaking countries, and existential phenomenology, which tends to dominate the field elsewhere, reject any form of Cartesian dualism.[5] Gilbert Ryle, a leading British analyst, has strongly attacked what he calls "the dogma of the ghost in the machine." And Maurice Merleau-Ponty, possibly France's greatest phenomenologist, defended a doctrine which looks very much like an updated form of hylomorphism. For him there are three kinds of behavior: the syncretic, the amovable, and the symbolic. We might perhaps put it more simply and speak of three levels in man: the level of reflex activity and of instincts, the level of learning, and the level of symbolic thinking. Or again, the physiological, the psychic, and the spiritual level. Each lower level stands to the next higher one in the same relation as data stand to their meaning, as materiality stands to the idea embodied in it. The data are not data if they do not possess some meaning, and there can be no meaning which is not embedded in some data. Each higher level presupposes the lower one; there can be no mind before the organism is ready to carry one and no spirit before the mind is capable of receiving it. I submit that this clearly implies delayed animation.

In my opinion there is a great amount of agreement between the contemporary antidualistic trend of philosophy and the hylomorphic conception of man. It is wise therefore to return to this conception or, at least, to accept the conclusions which follow from it. One of these conclusions is that the embryo is certainly not a human person during the early stages of pregnancy, and that, consequently, it is not immoral to terminate pregnancy during this time, provided there are serious reasons for such an intervention.

Let me insist on this restriction: the opinion which I have defended may lead to abuses, to abortions performed under flimsy pretexts. I would be among the first to deplore and condemn such abuses. Although a prehuman embryo cannot demand from us the absolute respect which we owe to the human person, it deserves a very great consideration, because it is a living being, endowed with a

---

[5] Among the few exceptions we must mention J. P. Sartre, whose dualism constitutes one of the weakest and most controversial aspects of his philosophy.

human finality, on its way to hominization. Therefore it seems to me that only very serious reasons should allow us to terminate its existence. Excesses will unavoidably occur, but they should not induce us to overlook the instances where sufficiently serious reasons exist for performing an abortion during the early stages of pregnancy.

The Scope of the Prohibition Against Killing

Philip E. Devine

A. Nonhumans, Robots, and Infants

. . . This and the following chapter will . . . be concerned with the scope of the prohibition against homicide and other moral rules protecting the interests of human beings or persons. What kinds of creatures, I shall be asking, are comprised within the class whose members the moral rule against homicide protects? What is the status of normal human fetuses and infants? of human defectives? of robots and androids? of dolphins and chimpanzees? Is it ever prima facie wrong to kill such creatures, and if so, need the justifications for killing them be as compelling as those required to warrant killing a normal adult human? These questions are important not only for the ethics of homicide, but for ethics generally, since if a creature has no right not to be killed, it cannot have any other serious rights in contexts where its interests and those of persons are in conflict. Such a conflict could always be resolved by killing the troublesome creature. . . .

In what follows, I distinguish three principles of interpretation determining the limits of the moral rule against homicide and other moral rules protecting distinctively human rights. One of these, the *species principle,* will be founded on the kinship or solidarity that obtains among members of the same species. It seems best understood as a more precise version of the "Standard Belief" which Roger Wertheimer attributes to nearly everyone: that what warrants the ascription of human moral status to a creature is simply that creature's being human.[1] (I say

Excerpted with permission of Cornell University Press from Philip E. Devine, *The Ethics of Homicide* (Copyright © 1978 by Cornell University), chaps. 2, 3. (The section on robots in Part A has been omitted.)

[1] Roger Wertheimer, "Philosophy on Humanity," in Robert L. Perkins, ed., *Abortion* (Cambridge, Mass., 1974).

a more precise version, since Wertheimer believes that one can deny that a biologically human creature is a member of "the family of man," although why he thinks this is not completely clear.) The second, the *present enjoyment* (or present possession) *principle,* rests on the ability of human beings to assert their personhood by appeals or resistance. And the third, the *potentiality principle,* rests on the uniquely rich kinds of action and experience of which human beings are capable, and the uniquely severe loss suffered when the prospect of such a life is frustrated, whether or not the organism whose existence has been ended or whose capacity for such life has been impaired has had some experience of it. The potentiality and present enjoyment principles seem best viewed as attempts to replace the Standard Belief with something thought more satisfactory. Our choice among these principles will determine our judgment of the moral status of fetuses, infants, and the moribund, and thus make a crucial difference to our judgments concerning abortion, infanticide, and euthanasia.[2]

1. The Species Principle

A first statement of the species principle as it applies to killing is as follows: those creatures protected by the moral rule against homicide are the members of the human species, and only the members of the human species. This version of the principle protects all human organisms, whatever their degree of maturity or decay, including fetuses and embryos, but not robots or nonhuman animals, whatever the attainments of such beings might be.

The species principle does not mean, as Joseph Fletcher thinks, that "we would be human if we have opposable thumbs, are capable of face-to-face coitus and have a brain weighing 1400 grams, whether a particular brain functions cerebrally or not."[3] Obviously a creature might be morally and biologically human while lacking one of these traits—say a child born without hands (and thus without thumbs)—and it is easy to imagine a species that met the suggested criteria without being in any sense human. Membership in a biological species is a complex matter, but scientists are now well able to recognize biological humanity in the fine structure of an organism, without reference to such things as opposable thumbs. Jérôme Lejeune puts the point nicely:

> Let us take the example of trisomy 21 [a chromosome disorder], observed by amniocentesis. Looking at the chromosomes and detecting the extra 21, we say

---

[2] Letting *T* be the complex of traits we think of as distinctively human, these principles may be stated as follows. *Species principle:* All biological humans (or all members of species characterized by *T*) have a serious right to life. *Present enjoyment principle:* All creatures which presently enjoy the possession of *T* have a serious right to life. *Potentiality principle:* All creatures which potentially possess (now or will in due course possess) *T* have a serious right to life.

[3] Joseph F. Fletcher, "Four Indicators of Humanhood—The Enquiry Matures," *Hastings Center Report,* Dec. 1974, p. 6.

very safely "The child who will develop here will be a trisomic 21." But this phrase does not convey all the information. We have not seen only the extra 21; we have also seen all the 46 other chromosomes and concluded that they were human, because if they had been mouse or monkey chromosomes, we would have noticed.[4]

In other words, even a human defective is a defective *human,* and this biological humanity is recognizable in the genetic structure of the organism even when the genetic structure itself is defective.

Some vagueness does afflict the species principle when it comes to deciding precisely when—at conception or shortly thereafter, when the unity and uniqueness of the nascent creature is secured—a human organism comes into existence, as well as how much breakdown is necessary before we say that a human organism has ceased to be. Ape-human hybrids and the like also pose a knotty problem. But none of these zones of vagueness render the principle unusable, nor do they provide any grounds for refusing to use the principle to condemn killing where the victim is unambiguously a human organism.

Finally, the species principle provides an adequate answer to the "acorn" argument, which has a surprising persistence in disputes about abortion.[5] Whatever may be the case with dormant acorns, a germinating acorn is, while not an oak *tree,* still a member of the appropriate species of oak. If oaks had a serious right to life in their own right, so would oak saplings and germinating acorns. And the same reply can be made to those who would argue about abortion from the premise that a caterpillar is not a butterfly.[6]

An unsound objection to the species principle is that it employs a biological category, that of the species, in the derivation of moral conclusions. This objection takes two forms: that such derivation is an illegitimate inference from an "is" to an "ought," and that to rely on such categories is to offend human dignity by subjecting human beings, like beasts, to the tyranny of animal nature. Neither version of the objection is plausible.

At most, what cannot be done in deriving an "ought" from an "is" is to assert an *entailment.* Modes of inference weaker than entailment cannot be barred as instances of the naturalistic fallacy lest all moral reasoning be made impossible. "X is a human organism; therefore X ought not to be killed" may be as good as any other significant moral inference. Of course one could treat this inference as elliptical, its missing premise being the moral rule against homicide as interpreted

---

[4]In Bruce Hilton et al., eds., *Ethical Issues in Human Genetics* (New York, 1973), p. 113.

[5]It is employed in Judith Jarvis Thomson, "A Defense of Abortion," *Philosophy & Public Affairs,* 1 (1971), 47–48, and in Marvin Kohl, *The Morality of Killing* (New York, 1974), p. 42. It also makes brief appearances in Roger Wertheimer, "Understanding the Abortion Argument," *Philosophy & Public Affairs,* 1 (1971), 74, 82.

[6]Lawrence C. Becker, "Human Being: The Boundaries of the Concept," *Philosophy & Public Affairs,* 4 (1975), esp. pp. 337–345.

in accordance with the species principle ("One ought not to kill a human organism"). But to spell out this argument in this way may be no more illuminating than treating inductive inference as deductive inference with the principle of induction as a suppressed premise. In any case, this reading does nothing to strengthen the objection to the species principle.

As for the version of this contention which turns on human dignity, the answer to it is best put in the form of a question. Why is it wounding to human dignity to recognize that human beings are, among other things, animals, and to call for some respect for the animal aspect of man's being? Is the sanctioning of unlimited assaults on the characteristic modes of coming to be and passing away of the human species more in keeping with respect for human dignity than the placing of restraints on such activity? To regard the according of moral significance to the animal aspect of man's existence as wounding to his dignity seems to make man's dignity contingent upon his being regarded as something he is not.

A more troubling charge is that of species chauvinism: the charge, that is, that the giving of a higher moral status to members of one's own species than to those of others is akin to regarding members of other races as subhuman. It would not be chauvinism in the strict sense to argue that between two intelligent species, members of one have no rights which members of the other are bound to respect, while each agent is morally required to respect the rights of members of his own species, in particular not to kill them unless he has a very compelling justification. It is, after all, considered worse (all other things being equal) to kill one's brother than a stranger, not because one's brother in himself is morally more worthy than the stranger, but because the relationship between brothers is itself morally significant. Nonetheless we would certainly want intelligent Martians to respect our rights, and might be prepared to respect theirs in return. And, if Martians were enough like human beings that the notion of human individuality could be extended to them, this respect for their rights would naturally take the form, *inter alia,* of regarding Martians as protected by our moral (and quite possibly our legal) rules against homicide.

But this line of thought can be accommodated by a modification of the species principle which does not alter its essential structure. According to this modification, what the moral rule against homicide protects is all members of intelligent species, including, but not limited to, the human. On this account determining whether a given creature is protected by the moral rule against homicide is a two-step process: first, identifying the species to which the creature belongs, and second, deciding whether this species is in fact intelligent. For members of the human species, the human species continues to play a somewhat paradigmatic role, in setting the standard of intelligence which must be approached or exceeded for a species to be considered intelligent, and the same is true for members of other intelligent species. A human being will ask whether Martians as a species are intelligent enough by human standards to be regarded as persons, and an intelligent Martian will make the corresponding inquiry concerning human beings.

In any case, all creatures protected by the original species principle are protected by the modified species principle as well.

Three problems of application arise for the modified species principle, of particular importance in assessing the claims which might be made on behalf of chimpanzees, whales, and dolphins. First, supposing one member of a species reaches the human level, what effect does this achievement have on the status of the other members of the species? Second, what kind of standards are to be employed in determining whether a given species is to be regarded as intelligent? Since we cannot, in answering these questions, rely on the considerations of lineage which settle nearly all questions of species membership, they will require very careful examination.

It seems that we want to regard an individual cat which has, through some chance or other, attained human intelligence as protected by the moral rule against homicide. To do so consistently with the species principle requires the adoption of one of two strategies: (1) the existence of such a cat renders the entire species *Felis domestica* an intelligent species, and all of its members protected by the moral rule against homicide (consider the plea such a cat might make on behalf of its less intelligent brethren)[7] or (2) the intelligence of our super-cat might be considered as producing a different species, consisting of him alone, although he is still capable of breeding fertilely with other, less favored, cats. (He may wish to disassociate himself from other cats, and feel humiliated by his bodily likeness to subhuman creatures.) The first of these strategies would be plausible for the claims of dolphins and the like, all of which at least come somewhat close to human intelligence. The second would be more plausible for the claims of cats and dogs.

The second question is what traits are decisive for regarding a given individual as rendering his species intelligent. Self-consciousness (or consciousness of oneself as a subject of conscious states) might be suggested, as a necessary condition of the desire to live.[8] Moral agency is another contender, since moral agents are presupposed by moral discourse as such. Finally, the use of language is the key to the rich kind of life enjoyed by human beings, so that it may be taken as what distinguishes the human from the subhuman. An attractive blend of these last two possibilities is participation in moral discourse: if we discover that Martians argue about the issues discussed in this book, we should be obliged to regard them for moral purposes as human.

The question of which traits are crucial is less important for the species than for other interpretations of the moral rule against homicide, since no attempt is

---

[7] This kind of strategy turns out to be crucial in Vecors (pseud.), *You Shall Know Them*, Rita Barisse, tr. (Boston, 1953).

[8] Michael Tooley thinks that adult polar bears for instance may be self-conscious ("In Defense of Abortion & Infanticide," p. 91). But the only workable criterion of self-consciousness that I can see is the use of a language involving something corresponding to the pronoun "I."

made to draw lines within the human species. But even here it may be crucial—especially on some interpretations of what it is to speak a language—to the status of some nonhumans such as chimpanzees. What seems to be the case is that the distinction between human and nonhuman rests not on any one trait, but on an interlocking set of traits, which will wax and wane as a whole.

Finally, we need to ask (supposing that the relevant traits admit of degree) how much of them is required to make a species one of the human level. (If they do not, we will still have to adjudicate borderline cases.) It is worth noticing that our standards can be more demanding here than for either of the species principle's two rivals. In order to reach minimally tolerable results, the present enjoyment principle will have to demand very little of a creature before treating it as a person; the potentiality principle can ask for more, since what the creature will attain in due course, not what it attains now, is the standard. But the species principle can demand the production of saints, philosophers, musicians, scientists, or whatever else is thought to be the highest embodiment of human nature, since the bulk of the species can gain their morally privileged status through the achievements of their best members, so long as there is not a sharp break between the capacities of the best of a species and members of that species generally. . . .

2. The Present Enjoyment Principle

. . . Caring for those who are persons on the species principle frequently places burdens on those who are persons on narrower principles of which an unwanted pregnancy may be taken as emblematic. It is therefore well worth asking whether a narrower version of the rule against homicide is possible, one, that is, which is not merely an *ad hoc* modification of the rule designed to allow us to kill those whose existence we find particularly burdensome.

An obvious possibility is to drop the reference to the species and to require that a creature be in present possession of distinctively human traits before the killing of such a creature will be deemed homicide. Assuming that what we value human beings for is their capacities for rational and social life, perhaps we should place the kind of value which grounds the moral rule against homicide only on those that (now) have these capacities. Or, again we may be impressed by the various ways human beings (and not animals) insist upon respect for their rights (including the right not to be killed), and feel that those who are incapable of making such appeals (or engaging in such resistance) do not deserve to be treated as persons. Let us call this principle the present enjoyment principle. . . .

3. Infanticide and Our Intuitions

The most striking conflict between the present enjoyment principle and our intuitions—the implication of the principle that infants have no right to live—arises in the specific context of debates about abortion. Many such debates have been conducted within limits imposed by agreed-upon judgments concerning contraception and infanticide. Contraception, it has been agreed, is a morally legitimate way of avoiding undesired parenthood, and infanticide is not. The participants in the controversy have limited themselves to arguing that abortion (or a practice on the borderline between contraception and abortion) is more closely analogous to contraception than to infanticide, or more closely analogous to infanticide than to contraception. But some defenders of abortion have conceded—or even, like Tooley, insisted on and argued for—what has hitherto been the principal contention of opponents of abortion, that abortion and infanticide are essentially the same, and maintained that there are no good grounds for regarding infanticide as a violation of anyone's right to live.

I shall be considering Tooley's views in some detail, since by his willingness to carry the case against fetal rights to its logical extreme, he manages to present the issues underlying the abortion debate with more than ordinary clarity. An examination of the arguments employed by those who have rested their defense of abortion on the fact that the fetus (and not the woman) is unable to envisage a future for itself, talk, enter into social relations, and so on, will show that their premises are brought to their logical conclusion in Tooley's articles.

I shall not here attempt a direct proof that Tooley is wrong, and that infants have a right to live, but shall limit myself to showing that Tooley's attempt to show that the infant cannot be correctly ascribed a right to live (i.e., accorded the protection of the moral rule against homicide) does not succeed. How serious a limitation this is on a moral case against infanticide depends on one's view of the relationship between moral principles formulated by philosophers and socially established moral intuitions of a relatively concrete sort. In my view, the concrete intuitions embodied in our laws and customs, at least insofar as they are shared by the philosopher in his prereflective moments, are entitled to at least as much weight as the moral principles he finds plausible when they are stated in an abstract manner. . . .

What I have done so far is to expound the species principle, and to state and give grounds for rejecting the present enjoyment principle. In particular, I have argued that there is no good reason to deny, as holders of the present enjoyment principle must, that infants have a right to live in principle no different from that enjoyed by adults. With this background, we are prepared to confront the question of abortion.

B. Fetuses

I now turn to an exposition of and defense of the potentiality principle, an attempt to do justice to the competing claims of the potentiality and species principles, and an argument that at least the central cases of abortion are morally unacceptable.

4. Abortion

I shall assume here that infants are protected by the moral rule against homicide. From this assumption it seems to follow immediately that fetuses, and other instances of human life from conception onward, are also so protected, so that, unless justified or mitigated, abortion is murder. For there seem to be only two possible grounds for asserting the humanity of the infant: (1) The infant is a member of the human species (species principle). (2) The infant will, in due course, think, talk, love, and have a sense of justice (potentiality principle). And both (1) and (2) are true of fetuses, embryos, and zygotes, as well as of infants. A zygote is alive (it grows) and presumably is an instance of the species *homo sapiens* (of what other species might it be?), and it will, if nothing goes wrong, develop into the kind of creature which is universally conceded to be a person.

But a number of arguments still have to be answered before the humanity or personhood of the fetus can be asserted with confidence. All of them are reflected in, and lend plausibility to, Joel Feinberg's remark: "To assert that a single-cell zygote, or a tiny cluster of cells, as such, is a complete human being already possessed of all the rights of a developed person seems at least as counter-intuitive as the position into which some liberals [defenders of abortion] are forced, that newly born infants have no right to continue living."[1] These arguments are (1) that if a fetus is a person because of its potential and its biological humanity, spermatazoa and ova must also be considered persons, which is absurd; (2) that personhood is something one acquires gradually, so that a fetus is only imperfectly a person; (3) that there is an adequately defensible dividing point between the human and the nonhuman, the personal and the nonpersonal, which enables us to defend abortion (or "early" abortion) without being committed to the defense of infanticide; and finally (4) that the opponent of abortion himself does not take seriously the humanity of the fetus, an argument *ad hominem*. Insofar as one relies on intuition to establish the wrongness of infanticide, one must come to terms with the contention that the assertion that a fetus is a person is itself counter-intuitive.

1. Michael Tooley argues that if it is seriously wrong to kill infants or fetuses because they potentially possess human traits, it must also be seriously wrong to prevent systems of objects from developing into an organism possessing self-consciousness, so that artificial contraception will be just as wrong as infanticide. But only organisms can have a right to life, although something more like an organism than a mere concatenation of sperm and egg might have a right to something like life. And the same point can be reached if we speak not in terms of a right to life but of a moral rule against certain kinds of killing, for only an organism can be killed.

There is another, more complicated, argument against the contention that a spermatozoon and an ovum, not united, might be protected by the moral rule

---

[1] Joel Feinberg, *The Problem of Abortion,* Introduction [*supra,* p. 4].

against homicide (or would be if infants and fetuses were). Since the moral rule against homicide is a rule that protects rights, it cannot obtain unless there is some specifiable individual[2] whose rights would be violated were it breached. A sperm conjoined with an ovum in this way is not in any sense an individual; therefore it cannot have any rights. For this reason the prevention of such a combination's being fruitful cannot be a violation of the moral rule against homicide. An ejaculation contains many more spermatazoa than could possibly be united with ova, and it is difficult to see the sperm-plus-ovum combinations which do not prevail as somehow deprived of something on which they have a claim.

But it is hard to reject all rights-claims made on behalf of inchoate subjects. It is commonly held to be prima facie wrong to exterminate entire species of animals, and such a wrong could be committed without destroying any individual animal (e.g., by rendering all members of the species sterile). It seems that many of us want to accord to the species as such a right to continue in existence as a species. (Compare the notion that genocide, the destruction of an entire race or ethnic group, is a crime over and above, and indeed apart from, the destruction of individual members of such a group.) How seriously we take talk of the rights of species depends on how seriously we take the interests of species. It will not do to refuse to admit the existence of such interests on the grounds that "a whole collection, as such, cannot have beliefs, expectations, wants, or desires,"[3] since such conditions are not necessary to the existence of interests. We can easily view the perpetuation of a species through its characteristic mode of reproduction as an act, not only of the individual organisms that engage in reproductive activity, but also of the species itself, acting through its members. It is thus possible to attribute an aim of preserving itself to the species as a whole and to see this aim as frustrated when a species becomes extinct.

If so, it seems also that human beings have at least a general duty to procreate, to the extent that it would be wrong to encompass, or to adopt maxims which entail, the dying-out of the human species. (What I have in mind are those who hold that truly virtuous or enlightened persons will abstain from sexual activity or reproduction, a view which has the result that the human species will be continued by fools or sinners, if by anyone.) Thus, it seems, unrealized human possibilities do have some sort of claim on us. Still, the distinction between an individual organism and an unrealized possibility of such an organism is surely great enough to block any attempt to bring such unrealized possibilities within the scope of the moral rule against homicide.

---

[2] "Individual: . . . An object which is determined by properties peculiar to itself and cannot be divided into others of the same kind" (OED). Thus bicycles, embryos of more than four weeks gestation, and infants are individuals, whereas water droplets, zygotes, and amoebas are not. Nor, by a natural extension of the same idea, are pairs of sperm and egg, since these can be split and rearranged to form other pairs.

[3] Joel Feinberg, "The Rights of Animals and Unborn Generations," in William T. Blackstone, ed., *Philosophy and Environmental Crisis* (Athens, Ga., 1974), p. 55.

One can reply similarly to the contention that, since every cell in the body is a potential person (by cloning), and no very great moral weight attaches to the cells in the body, no very great moral weight attaches to potential persons. But even with cloning, an ordinary human cell is not only a merely potential person: it is also a merely potential organism. Belief that creatures which are potentially personal are persons is not the same as believing that anything from which such a creature might arise is also a person. One might, in view of the possibility of cloning, argue that a one-celled zygote is only a potential organism, essentially no different from an ovum or an ordinary cell; but the embryo and the fetus are clearly actual organisms, even if they are supposed to be merely potential persons. Hence, if to be potentially personal is to be a person, they are actual persons as well.

Spermatozoa and ova might be said to be living individuals in a sense. But it is clear that a spermatozoon cannot be considered a member of the human species or a being potentially possessing the traits we regard as distinctively human in the way a fetus or infant can. A developed human being issuing from a sperm alone is a possibility far outside the normal powers of the spermatozoon in the way a developed human being issuing from a fetus or infant is not outside the normal powers of those creatures.

The case of the ovum is more complicated, since parthenogenesis, reproduction from ovum alone, takes place in at least some species. But, apart from considerations involving twinning and recombination (to be discussed below), fertilization still remains a relatively bright line available for distinguishing prehuman organic matter from the developing human organism. Finally, we must remember that sperm and ovum are biologically parts of *other* human individuals (the parents).

2. Perhaps, however, it is a mistake to look for a bright line between prehuman organic matter and a developing human being or person. Perhaps personhood is a quality the developing human creature acquires gradually. This suggestion will always have a considerable appeal to the moderate-minded. For it avoids the harshness, or seeming harshness, of those who would require great suffering on the part of the woman carrying a fetus for the sake of that fetus's rights, while avoiding also the crudity of those who regard abortion as of no greater moral significance than cutting one's toenails, having a tooth pulled, or swatting a fly. Moreover, that abortion is morally less desirable the closer it is to birth—and not simply because a late abortion is more likely to harm the woman—is one of the few intuitions widely shared on all sides of the abortion controversy, and thus not to be despised. That abortion should become harder and harder to justify as pregnancy proceeds, without being ever as hard to justify as is the killing of a person, is a suggestion which ought therefore to be given the most serious attention.

The gradualist suggestion raises a problem of quite general scope. Not only as regards the distinction between prehuman organic matter and a human person, but also as regards that between human beings and brute animals,[4] and that between a dying person and a corpse,[5] our thought is pulled in two different directions. On the one hand, we find it natural to look for sharp, if not radical, breaks between different kinds of being, for evolutionary quanta so to speak. On the other hand, we are suspicious of sharp breaks and look for continuities at every point in nature. On a merely theoretical level, Kant's suggestion—that we regard the principle of continuity and the principle of speciation as regulative ideals or heuristic principles which, although contradictory if asserted together, are nonetheless useful in prompting the advance of knowledge; in other words, that we should look for both continuities and gaps[6]—is most attractive. But it is of very little use to us here.

For what we are looking for is a way of making abortion decisions that offers some hope of rational agreement. And there seems to be no stable, nonarbitrary way of correlating stages of fetal development with justifying grounds. At the stage of development when the embryo most closely resembles a fish, the moderate on the abortion question will want to ascribe it stronger rights than he does fish, but weaker rights than he does full human beings. And the moderate, as I conceive him, regards an infant as a human person, though the difference between a human infant and an infant ape is not palpable. Turning to "indications," it is far from clear why incestuous conception, for instance, plays the kind of role it does in justifying abortion to many moderates.[7]

There is a form of the moderate position which seems to escape this line of attack. Marvin Kohl defines and defends a "moderate feminist" view of abortion, according to which "a living potential human being has the prima facie right to life but . . . the actual right may be reasonably denied in cases of abortion on request."[8] In other words, although the killing of a fetus requires justification, any reason which might prompt a woman to request an abortion is sufficient.

---

[4] See Mortimer Adler, *The Difference of Man and the Difference It Makes* (New York, 1967). As Adler notices, the belief that man differs radically from brute animals would not be refuted by a discovery that dolphins (say) were not brute animals after all.

[5] See Robert Morison, "Death: Process or Event?" and Leon R. Kass, "Death as an Event: A Commentary on Robert Morison," both in Richard W. Wertz, ed., *Readings on Ethical and Social Aspects of Bio-medicine* (Englewood Cliffs, N.J., 1973), pp. 105–109, 109–113.

[6] Immanuel Kant, *Critique of Pure Reason,* A 650ff., B 678ff., Norman Kemp Smith, tr. (London, 1963).

[7] The anomalous role of incest in the abortion discussion is pointed out by Roger Wertheimer, "Understanding the Abortion Argument," *Philosophy & Public Affairs,* 1 (1971), 90. One moderate writer goes so far as to sanction abortion against the woman's will where the pregnancy is incestuous in origin (George Huston Williams, "The Sacred Condominium," in John T. Noonan, Jr., ed., *The Morality of Abortion* [Cambridge, Mass., 1970], pp. 164–165). Cf. pp. 167–168 (compulsory abortion at the husband's option in cases of adulterous conception).

[8] Marvin Kohl, *The Morality of Killing* (New York, 1974), p. 52, n. 4; p. 67. . . .

Kohl concedes that there is nothing in his view to prevent a woman from having an abortion for no reason at all, or more precisely, nothing in his view to permit Kohl to disapprove such abortions. But he sees no need for such a preventative. To suppose that a significant number of women will have frivolous abortions, thinks Kohl, is to be guilty of "the most deadly anti-women bias of all, namely: that unless women are carefully controlled they will kill their own progeny wihout reason because they are not fully rational creatures." In this way, Kohl combines a moderate assessment of the fetus with an avoidance of line-drawing. The issue of how much justification is required for killing a fetus is left to the good sense and discretion of the pregnant woman.

There are three answers to Kohl here: one qualitative, one quantitative, and one conceptual. The qualitative point is that while it is of course extremely unlikely that a woman will have an abortion for a lark, there is also evidence that women and couples (I do not know what Kohl considers a significant number) will sometimes request abortions for uncompelling reasons. There have been reports of women having abortions because the child turned out to be of the "wrong" sex, and because a one-in-twenty chance of a cleft lip was diagnosed.[9] Quantitatively, where permissive attitudes toward abortion prevail, the number of abortions has been known to exceed the number of live births. To defend such results one has to abandon all pretense of moderation about abortion and contend that the fetus has no right to live, even a prima facie one, against its mother. For—and this is the conceptual point—there is a connection between the concept of a right and the maxim that no one shall be judge in his own cause. I should remark in conclusion that I do not regard either women or men as fully rational beings. A writer on ethics who denies the irrational (even perverse) side of the human make-up, including his own, is doomed to irrelevance. In any case, questions of sexual bias, however important they may be in other contexts, are of very little relevance here. For the unborn, at least as much as women, may be victims of prejudice.

Moreover, if personhood or humanity admits of degrees before birth, then it would seem that it must admit of degrees after birth as well. And even if we can manage to block such inferences as that kings are more persons than peasants, Greeks than barbarians, men than women (or women than men), or those with Ph.D.'s than those with M.A.'s, according to this theory we should still expect that adults will be considered more fully human than children. But few hold and fewer still teach that a ten-year-old child[10] can be killed on lighter grounds than an adult. Indeed the killing of small children is often considered worse than the killing of adults. (Although a parent who kills his child is likely to receive a less

---

[9] See Paul Ramsey, "Screening: An Ethicist's View," in Bruce Hilton et al., *Ethical Issues in Human Genetics* (New York, 1975), p. 154, citing Robert W. Stock, "Will the Baby Be Normal?" *New York Times Magazine,* March 2, 1969.

[10] If the child were under ten, G. R. Grice would presumably think he could be (*Grounds of Moral Judgement* [Cambridge, Eng., 1967], pp. 147–150).

severe sentence than someone who kills an adult, this remnant of the *patria potestas* is the result of excuse or mitigation rather than of justification.)[11]

Some philosophers, it is true, might contend that there are degrees of humanity, but that full-fledged humanity is attained well before the age of ten. The question then is at what point full-fledged humanity is attained. Tooley's suggestion—twenty-four hours after birth—is clearly dictated by considerations of convenience rather than by the nature of the newborn. Some might say that first use of speech is a plausible criterion, but the development of linguistic capacities is a process, if anything is, not completed, if ever, until much later in a human being's development than his tenth birthday. If one wishes to fix a point after birth when someone becomes a full-fledged person, it could seem plausible to some thinkers to choose a point after the age of ten—when the nervous system is fully developed, at puberty, or at the conventional age of majority. In any case, the gradualist does not avoid the central problem—that of determining when we have a person in the full sense on our hands.

It has also been argued that a graduation from personhood into nonpersonhood can be observed at the end of life.[12] But the consequences of such a view are scarcely tolerable. For what the analogy with abortion leads to is the killing of old people (1) without their consent, and (2) for the sake of relieving *others* of the burden they pose. Whatever our conclusion might be concerning voluntary euthanasia, and whatever difficulties there might be in fixing a precise moment of death, we cannot admit that anyone who is humanly conscious, or will or may regain human consciousness, is anything but a full-fledged person. This point can be restated in more technical terms as follows. The concept of a person is normally both open-textured and flexible in its application—a corporation for instance may be treated legally as a person for some purposes and not for others. But when the concept of a person is given one particular use, to mark out those creatures whose existence and interests are to be given special protection in the court of morality, there are special reasons weighing in the direction of clarity and rigidity. Whatever the extent to which the interest of a given person might legitimately be sacrificed for the good of the community, it seems intolerable that a creature should be regarded as not a person—and hence of next to no account in moral deliberation—simply because it is or appears to be in the interest of others to so regard that creature. At any rate, to proceed in such a manner would be to overthrow some of the most fundamental elements of our moral tradition.

The difference between early and late abortion is best accounted for, I believe, not by the more nearly human status of the mature fetus as compared with the younger one, but rather by the closer imaginative and emotional link between the

---

[11] There does not appear to be any information on the sentencing of those, other than their parents, who kill children, since statistics on punishment are gathered according to the characteristics of the offender rather than those of the victim.

[12] This is the argument made in Morison.

mature fetus and a born child and hence between such a creature and an adult human than is the case for a young fetus or embryo. Hence, while whatever norms are appropriate to our treatment of fetuses might be applied with greater strictness to them when they are mature than when they are young, nonetheless the fundamental moral status of all fetuses might still be the same.

We might also be faced with a gray area, not an area in which the unborn creature is gradually becoming a person, but one in which its status as a person or as prehuman organic matter (like an ovum) is open to reasonable doubt. The question for interventions in such a gray area would be on which side—of excessive risk or excessive caution—we prefer to err, and the decision might well depend on which end of the gray area we were at, just as the justifiability of firing a gun at an unidentified animal depends on how likely it is that it is a human being rather than a dangerous beast, without its being necessary to invoke the possibility that it might be something in between. In such cases the doctrine called probablism—that the agent is entitled to take the benefit of an honest doubt—and its rivals in the history of casuistry[13] become of relevance. It would seem that one's decision must be based not only on the strength of the doubts in question, but also on the relative importance of the interests at stake, so that even a fairly small possibility that what one is doing is taking the life of a person requires interests of considerable importance to override it.

Germain Grisez takes a more stringent view of this issue. He argues that if someone kills an embryo, not knowing whether or not it is a person (but having some reason to suppose that it is), he is in no different a moral posture than someone who kills what he knows is a person. In his own words, "to be willing to kill what for all we know might be a person is to be willing to kill it if it is a person." And he observes of possibly or probably abortifacient methods of birth control: "If one is willing to get a desired result by killing, and does not know whether he is killing or not, he might as well know that he is killing."[14] (This last case is an extremely complex one, since several layers of doubt may be superimposed upon one another: whether the method chosen results in the destruction of zygotes, whether there is a moral distinction between the prevention of implantation and the outright killing of the zygote, and whether the zygote is a human person within the meaning of the moral rule against homicide. This last doubt is itself complex, having factual, conceptual, and moral elements difficult or impossible to disentangle from one another.)

It does seem to me, however, that there is some difference, although not a large one or one it is desirable to emphasize, even between someone who says, "I know I am killing a person" and someone who says, "I may be killing a person, and

---

[13] One of these rivals is "tutiorism," the view that one must not act unless one is sure beyond a reasonable doubt that one's action is right. There is also a range of intermediate positions.

[14] Germain Grisez, *Abortion* (New York, 1970), pp. 306, 344. Both passages are in italics in the text.

I'd just as soon not find out whether I am." The latter might, after all, find out what he is doing despite himself, and stop doing it. But someone who says, "I may be killing a person, but I'm not satisfied that I am, and if you satisfy me, I'll stop" is in neither of these positions. (He may still be *wrong,* of course.)

3. We are now prepared to address the question of the homicidal character of abortion head on. If we assume the personhood of the human infant when born, is there a point later than fertilization when the life of a human person may be said to begin?

a. One possible dividing point is that stage at which twinning, and the combination of two developing zygotes to form one organism, is no longer possible. If something which we could not help but regard as a person were to split, or merge with another person, in such a manner, we would be compelled, in order to ascertain what (if anything) was the continuation of our original person, to rely on such criteria as memory and character. Bodily continuity would not give an unambiguous result. But since a developing zygote has neither memory nor character, we are left without means of resolving questions of personal identity. The potentiality of acquiring memory or character may suffice to ground a claim of personhood, but only with an organism whose unity and uniqueness is firmly secured.

One can hardly leave the question in this state, however, since the question of dividing (and fusing) selves cuts very deep into the contested question of personal identity. Faced with the possibility of a dividing self, there are, I think, three different possible responses. One can employ such a possibility to undermine our idea of a person, of one being persisting throughout the human life span.[15] Such a course would seem to overthrow a great deal of our moral universe, not least our ethics of homicide. A second strategy is the heroic course of regarding the self before a division as in fact two selves, so that each subsequent self will have the whole pre-split history as part of its past. The implausibility of this position need hardly be labored. The third possibility treats the question of who a given person is (in split cases) as relative to the temporal perspective from which the question is asked. Asked from before the split, the question leads us to pick out a Y-shaped "lifetime," including the pre-split self, and both subsequent branches. Asked from the perspective of afterwards, the question leads us to pick out one of the post-split selves, including the pre-split self as part of its history. The labored quality of this solution means that it can coexist with our concept of a person only when splits remain extraordinary (or a mere possibility): it is a precondition of the kind of language of selves that we have that selves normally neither split nor fuse.[16] Hence there is a legitimate presumption against positions

---

[15] So, following Hume, Derek Parfit, "Personal Identity," *Philosophical Review,* 80 (1971), 13–27.

[16] These strategies are taken from John Perry, "Can the Self Divide?" *Journal of Philosophy,* 69 (1972), 463–488.

The Scope of the Prohibition Against Killing

which require us to admit splitting or fusing selves, and hence also the capacity for fission and fusion enjoyed by the one-celled zygote is a legitimate moral difference between it and an infant or older embryo which warrants our regarding it as not a person. It hardly seems plausible to regard a distinction linked to our very concept of a person as arbitrary.

If this cut-off point is accepted, we are committed to the existence of bits of human biological material which are neither human organisms, nor parts of human organisms, but things which are becoming human organisms. But this of itself provides no warrant for extending the category of "human becoming" to embryos and fetuses generally.[17] For the behavior of the zygote is quite clearly an anomaly, and any way we choose to deal with it is going to produce some degree of conceptual discomfort. At least where the context is an ethical one, the category of "human becoming" seems to be the least uncomfortable way of dealing with the problem. But being an embryo can still be part of the life cycle of members of the human species, as being a caterpillar is part of the life cycle of members of various species of butterfly. For the justification present in the zygotic case for introducing an anomalous concept is not present in the embryonic one.

b. A plausible but troublesome dividing point is suggested by a difficulty of persuasion which the opponent of abortion commonly faces: the invisibility of his client, the fetus. (Consider the frequent occurrence of abortion in lists of crimes without victims.) This difficulty is met, at least in part, by photographs of fetuses *in utero* and of the results of abortion now widely available. But such persuasive devices have a very important limitation: they are of use only when the unborn creature has some semblance of human form.

This line of reasoning suggests that a necessary criterion of personhood is the possibility that the creature regarded as a person be the object of at least a modicum of human sympathy, and that such sympathy cannot in principle be extended to embryonic life lacking any semblance of human form even when the standard of comparison is an infant rather than an adult. (Capacity to evoke sympathy is not of course a sufficient condition for personhood, since we can and do feel sympathy for dogs and horses.) One might buttress this suggestion by noticing its affinities with the historically important distinction between the formed and the unformed fetus[18] and by citing such remarks as that "only of a living human being and what resembles (behaves like) a living human being can one say: it has sen-

---

[17] The move to which I am objecting is made by Lawrence C. Becker, "Human Being: The Boundaries of the Concept," *Philosophy & Public Affairs,* 4 (1975), esp. p. 340.

[18] For a history of this distinction, see John T. Noonan, Jr., "An Almost Absolute Value in History," in *The Morality of Abortion,* pp. 6, 10, 15, 17, 20, 26–27.

[19] Ludwig Wittgenstein, *Philosophical Investigations,* tr. G. E. M. Anscombe (New York, 1966), sec. 281. Cf. secs. 283, 420, p. 226.

sations; it sees; is blind; hears; is deaf; is conscious or unconscious."[19] Further support might be drawn from the psychological observation that fellow-feeling precedes a sense of justice, sympathy a willingness to accord rights.[20] For versions of the case against abortion, like John T. Noonan, Jr.'s latest attempt,[21] which lean heavily on the response to the fetus that is possible by the educated imagination, the appearance of a human-like form would seem to be the crucial dividing point.

On the other hand, it is essential that the limitation on human sympathy in question be in some sense intrinsic and inherent. To allow merely contingent limitations upon our sympathy to delimit those who are entitled to rights would be to sanction every kind of prejudice. One cannot for instance justify—though one can of course *explain*—the difficulty many people have in regarding the fetus as an object of serious moral concern by appealing to the limited nature of the encounters mature humans have with it.[22] At least, when such concern is *possible,* sufficient basis for regarding such concern as appropriate is provided by the consideration that the fetus is a member of the human species which will in due course do the things we normally think of as human. And I know of no way of proving that fellow-feeling for zygotes is impossible, apart from a showing (not available without independent reasons for not regarding the nascent human organism as a person) that such sympathy is so radically inappropriate as to be humanly unintelligible. Certainly some people have believed, if only because the logic of their argument required (or appeared to require) it, that zygotes were human persons.

Supposing fellow-feeling for zygotes to be impossible (in the relevant sense of "impossible"), we are faced with the question of at what point fellow-feeling for the nascent human organism becomes a possibility. And the answer to this question may well depend on the mood in which we approach the data (in particular the photographs). In any case, the latest cut-off point which seems at all defensible on this kind of ground is six weeks. After that point, while one might have difficulty feeling sympathy for a fetus (or indeed an infant or an adult of another race), there seems to be no way of maintaining that such sympathy is impossible or unintelligible.

c. None of the other proposed intra-uterine dividing points is in the end credible. The beginning of heart or brain activity gains its plausibility from the criteria

---

[20] John Rawls, *A Theory of Justice* (Cambridge, Mass., 1972), pp. 490–491.

[21] John T. Noonan, Jr., *How to Argue about Abortion* (New York, 1974).

[22] See Wertheimer, and Ronald Green, "Conferred Rights and the Fetus," *Journal of Religious Ethics,* Spring 1974 (contrasting the sympathy-arousing circumstances in which we view newborn infants). Green sees that the situation of doctors and nurses—who are asked actually to *perform* abortions—is rather different (pp. 70ff.). His response to their problem seems to be to counsel self-deception.

of death, but the cessation of such activity is a criterion of death only because it is irreversible: when, as in the embryonic case, such activity will begin in due course, there is no reason to regard its absense as decisive on the personhood issue. Growth alone, combined with the possibility of future activity, seems sufficient to justify the finding that the distinctively human kind of life is present, unless we are able to find some other reason for denying the immature embryo the status of a person, or are prepared to revert to the present enjoyment principle and treat infants as well as fetuses as subpersonal.

Writing in defense of a brain-activity criterion, Baruch Brody asks:

> Imagine the following science-fiction case: imagine that medical technology has reached the stage at which, when brain death occurs, the brain is removed, "liquefied," and "recast" into a new functioning brain. The new brain bears no relation to the old one (it has none of its memory traces and so on). If the new brain were put back into the old body, would the same human being exist or a new human being who made use of the body of the old one? I am inclined to suppose the latter. But consider the entity whose body has died. Is he not like the fetus? Both have the potential for developing into an entity with a functioning brain (we shall call this a weak potential) but neither now has the structure of a functioning brain. [23]

The answer is that there is this crucial distinction between the two sorts of "weak potential." The weak potential of the fetus includes genetic information, with which the fetus will, in due course, generate a brain of its own. The weak potential of a brain-dead individual is merely the capacity to sustain a brain which can be imposed upon it from the outside.

Of course the absence of brain activity means that the unborn organism is not conscious, but once again this lack of consciousness, being merely temporary, has no decisive moral weight. Conversely, the responses to stimuli observed in very young embryos do not of themselves establish personhood—that must rest on the capacity for distinctively human development—whether or not these responses indicate consciousness in the usual sense. They do, however, like human form, provide a possible basis for sympathy.

d. Quickening has moral relevance of a secondary sort, since it affects the way a woman perceives the life within her, and hence also the social results of the widespread practice of abortion. But it does not represent any biologically or morally significant stage in the development of the fetus itself.

The decisive objection to viability is not that it is unclear precisely when a given fetus is capable of prolonged life outside the womb—with the result that legal definitions of viability are often too late. It is not necessary to demand that the line between persons and nonpersons be perfectly precise, so long as it is clear

---

[23] Baruch Brody, *Abortion and the Sanctity of Human Life* (Cambridge, Mass., 1975), pp. 113–114.

enough to enable us to make intelligent decisions regarding abortion and other such issues; it is necessary to demand only that it not be arbitrary. Nor is it decisive that viability is relative to medical technology. (So, on many views, is death.) The decisive objection to viability is that there is no reason to suppose that the fact that a given creature cannot live outside a given environment provides a reason why depriving it of that environment should be morally acceptable. (And the independent viability of even a born human being is of course a highly relative matter.) The moral significance of viability, like that of quickening, is secondary. It results from our ability to relieve a woman of a burdensome pregnancy while preserving the fetus alive—by premature birth rather than abortion in the usual sense. But the relevance of this point is limited, since prematurity has its hazards.

e. Although birth is given considerable significance by our law and conventional morality (otherwise this section would not have to be written), it is still difficult to see how it can be treated as morally decisive. Considered as a shift from one sort of dependency to another, I believe it has little moral importance. The severance of the umbilical cord removes the child, not from the body of his mother, but from the placenta, an organ of his own for which he has no further use. The social and administrative importance of birth is well accounted for in terms of practicality and discretion irrelevant to the abortion issue. One example is the reckoning of United States citizenship from birth rather than conception; another is the practice of not counting fetuses in the census.

And the grounds given by H. Tristram Engelhardt for distinguishing between fetus and infant, "that the mother-fetus relationship is not an instance of a generally established social relation," whereas "the infant, in virtue of being able to assume the role 'child,' is socialized in terms of this particular role, and a personality is *imputed* to it,"[24] are in fact an argument for drawing the line sometime, say twenty-four hours, after birth. It would be possible to postpone the imputation of personality (signalized by naming) for such a period in order to look for defects and decide whether to kill the infant or spare it. On the assumption, argued for in [*b*], that newborn infants are persons, Engelhardt's argument must therefore be rejected.

Finally, treating birth as the dividing point between the human and the nonhuman places a rationally indefensible premium on modes of abortion designed to kill the unborn infant within the womb, since once removed from the womb a fetus is born, and thus human by the suggested criterion, and is therefore entitled to be kept alive if prospects of success exist. Some might try to get around this by stipulating that whether a creature of the human species counts as an infant (with a right to life) or an abortus (which doesn't have one) depends on the intentions with which it is delivered. This kind of proposal seems quite arbitrary, however.

---

[24] H. Tristram Engelhardt, "Viability, Abortion, and the Difference between a Fetus and an Infant," *American Journal of Obstetrics and Gynecology,* 116 (1973), 432.

4. A final objection to the claim that abortion is homicide is the argument *ad hominem*. Ralph B. Potter, Jr., phrases this objection:

> Neither the church nor the state nor the family actually carries out the practices logically entailed by the affirmation that the fetus is fully human. The church does not baptize the outpouring spontaneously aborted soon after conception. Extreme unction is not given. Funeral rites are not performed. The state calculates age from date of birth, not of conception, and does not require a death or a burial or a birth certificate nor even a report of the demise of a fetus aborted early in pregnancy. Convicted abortionists are not subjected to penalties for murder. The intensity of grief felt within a family over a miscarriage is typically less than that experienced upon the loss of an infant, an older child, or an adult.[25]

But alongside the indications of a less than personal status for the fetus in our laws and customs listed by defenders of abortion, there have been many indications of fetal personhood. Since Potter mentions baptism, it is worth remarking that the Roman Catholic Church ordains the baptism of embryos of whatever degree of maturity, although problems of feasibility naturally arise in cases close to conception because the nascent organism is so small. And Protestants who do not baptize fetuses need not be expressing a lesser evaluation of unborn life, but only a non-Catholic baptismal theology. (Certainly many Protestants have condemned abortion, as have many non-Christians, who of course do not baptize anyone.)

There have been many indications that the fetus has been considered a person in the law of torts and the law of property. One might also notice the holding of a New York court that a fetus is a patient for the purposes of the doctor-patient testimonal privilege,[26] as well as the traditional reluctance to execute a pregnant woman and the accompanying feeling that the killing of a pregnant woman is a peculiarly reprehensible act. And men and women sometimes feel significant grief over the loss of an unborn child. Even contemporary sensibility has little difficulty personalizing a fetus—calling it a "baby," and using the pronouns "he" and "she"—in the context, say, of instruction in the facts of reproduction or in the techniques of prenatal care. Finally, the existence of inherited norms forbidding abortion itself testifies to a recognition of fetal rights.[27]

Some (although hardly all) of the above features of our laws and customs might be explained in other terms. A fetus might be treated as a person with a condition subsequent,[28] in other words as having rights (now), subject to the rebuttable

---

[25] Ralph B. Potter, Jr., "The Abortion Debate," in Donald R. Cutler, ed., *Updating Life and Death* (Boston, 1969), p. 117.

[26] *Jones* v. *Jones,* 114 N.Y.S. 2d 820 (1955).

[27] See also the testimony from art and literature eloquently mustered by Noonan, *How to Argue Abortion,* pp. 17–19.

[28] This suggestion is due to William T. Barker.

expectation that it will mature. So artificial a concept—while no doubt acceptable in law—should not be introduced into morality without very compelling justification. A few might tend to think of a fetus as a person when its interests and those of its mother work together (for instance in the getting of food stamps),[29] while doubting its status only when the mother herself desires to be rid of her child. But it is difficult to see how this could be justified.

Moreover, the practices that seem to point away from fetal personhood can be explained in other ways. To the extent that funeral practices are designed to deal with a severed relationship, they are not necessary when no such relationship has been established. The same can be said of the rule of inheritance cited by Joel Feinberg as counting against fetal personhood: "A posthumous child . . . may inherit; but if he dies in the womb, or is stillborn, his inheritance fails to take effect, and no one can claim through him, though it would have been different if he lived for an hour after birth."[30] It can be explained in part as a special rule of intestate succession designed (inter alia) to guarantee that spurious or doubtful pregnancy will not confuse inheritance. The disposition of its property is in any case a matter of indifference to a dead fetus. Finally, the reluctance of the courts to treat the fetus as a human person in criminal-law contexts other than abortion requested by a pregnant woman[31] can be explained as reflecting an unwillingness of courts to read criminal statutes more broadly than their language requires.

Nor is it necessary that the opponent of abortion insist that abortion be treated, legally or socially, as murder. The difficult situation pregnancy often poses for a woman, and the difficulty many people feel in regarding the fetus as a human person—in particular the understandable difficulty some women have in regarding the fetus as a person separate from themselves—suffice to mitigate abortion to a moral analogue of (voluntary) manslaughter. Another analogy is the special offense of infanticide which exists in a number of jurisdictions.[32] On the other hand, while these mitigating circumstances are quite powerful when the well-being of another human being—the mother—is at stake, the opponent of abortion need have no hesitation in regarding as murder (and demanding the severest punishment for) the killing of embryos where what is at stake is only scientific curiosity—for instance when embryos conceived in vitro are disposed of, or when embryos are conceived in vitro with the intent that they should be so disposed of if they survive.

---

[29] See for instance Burns v. Alcala, 95 S. Ct. 1180, 1187–1189 (Marshall, J., dissenting). Justice Marshall was part of the majority in the abortion decisions.

[30] John Salmond, Jurisprudence, 11th ed., p. 355, quoted in Problems of Abortion, p. 7. Notice the pronouns, however.

[31] Keeler v. Superior Court, 470 P. 2d 617 (Calif., 1970) (killing of unborn child by woman's estranged husband not murder), State v. Dickinson, 28 Ohio St. 65 (1970) (vehicular homicide). The Keeler holding has been reversed by statute, California Penal Code, sec. 187 (feticide under some circumstances murder).

[32] Compare Kant's remarks on bastard infanticide in the Metaphysical Elements of Justice, John Ladd, tr. (New York, 1965), p. 106.

The Scope of the Prohibition Against Killing

When conventional morality is ambiguous, the rational course is to resolve its ambiguities in the most coherent way possible. And the result of so doing is to ascribe a right to live to the fetus or embryo from the sixth week of gestation at the very latest, since this is the latest point at which the possibility of arousing sympathy might be said to begin. It should be added that, where there is even some probability that the life at stake in a decision is that of a human person, some morally persuasive reason, even if not so grave a one as is required to warrant what is clearly homicide, is required if that life is to be rightly taken. . . .[33]

Postscript, 1982

The Ethics of Homicide now seems to me in error on one point. In that book, I took very seriously the suggestion that "a necessary condition of personhood is the possibility that the creature regarded as a person be the object of at least a modicum of sympathy." And thus I concluded that a rational reconstruction of conventional morality would "ascribe a right to live to the fetus or embryo from the sixth week of gestation at the very latest, since this is the latest point at which the possibility of arousing sympathy may be said to begin." My present view, however, is that sympathy is too fickle an emotion to provide a usable criterion of personhood. In particular the enormous variety of modes of life pursued by human beings, and the difficulty I might feel in sympathizing with those whose mode of life I am disposed to regard as defective or degraded, convinces me that, where the right not to be killed is in question, sympathy is not a reliable guide. There remains the question whether, in view of the ability of human zygote to split or merge, the appropriate cut-off point is not about two weeks after conception. It is sobering that so narrow an issue should turn on metaphysical issues of bewildering intricacy.

---

[33] Editor's note: I have regretfully omitted the concluding section of this chapter on "Human Vegetables."

Understanding the Abortion Argument

Roger Wertheimer

A t what stage of fetal development, if any, and for what reasons, if any, is abortion justifiable? Each part of the question has received diverse answers, which in turn have been combined in various ways.

According to the liberal, the fetus should be disposable upon the mother's request until it is viable; thereafter it may be destroyed only to save the mother's life. To an extreme liberal the fetus is always like an appendix, and may be destroyed upon demand anytime before its birth. A moderate view is that until viability the fetus should be disposable if it is the result of felonious intercourse, or if the mother's or child's physical or mental health would probably be gravely impaired. This position is susceptible to wide variations. The conservative position is that the fetus may be aborted before quickening but not after, unless the mother's life is at stake. For the extreme conservative, the fetus, once conceived, may not be destroyed for any reason short of saving the mother's life.

This last might be called the Catholic view, but note that it, or some close variant of it, is shared by numerous Christian sects, and is or was maintained by Jews, by Indians of both hemispheres, by a variety of tribes of diverse geographical location and cultural level, and even by some contemporary atheistical biochemists who are political liberals. Much the same can be said of any of the listed positions. I call attention to such facts for two reasons. First, they suggest that the abortion issue is in some way special, since, given any position on abortion and any position on any other issue, you can probably find a substantial group of people who have simultaneously held both. Second, these facts are regularly denied or distorted by the disputants. Thus, liberals habitually argue as though extreme conservatism were an invention of contemporary scholasticism with a mere century of popish heritage behind it. This in the face of the fact that

This is a shortened version of Roger Wertheimer, "Understanding the Abortion Argument," in *Philosophy & Public Affairs,* vol. 1, no. 1 (Copyright © 1971 by Princeton University Press), pp. 67–95. Reprinted by permission of Princeton University Press.

that position has had the force of law in most American states for more than a century, and continues to be law even in states where Catholicism is without influence. We shall see that these two points are not unrelated.

Now, it is commonly said that the crux of the controversy is a disagreement as to the *value* of fetal life in its various stages. But I submit that this subtly but seriously misdescribes the actual arguments, and, further, betrays a questionable understanding of morality and perhaps a questionable morality as well. Instead, I suggest, we had best take the fundamental question to be: When does a human life begin?

First off I should note that the expressions "a human life," "a human being," "a person" are virtually interchangeable in this context. As I use these expressions, except for monstrosities, every member of our species is indubitably a person, a human being at the very latest at birth. The question is whether we are human lives at any time before birth. Virtually everyone, at least every party to the current controversy, *actually* does agree to this. However, we should be aware that in this area both agreement and disagreement are often merely verbal and therefore only apparent. For example, many people will say that it takes a month or even more after birth for the infant to become a person, and they will explain themselves by saying that a human being must have self-consciousness, or a personality. But upon investigation this disagreement normally turns out to be almost wholly semantic, for we can agree on all the facts about child development, and furthermore we can agree, at least in a general way, in our moral judgments on the care to be accorded the child at various stages. Thus, though they deny that a day-old infant is a person, they admit that its life cannot be forfeited for any reason that would not equally apply to a two-year-old.

On the other hand, significant disagreements can be masked by a merely verbal agreement. Sometimes a liberal will grant that a previable fetus is a human being, but investigation reveals that he means only that the fetus is a potential human being. Or he may call it human to distinguish it from canine and feline fetuses, and call it alive or living in opposition to dead or inert. But the sum of these parts does not equal what he means when he uses the phrase "a human life" in connection with himself and his friends, for in that extended sense he could equally apply that expression to human terata, and, at least in extreme cases, he is inclined to deny that they are human lives, and to dispose of them accordingly.

Implicit in my remarks is the suggestion that one way to find out how someone uses the expression "human being" and related ones is by looking at his moral judgments. I am suggesting that this is a way, sometimes the only way, of learning both what someone means by such expressions and what his conception of a human being is. It seems clear enough that given that a man has a certain set of desires, we can discern his conception of something, X, by seeing what kinds of behavior he takes to be appropriate regarding X. I am saying that we may have to look at his *moral* beliefs regarding X, especially if X is a human being. And I want to say further that while some moral judgments are involved in determining whether the fetus is a human being, still, the crucial question about the fetus is not "How much is it worth?" but "What is it?"

The defense of the extreme conservative position runs as follows. The key premise is that a human fetus is a human being, not a partial or potential one, but a full-fledged, actualized human life. Given that premise, the entire conservative position unfolds with a simple, relentless logic, every principle of which would be endorsed by any sensible liberal. Suppose human embryos are human beings. Their innocence is beyond question, so nothing could justify our destroying them except, perhaps, the necessity of saving some other innocent human life. That is, since similar cases must be treated in similar ways, some consideration would justify the abortion of a prenatal child if and only if a comparable consideration would justify the killing of a postnatal child.

This is a serious and troubling argument posing an objection in principle to abortion. It is the *only* such argument. Nothing else could possibly justify the staggering social costs of the present abortion laws.

It should be unmistakably obvious what the Catholic position is. Yet, and this deserves heavy emphasis, liberals seem not to understand it, for their arguments are almost invariably infelicitous. The Catholic defense of the status quo is left unfazed, even untouched, by the standard liberal critique that consists of an inventory of the calamitous effects of our abortion laws on mother and child, on family, and on society in general. Of course, were it not for those effects we would feel no press to be rid of the laws—nor any *need* to retain them. That inventory does present a conclusive rebuttal of any of the piddling objections conservatives often toss in for good measure. But still, the precise, scientific tabulations of grief do not add up to an argument here, for sometimes pain, no matter how considerable and how undesirable, may not be avoidable, may not stem from some injustice. I do not intend to understate that pain; the tragedies brought on by unwanted children are plentiful and serious—but so too are those brought on by unwanted parents, yet few liberals would legalize parricide as the final solution to the massive social problem of the permanently visiting parent who drains his children's financial and emotional resources. In the Church's view, these cases are fully analogous: the fetus is as much a human life as is the parent; they share the same moral status. Either can be a source of abiding anguish and hardship for the other and sometimes there may be no escape. In this, our world, some people get stuck with the care of others, and sometimes there may be no way of getting unstuck, at least no just and decent way. Taking the other person's life is not such a way.

The very elegance of the Catholic response is maddening. The ease with which it sweeps into irrelevance the whole catalogue of sorrow has incited many a liberal libel of the Catholic clergy as callous and unfeeling monsters, denied domestic empathy by their celibacy and the simplest human sympathies by their unnatural asceticism. Of course, slander is no substitute for argument—that's what the logic books say—and yet, we cast our aspersions with care, for they must deprive the audience of the *right* to believe the speaker. What wants explanation, then, is why the particular accusation of a *warped sensibility* seems, to the liberal, both just and pertinent. I shall come back to this. For the moment, it suffices to record that the liberal's accusation attests to a misunderstanding of the Catholic defense, for it is singularly inappropriate to label a man heartless who wants only to protect innocent human lives at all costs.

There is a subsidiary approach, a peculiarly liberal one, which seeks to disarm the Catholic position not by disputing it, but by conceding the Catholic's right to believe it and act accordingly. The liberal asks only that Catholics concede him the same freedom, and thus abandon support of abortion laws. The Catholic must retort that the issue is not, as the liberal supposes, one of religious ritual and self-regarding behavior, but of minority rights, the minority being not Catholics but the fetuses of all faiths, and the right being the right of an innocent human being to life itself. The liberal's proposal is predicated on abortion being a crime without a victim, but in the Catholic view the fetus is a full-scale victim and is so independent of the liberal's recognition of that fact. Catholics can no more think it wrong for themselves but permissible for Protestants to destroy a fetus than liberals can think it wrong for themselves but permissible for racists to victimize blacks. Given his premise, the Catholic is as justified in employing the power of the state to protect embryos as the liberal is to protect blacks. I shall be returning to this analogy, because the favored defense of slavery and discrimination takes the form of a claim that the subjugated creatures are by nature inferior to their masters, that they are *not fully human.*

Now, why do liberals, even the cleverest ones, so consistently fail to make contact with the Catholic challenge? After all, as I have made plain, once premised that the fetus is a person, the entire conservative position recites the common sense of any moral man. The liberal's failure is, I suggest, due to that premise. He doesn't know how to respond to the argument, because he cannot *make sense* of that premise. To him, it is not simply false, but wildly, madly false, it is nonsense, totally unintelligible, literally unbelievable. Just look at an embryo. It is an amorphous speck of apparently coagulated protoplasm. It has no eyes or ears, no head at all. It can't walk or talk; you can't dress it or wash it. Why, it doesn't even qualify as a Barbie doll, and yet millions of people call it a human being, just like one of us. It's as though someone were to look at an acorn and call it an oak tree, or, better, it's as though someone squirted a paint tube at a canvas and called the outcome a painting, a work of art—and people believed him. The whole thing is precisely that mad—and just that sane. The liberal is befuddled by the conservative's argument, just as Giotto would be were he to assess a Pollock production as a *painting.* If the premises make no sense, then neither will the rest of the argument, except as an exercise in abstract logic.

The Catholic claim would be a joke were it not that millions of people take it seriously, and millions more suffer for their solemnity. Liberals need an explanation of how it is possible for the conservatives to believe what they say, for after all, conservatives are not ignorant or misinformed about the facts here—I mean, for example, the facts of embryology. So the liberal asks, "How *can* they believe what they say? How *can* they even make sense of it?" The question is forced upon the liberal because his conception of rationality is jeopardized by the possibility that a normal, unbiased observer of the relevant facts could really accept the conservative claim. It is this question, I think, that drives the liberal to attribute the whole antiabortion movement to Catholicism and to the Roman clergy in particular. For it is comforting to suppose that the conservative beliefs could take root only in a mind that had been carefully cultivated since infancy to support every extravagant dogma of an arcane theology fathered by the victims of unnatural and unhealthy lives. But, discomforting though it may be, people, and not just Catholics, can and sometimes do agree on all the facts about embryos and still disagree as to whether they are persons. Indeed, apparently people can agree on *every* fact and still disagree on whether it is a fact that embryos are human beings. So now one might begin to wonder: What sort of fact is it?

I hasten to add that not only can both parties agree on the scientific facts, they need not disagree on any supernatural facts either. The conservative claim does not presuppose that we are invested with a soul, some sort of divine substance, at or shortly after our conception. No doubt it helps to have one's mind befogged by visions of holy hocus-pocus, but it's not necessary, since some unmuddled atheists endorse a demythologized Catholic view. Moreover, since ensoulment is an unverifiable occurrence, the theologian dates it either by means of some revelation—which, by the way, the Church does not (though some of its parishioners may accept the humanity of embryos on the Church's say-so)—or by means of the same scientifically acceptable data by which his atheistical counterpart gauges the emergence of an unbesouled human life (e.g., that at such and such a time the organism is capable of independent life, or is motile.)

The religious position derives its plausibility from independent secular considerations. It serves as an expression of them, not as a substitute for them. In brief, here as elsewhere, talk about souls involves an unnecessary shuffle. Yet, though unnecessary, admittedly it is not without effect, for such conceptions color our perceptions and attitudes toward the world and thereby give sense and substance to certain arguments whose secular translations lack appeal. To take a pertinent instance, the official Church position (not the one believed by most of the laity or used against the liberals, but the official position) is that precisely because ensoulment is an unverifiable occurrence, we can't locate it with certainty, and hence abortion at any stage involves the *risk* of destroying a human life. But first off, it is doubtful whether this claim can support the practical conclusions the Catholic draws. For even if it is true, is abortion an *unwarrantable* risk? Always? Is it morally indefensible to fire a pistol into an uninspected barrel? After all, a child *might* be hiding in it. Secondly, though this argument has no attractive secular version, still, it derives its appeal from profane considerations. For what is it that so much as makes it seem that a blastocyst *might* be a person? If the conception of being besouled is cut loose from the conception of being human *sans* soul, then a human soul might reside in anything at all (or at least any living thing), and then the destruction of anything (or any living thing) would involve the risk of killing someone.

I have said that the argument from risk has no secular counterpart. But why not? Well, for example, what sense would it make to the liberal to suppose that an embryo *might* be a person? Are there any discoveries that are really (not just logically) possible which would lead him to admit he was mistaken? It is not a *hypothesis* for the liberal that embryos are not persons; *mutatis mutandis* for the conservative.

At this juncture of the argument, a liberal with a positivistic background will announce that it's just a matter of definition whether the fetus is a person. If by this the liberal means that the question "Is a fetus a person?" is equivalent to "Is it proper to call a fetus a person?"—that is, "Is it true to say of a fetus, 'It is a person'?"—then the liberal is quite right and quite unhelpful. But he is likely to add that we can define words any way we like. And that is either true and unhelpful or flatly false. For note, both liberals and conservatives think it wrong to kill an innocent person except when other human lives would be lost. So neither party will reform its speech habits regarding the fetus unless that moral principle is reworded in a way that vouchsafes its position on abortion. Any stipulated definition can be recommended only by appealing to the very matters under dispute. Any such definition will therefore fail of universal acceptance and thus only mask the real issues, unless it is a mere systematic symbol switch. In brief, agreement on a definition will be a consequence of, not a substitute for, agreement on the facts.

A more sophisticated liberal may suggest that fetuses are borderline cases. Asking whether fetuses are persons is like asking whether viruses are living creatures; the proper answer is that they are like them in some ways but not in others; the rules of the language don't dictate one way or the other, so you can say what you will. Yet this suggests that we share a single concept of a human being, one with a fuzzy or multifaceted boundary that would make any normal person feel indecision about whether a fetus is a human being, and would enable that person, however he decided, to understand readily how someone else might decide otherwise. But at best this describes only the minds of moderates. Liberals and conservatives suffer little indecision, and, further, they are enigmatic to one another, both intellectually and as whole persons. And finally, precisely because with the virus you can say what you will, it is unlike the fetus. As regards the virus, scientists can manage nicely while totally ignoring the issue. Not so with the fetus, because deciding what to call it is tantamount to a serious and unavoidable moral decision.

This last remark suggests that the fetus' humanity is really a moral issue, not a factual one at all. But I submit that if one insists on using that raggy fact-value distinction, then one ought to say that the dispute is over a matter of fact in the sense in which it is a fact that the Negro slaves were human beings. But it would be better to say that this dispute calls that distinction into question. To see this, let us look at how people actually argue about when a human life begins.

The liberal dates hominization from birth or viability. The choice of either stage is explicable by reference to some obvious considerations. At birth the child leaves its own private space and enters the public world. And he can be looked at and acted upon and interacted with. And so on. On the other hand, someone may say viability is the crucial point, because it is then that the child has the capacity to do all those things it does at birth; the sole difference is a quite inessential one of geography.

Now note about both of these sets of considerations that they are not used as proofs or parts of proofs that human life begins at birth or at viability. What would the major premise of such a proof be? The liberal does not—nor does anyone else—have a rule of the language or a definition of "human life" from which it follows that if the organism has such and such properties, then it is a human life. True, some people have tried to state the essence of human life and argue from that definition, but the correctness of any such definition must first be tested against our judgments of particular cases, and on some of those judgments people disagree; so the argument using such a definition which tries to settle that disagreement can only beg the question. Thus, it seems more accurate to say simply that the kinds of considerations I have mentioned explain why the liberal chooses to date human life in a certain way. More accurately still, I don't think the liberal chooses or decides at all; rather, he looks at certain facts and he responds in a particular way to those facts: he dates human life from birth or from viability— and he acts and feels accordingly. There is nothing surprising in such behavior, nor anything irrational or illegitimate.

All this can be said of any of the considerations that have been used to mark the beginning of a human life.

Liberals always misplace the attractions of fertilization as the critical date when they try to argue that if you go back that far, you could just as well call the sperm or the egg a human being. But people call the zygote a human life not just because it contains the DNA blueprint which determines the physical development of the organism from then on, and not just because of the potential inherent in it, but also because it and it alone can claim to be the beginning of the spatio-temporal-causal chain of the physical object that is a human body. And though I think the abortion controversy throws doubt on the claim that bodily continuity is the *sole* criterion of personal identity, I think the attractions of that philosophical thesis are of a piece with the attractions of fertilization as the point marking the start of a person. Given our conceptual framework, one can't go back further. Neither the sperm nor the egg could be, by itself, a human being, any more than an atom of sodium or an atom of chlorine could by itself properly be called salt. One proof of this is that *no one* is in the least inclined to call a sperm or an egg a human life, a fact acknowledged by the liberal's very argument, which has the form of a *reductio ad absurdum*.

These are some of the considerations, but how are they actually presented? What, for example, does the liberal say and do? Note that his arguments are usually formulated as a series of rhetorical questions. He points to certain facts, and then, quite understandably, he expects his listeners to respond in a particular way—and when they don't, he finds their behavior incomprehensible. First he will point to an infant and say, "Look at it! Aren't you inclined to say that it is one of us?" And then he will describe an embryo as I did earlier, and say, "Look at the difference between it and us! Could you call that a human being?" All this is quite legitimate, but notice what the liberal is doing. First, he has us focus our attention on the *earliest stages* of the fetus, where the contrast with us is greatest. He does not have us look at the fetus shortly before viability or birth, where the differences between it and what he is willing to call a human being are quite minimal. Still, this is not an unfair tactic when combating the view that the fertilized egg is a human life. The other side of this maneuver is that he has us compare the embryo with *us adults*. This seems fair in that we are our own best paradigms of a person. If you and I aren't to be called human beings, then what is? And yet the liberal would not say that a young child or a neonate or even a viable fetus is to be called a human life only in an extended sense. He wants to say that the infant at birth or the viable fetus is a one hundred percent human being, but, again, the differences between a neonate and a viable fetus or between a viable fetus and a soon-to-be-viable fetus are not impressive.

The liberal has one other arrow in his meager quiver. He will say that if you call an embryo a human life, then presumably you think it is a valuable entity. But, he adds, what does it have that is of any value? Its biochemical potential to become one of us doesn't ensure that it itself is of any real value, especially if neither the mother nor any other interested party wants it to fulfill that potential.

When liberals say that an embryo is of no value if no one has a good reason to want to do anything but destroy it, I think they are on firm ground. But the conservative is not saying that the embryo has some really nifty property, so precious that it's a horrid waste to destroy it. No, he is saying that the embryo is a human being and it is wrong to kill human beings, and that is why you must not destroy the embryo. The conservative realizes that, unless he uses religious premises, premises inadmissible in the court of common morality, he has no way of categorically condemning the killing of a fetus except by arguing that a fetus is a person. And he doesn't call it a human being because its properties are valuable. The properties it has which make it a human being may be valuable, but he does not claim that it is their value which makes it a human being. Rather, he argues that it is a human being by turning the liberal's argument inside out.

The conservative points, and keeps pointing, to the similarities between each set of successive stages of fetal development, instead of pointing, as the liberal does, to the gross differences between widely separated stages. Each step of his argument is persuasive, but if this were all there was to it, his total argument would be no more compelling than one which traded on the fuzziness of the boundaries of baldness and the arbitrariness of any sharp line of demarcation to conclude that Richard M. Nixon is glabrous. If this were the whole conservative argument, then it would be open to the liberal's *reductio* argument, which says that if you go back as far as the zygote, the sperm and the egg must also be called persons. But in fact the conservative can stop at the zygote; fertilization does seem to be a nonarbitrary point marking the inception of a particular object, a human body. That is, the conservative has independent reasons for picking the date of conception, just like the liberal who picks the date of birth or viability, and unlike the sophist who concludes that Nixon is bald.

But we still don't have the whole conservative argument, for on the basis of what has been said so far the conservative should also call an acorn an oak tree, but he doesn't, and the reason he uses is that, as regards a human life, it would be *morally* arbitrary to use any date other than that of conception. That is, he can ask liberals to name the earliest stage at which they are willing to call the organism a human being, something which may not be killed for any reason short of saving some other human life. The conservative will then take the stage of development immediately preceding the one the liberals choose and challenge them to point to a difference between the two stages, a difference that is a morally relevant difference.

Suppose the liberal picks the date of birth. Yet a newborn infant is only a fetus that has suffered a change of address and some physiological changes like respiration. A neonate delivered in its twenty-fifth week lies in an incubator physically less well developed and no more independent than a normal fetus in its thirty-seventh week in the womb. What difference is there that can be used to justify killing the prenatal child where it would be wrong to kill the postnatal child?

Or suppose the liberal uses the date of viability. But the viability of a fetus is its capacity to survive outside the mother, and *that* is totally relative to the state of the available medical technology. In principle, eventually the fetus may be deliverable at any time, perhaps even at conception. The problems this poses for liberals are obvious, and in fact one finds that either a liberal doesn't understand what viability really is, so that he takes it to be necessarily linked to the later fetal stages; or he is an extreme liberal in disguise, who is playing along with the first kind of liberal for political purposes; or he has abandoned the viability criterion and is madly scurrying about in search of some other factor in the late fetal stages which might serve as a nonarbitrary cutoff point. But I am inclined to suppose that the conservative is right, that going back stage by stage from the infant to the zygote one will not find any differences between successive stages significant enough to bear the enormous moral burden of allowing wholesale slaughter at the earlier stage while categorically denying that permission at the next stage.

The full power and persuasiveness of the conservative argument is still not revealed until we uncover its similarities to and connections with any of the dialectical devices that have been used to widen a man's recognition of his fellowship with all the members of his biological species. It is a matter of record that men of good will have often failed to recognize that a certain class of fellow creatures were really human beings just like themselves.

To take but one example, the history of Negro slavery includes among the white oppressors men who were, in all other regards, essentially just and decent. Many such men sincerely defended their practice of slavery with the claim that the Negro was not a member of the moral community of men. Not only legally, but also conceptually, for the white master, the Negro was property, livestock. He would be inclined to, and actually did, simply point to the Negroes and say: "Look at them! Can't you see the differences between them and us?" And the fact is that at one time that argument had an undeniable power, as undeniable as the perceptual differences it appealed to. Check your own perceptions. Ask yourself whether you really, in a purely phenomenological sense, *see* a member of another race in the same way you see a member of your own. Why is it that all Chinamen look alike and are so inscrutable? Add to the physiological facts the staggering cultural disparities dividing slave and master, and you may start to sense the force of the master's argument. What has been the rebuttal? We point to the similarities between Negro and white, and then step by step describe the differences and show about each one that it is not a morally relevant difference, not the kind of difference that warrants discriminating against a Negro.

The parallels with the abortion controversy are palpable. Let me extend them some more. First, sometimes a disagreement over a creature's humanity does turn on beliefs about subsidiary matters of fact—but it need not. Further, when it does not, when the disagreement develops from differing responses to the same data, the issue is still a factual one and not a matter of taste. It is not that one party prefers or approves of or has a favorable attitude or emotion toward some property, while the other party does not. Our response concerns what the thing is, not whether we like it or whether it is good. And when I say I don't *care* about the color of a man's skin, that it's not *important* to me, I am saying something quite different than when I say I don't care about the color of a woman's hair. I am saying that this property cannot be used to justify discriminatory behavior or social arrangements. It cannot be so used because it is irrelevant; neither black skin nor white skin is, in and of itself, of any value. The slaveholder's response is not that white skin is of intrinsic value. Rather, he replies that people with naturally black skin are niggers, and that is an inferior kind of creature. So too, the liberal does not claim that infants possess some intrinsically valuable attribute lacked by prenatal children. Rather, he says that a prenatal child is a fetus, not a human being.

In brief, when seen in its totality the conservative's argument *is* the liberal's argument turned completely inside out. While the liberal stresses the differences between disparate stages, the conservative stresses the resemblances between consecutive stages. The liberal asks, "What has a zygote got that is valuable?" and the conservative answers, "Nothing, but it's a human being, so it is wrong to abort it." Then the conservative asks, "What does a fetus lack that an infant has that is so valuable?" and the liberal answers, "Nothing, but it's a fetus, not a human being, so it is all right to abort it." The arguments are equally strong and equally weak, for they are the *same* argument, an argument that can be pointed in either of two directions. The argument does not itself point in either direction: it is *we* who must point it, and we who are led by it. If you are led in one direction rather than the other, that is not because of logic, but because you respond in a certain way to certain facts.

Recall that the arguments are usually formulated in the interrogative, not the indicative, mood. Though the answers are supposed to be absolutely obvious, they are not comfortably assertible. Why? Because an assertion is a truth claim which invites a request for a proof, but here any assertible proof presupposes premises which beg the question. If one may speak of proof here, it can lie only in the audience's response, in their acceptance of the answer and of its obviousness. The questions convince by leading us to appreciate familiar facts. The conclusion is validated not through assertible presuppositions, but through our acknowledgment that the questions are *rhetorical*. You might say that the conclusion is our seeing a certain aspect: e.g., we see the embryo as a human being. But this seems an unduly provocative description of the situation, for what is at issue is whether such an aspect is there to be seen.

Evidently, we have here a paradigm of what Wittgenstein had in mind when he spoke of the possibility of two people agreeing on the application of a rule for a long period, and then, suddenly and quite inexplicably, diverging in what they call going on in the same way. This possibility led him to insist that linguistic communication presupposes not only agreement in definitions, but also agreement in judgments, in what he called forms of life—something that seems lacking in the case at hand. Apparently, the conclusion to draw is that it is not true that the fetus is a human being, but it is not false either. Without an agreement in judgments, without a common response to the pertinent data, the assertion that the fetus is a human being cannot be assigned a genuine truth-value.

Yet, we surely want to say that Negroes are and always have been full-fledged human beings, no matter what certain segments of mankind may have thought, and no matter how numerous or unanimous those segments were. The humanity of the slaves seems unlike that of the fetus, but not because by now a monolithic majority recognizes—however grudgingly—the full human status of Negroes, whereas no position regarding the fetus commands more than a plurality. The mere fact of disagreement in judgments or forms of life would not render unsettleable statements about the humanity of fetuses, otherwise the comparable statements about Negroes, or for that matter whites, would meet a similar fate. What seems special about the fetus is that, apparently, we have no vantage point from which to criticize opposing systems of belief.

It will be said by some that a form of life is something not really criticizable by or from an opposing form of life. In this instance the point is without practical relevance, since the differences between the disputants are not so systematic and entire as to block every avenue of rational discussion. Clearly, their communality is very great, their differences relatively isolated and free-floating.

At this stage of the dispute over a creature's humanity, I stand to the slaveholder in roughly the same relation I stand to the color-blind man who judges this sheet of paper to be gray. Our differing color judgments express our differing immediate responses to the same data. But his color judgment is mistaken because his vision is defective. I criticize his judgment by criticizing him, by showing him to be abnormal, deviant—which is not the same as being in the minority. In a like manner we criticize those basic beliefs and attitudes which sanction and are sustained by the slaveholder's form of life. We argue that his form of life is, so to speak, an accident of history, explicable by reference to special socio-psychological circumstances that are inessential to the natures of blacks and whites. The fact that Negroes *can* and, special circumstances aside, naturally *would* be regarded and treated no differently than Caucasians is at once a necessary and a sufficient condition for its being right to so regard and treat them. Thus, while we may in large measure understand the life-style of the slaveholder and perhaps withhold condemnation of the man, we need not and should not condone his behavior.

Liberals and conservatives rail at each other with this same canonical schema. And if, for example, antiabortionism required the perverting of natural reason and normal sensibilities by a system of superstitions, then the liberal could discredit it—but it doesn't, so he can't. As things stand, it is not at all clear what, if anything, is the normal or natural or healthy response toward the fetus; it is not clear what is to count as the special historical and social circumstances, which, if removed, would leave us with the appropriate way to regard and treat the fetus. And I think that the unlimited possibility of natural *responses* is simply the other side of the fact of severely limited possibilities of natural *relationships* with the fetus. After all, there isn't much we can do with a fetus; either we let it out or we do it in. I have little hope of seeing a justification for doing one thing or the other unless this situation changes. As things stand, the range of interactions is so minimal that we are not compelled to regard the fetus in any particular way. For example, respect for a fetus cannot be wrung from us as respect for a Negro can be and is, unless we are irretrievably warped or stunted.

We seem to be stuck with the indeterminateness of the fetus' humanity. This does not mean that, whatever you believe, it is true or true for you if you believe it. Quite the contrary, it means that, whatever you believe, it's not true—but neither is it false. You believe it, and that's the end of the matter.

But obviously that's not the end of the matter; the same urgent moral and political decisions still confront us. But before we run off to make our existential leaps over the liberal-conservative impasse, we might meander through the moderate position. I'll shorten the trip by speaking only of features found throughout the spectrum of moderate views. For the moderate, the fetus is not a human being, but it's not a mere maternal appendage either; it's a human fetus, and it has a separate moral status just as animals do. A fetus is not an object that we can treat however we wish, neither is it a person whom we must treat as we would wish to be treated in return. Thus, *some* legal prohibitions on abortion *might* be justified in the name of the fetus *qua* human fetus, just as we accord some legal protection to animals, not for the sake of the owners, but for the benefit of the animals themselves.

Ultimately, most liberals and conservatives are, in a sense, only extreme moderates. Few liberals really regard abortion, at least in the later stages, as a bit of elective surgery. Suppose a woman had her fifth-month fetus aborted purely out of curiosity as to what it looked like, and perhaps then had it bronzed. Who among us would not deem both her and her actions reprehensible? One might refuse to outlaw the behavior, but still, clearly we do not respond to this case as we would to the removal of an appendix or a tooth. Similarly, in my experience few of even the staunchest conservatives consistently regard the fetus, at least in the earlier stages, in the same way as they do a fellow adult. When the cause of grief is a miscarriage, the object of grief is the mother; rarely does anyone feel pity or sorrow for the embryo itself. Nevertheless, enough people give enough substance to the liberal and conservative positions to justify describing them as I have done as views differing in kind rather than degree.

The moderate position is as problematic as it is popular. The moderate is driven in two directions, liberalism and conservatism, by the very same question: Why do you make these exceptions and not those?

The difficulty here is comparable to that regarding animals. There are dogs, pigs, mosquitoes, worms, bacteria, etc., and we kill them for food, clothing, ornamentation, sport, convenience, and out of simple irritation or unblinking inadvertence. We allow different animals to be killed for different reasons, and there are enormous differences between people on all of this. In general, for most of us, the higher the evolutionary stage of the species or the later the developmental stage of the fetus, the more restricted our permission to kill. But it is far more complicated than that, and anyone with a fully consistent, let alone principled, system of beliefs on these matters is usually thought fanatical by the rest of us.

To stabilize his position, the moderate would have to *invent* a new set of moral categories and principles. A happy amalgamation of the ones we have won't do, because our principles of justice apply solely to the relations between persons. But *how* is one to invent new categories and principles? I'm not sure it can be done, especially with the scanty building materials available. Again, our interactions with fetuses are extremely limited and peripheral, which is why our normative conceptual machinery in this area is so abbreviated, unformed, and up for grabs.

But perhaps this could be otherwise. Close your eyes for a moment and imagine that, due to advances in medical technology or mutation caused by a nuclear war, the relevant cutaneous and membranous shields became transparent from conception to parturition, so that when a mother put aside her modesty and her clothing the developing fetus would be in full public view. Or suppose instead, or in addition, that anyone could at any time pluck a fetus from its womb, air it, observe it, fondle it, and then stick it back in after a few minutes. And we could further suppose that this made for healthier babies, and so maybe laws would be passed requiring that it be done regularly. And we might also imagine that gestation took nine days rather than nine months. What then would we think of aborting a fetus? What would *you* think of aborting it? And what does that say about what you *now* think?

In my experience, when such imaginative exercises are properly presented, people are often, not always, moved by them, different people by different stories. They begin to talk about all of it somewhat differently than they had before, and less differently from each other. However, the role of such conjectures in or as arguments is far from clear. I don't think we discover the justifications for our beliefs by such a procedure. A liberal who is disturbed by the picture of a transparent womb may be acquiring some self-knowledge; he may come to realize how much power being visible and being hidden have for us and for him, and he may make a connection between this situation and the differing experiences of an infantryman and a bombardier. But surely the fetus' being hidden was not the liberal's *reason* for thinking it expendable.

Nor is it evident that such *Gedanken* experiments reveal the causes of our beliefs. Their results seem too unreliable to provide anything but the grossest projections as to how we would in fact react in the imagined situations. When I present myself with such science fiction fantasies, I am inclined to respond as I do to a question posed by Hilary Putnam[1]: If we build robots with a psychology isomorphic with ours and a physical structure comparable to ours, should we award them civil rights? In contrast to Putnam, who thinks we can now give a more disinterested and hence objective answer to this question, I would say that our present answer, whatever it is, is so disinterested as to count for nothing. It seems to me that such questions about the robot or the fetus can't be answered in advance. This seems so for much the same reason that some things, especially regarding moral matters, can't be told to a child. A child can of course hear the words and operate with them, but he will not really understand them without undergoing certain experiences, and maybe not even then. Odd as it may sound, I want to know exactly what the robot looks like and what it's like to live with it. I want to know how in fact we—how I—look at it, respond to it, and feel toward it. Hypothetical situations of this sort raise questions which seem answerable only when the situation is realized, and perhaps then there is no longer a real question.

I am suggesting that what our natural response to a thing is, how we naturally react to it cognitively, affectively, and behaviorally, is partly definitive of that thing, and is therefore partly definitive of how we ought to respond to that thing. Often only an actual confrontation will tell us what we need to know, and sometimes we may each respond differently, and thus have differing understandings.

Moreover, the relation of such hypothetical situations to our actual situation is problematic. My hunch is that if the fetal condition I described were realized, fewer of us would be liberals and more of us would be conservatives and moderates. But suppose that in fact we would all be hidebound conservatives and that we knew that now. Would a contemporary liberal be irrational, unjustified, or

---

[1]Hilary Putnam, "Robots: Machines or Artificially Created Life?" *The Journal of Philosophy*, vol. 61, no. 21 (1964): 668–691.

wicked if he remained adamant? Well, if a slaveholder with a conscience were shown why he feels about Negroes as he does, and that he would regard them as his equals if only he had not been reared to think otherwise, he might change his ways, and if he didn't I would unhesitatingly call him irrational and his behavior unjustified and wicked.

But now suppose that dogs or chimps could and did talk so that they entered our lives in more significant roles than those of experimental tools, friendly playthings, or faithful servants, and we enacted antivivisectionist legislation. If we discovered all this now, the news might deeply stir us, but would we necessarily be wrong if we still used animals as we do? Here, so I am inclined to think, we might sensibly maintain that in the hypothetical case the animals and their relations with us are essentially and relevantly different from what they now are. The capacities may exist now, but their realization constitutes a crucial change like that from an infant to an adult, and unlike that from a slave to a citizen. We would no more need to revise our treatment of animals than we need to apply the same principles of reciprocity to children and adults.

In the abortion case my instincts are similar but shakier. Yet I think that the adamant liberal could reply that what is special about fetuses, what distinguishes them from babies, slaves, animals, robots, and the rest, is that they essentially are and relate to us as bundles of potentialities. So, obviously, if their potentialities were actualized, not singly or partially, but in sufficient number and degree, we would feel differently. But to make them and their situation in respect to us different enough so that we would naturally regard them as human beings, they would have to become what they can become: human beings. In the hypothetical situation, they are babies in a biological incubator, and therefore that situation is irrelevant to our situation. In brief, an argument based on such a situation only restates the conservative's original argument with imaginary changes instead of the actual set of changes which transforms the fetus into a human child.

Viability and the Morality of Abortion

Alan Zaitchik

I t is common for fetal "viability" to be dismissed out of hand as a morally arbitrary or problem-ridden criterion for fetal "personhood." In this essay I want to examine and reject one particular reason often advanced in support of this claim, namely that future medical-technological progress is almost certain to someday render a fetus viable at the earliest stages of pregnancy, perhaps even at conception. Roger Wertheimer writes that "the viability of a fetus is its capacity to survive outside the mother, and *that* is totally relative to the state of available medical technology. In principle, eventually the fetus may be deliverable at any time, perhaps even at conception. The problems this poses for liberals are obvious . . . ."[1] But what exactly are these "obvious problems"? I shall argue that no obvious problems, perhaps no problems whatsoever, follow from the *mere* fact that someday even a fertilized ovum may be viable.

First we must clearly understand what is meant by "viability" and why some, including the United States Supreme Court,[2] have thought viability to be morally significant. Only then can we evaluate the force of "the objection from future medical technology" (hereafter called "the Objection").

From *Philosophy & Public Affairs,* vol. 10, no. 1 (Copyright © 1981 by Princeton University Press), pp. 18–26. Reprinted by permission of Princeton University Press.

[1]Roger Wertheimer, "Understanding the Abortion Argument," *Philosophy & Public Affairs,* vol. 1, no. 1 (Fall 1971), abridged and reprinted in Joel Feinberg, ed., *The Problem of Abortion* (Belmont, Calif.: Wadsworth Publishing Co., 1973), p. 43. Since all the references below are found in the Feinberg collection, I shall use the pagination in Feinberg throughout. Wertheimer's objection is echoed by others; see, for example, John Noonan, Jr., "An Almost Absolute Value in History," *Problem of Abortion,* p. 9, excerpted from John T. Noonan, Jr., *The Morality of Abortion: Legal and Historical Perspectives* (Cambridge, Mass.: Harvard University Press, 1970).

[2]See the Majority Opinion in Roe v. Wade (1973) prepared by Justice H. A. Blackman, *Problem of Abortion,* pp. 192–98. I accept D. Callahan's interpretation of the court's decision as "a definitive declaration of the nonpersonhood of the pre-viable fetus" (*Problem*

I

When it is said that around the end of the second trimester of pregnancy a fetus is viable, it is not being said that the fetus could be *delivered* at that point (and then sustained in an incubator). The fact is that, given current medical techniques, it is often impossible to induce labor or surgically remove a fetus without doing it permanent damage, even though it would be possible to sustain it in an incubator if it somehow managed to be maturely born. Viability, then, does not mean deliverability.[3]

Another thing that viability does *not* mean is this: were the fetus somehow ejected intact from its mother's body it *would* be saved and sustained through artificial means. This sense of "viability" depends upon such factors as the fetus' geographical location (is it near a hospital with an incubator or is it in the middle of the desert?) and the fetus' socioeconomic background (would anyone be both interested in and financially capable of providing it with medical care?). Clearly enough those who want to assign moral significance to viability do not want viability to depend upon morally arbitrary factors such as geography or socioeconomic status. No one would want to say that by flying from Cambridge to Calcutta a woman suddenly gained the right to destroy a formerly "viable" but now "pre-viable" fetus, or that the fetus suddenly ceased to be a person or human, or that it suddenly lost a "right to life." So when we say that a viable fetus is one which could be saved through artificial means, given the current "state of available medical technology" (Wertheimer) we do not mean medical technology

---

of Abortion [first ed.], p. 195). As we shall see, however, one needn't hold the pre-viable fetus to be a nonperson and the viable fetus to be a person just because one views viability to be "morally significant," that is to make a difference as regards which abortions are morally permissible and which are not. Incidentally, it must be noted that today abortions are not performed after fetal viability; in a few years this will no doubt change, partly because medical techniques will facilitate safe abortions in later stages of pregnancy and partly because technological progress will "push back" viability into earlier stages of pregnancy.

[3]If viability did mean deliverability then the "radical feminist" position, which holds that a woman has a right to an abortion even after viability, would be invalid. For in that case the woman would be credited not with a right to "be rid of" the fetus but with a right to have the fetus "gotten rid of," that is, a right to have the fetus destroyed rather than delivered and adopted and cared for by others. And although some might say that the state (or society) could have a compelling interest or right to destroy rather than deliver and care for certain deliverable fetuses, I think almost no one would want to assign the woman an exclusive decisive right to make this decision. It is clear, therefore, that the term "viability" is used in a sense different from that of "deliverability."

Consequently it is misleading of Wertheimer to formulate the Objection as resting upon the eventual *deliverability* of a fertilized ovum (see the quote from Wertheimer at the beginning of this paper). Noonan, too, makes this mistake: "The perfection of artificial incubation may make the fetus viable at any time: it may be removed and artificially sustained" (*Problem of Abortion*, p. 10). This wrongly suggests that viability is "removability *cum* sustainability."

actually available to the particular fetus in question; we mean medical technology *in principle available,* perhaps only somewhere else in the world and only to the wealthy.

So much for what "viability" means; how is this notion used in the controversy over the morality of abortions? Wertheimer and Noonan both assume that it is the "liberal" who uses the distinction between "pre-viable" and "viable," but in fact we can easily imagine a "conservative" application of the distinction. For unlike the "arch-conservative," the "conservative" might allow abortions to save the mother's life—but only before the fetus reaches viability. Or the conservative might allow abortions where the fetus is expected to die shortly after its (eventual) birth, provided that the diagnosis is made and the abortion is performed before the fetus becomes viable. If the Objection holds against the liberal's use of viability it presumably holds against the conservative's application as well. A quite general characterization of the Objection is thus: "How can you (the liberal, the conservative, and so on) hold that an abortion is permissible (in certain circumstances) if the fetus is not yet viable, but is impermissible (in those same circumstances) if the fetus is viable? For viability is relative to the current state of medical technology and will change in the years to come." Nothing in the Objection depends specifically on the question of whether a liberal or conservative use is being made of viability.

Nonetheless, it is convenient to simplify our discussion by pretending that only the liberal is concerned to defend the moral significance of viability from the thrust of the Objection. It is convenient to make this simplification not only because it saves us from having to write "or the conservative" every time we write "liberal," but also because it proves easiest to formulate just *why* the liberal allows abortions in (almost?) all circumstances before viability—namely, that the liberal does not see the pre-viable fetus as a person—and *why* the liberal denies a woman the right to decide on an abortion after viability—namely, that the liberal does see the viable fetus as a person. Furthermore, the claim that the fetus at this or that stage is or is not a person looks to be a very important judgment, and so we expect the Objection to be strongest when directed against the liberal. For the Objection maintains that viability is a morally insignificant cutoff point upon which no important moral distinctions should rest. So if we can rebut the Objection in the liberal's case we shall be confident that the Objection fails vis-à-vis the conservative as well.

Now I think it is clear that the intuitive basis of the liberal's use of the viability notion is simply this. When a fetus has reached the stage of viability, then even though it is *in fact* still inside and part of a woman's body, and even though it is *in fact* many miles and dollars removed from the nearest incubator—that is, although it *would* in all likelihood not enjoy the benefits of current medical technology even if it were prematurely born—nonetheless we can easily *imagine* it already outside its mother's body doing well in an artificial incubator. It is only due to this particular fetus' "bad luck" that it is still trapped inside the body of a woman who wants it destroyed. So it is natural to view the viable fetus as something more than a mere part of its mother's body; it is natural to view it as a person. *For it is only due to this fetus' bad luck that it is not already a person.*

None of this can be said about the pre-viable fetus, argues the liberal. If the pre-viable fetus were suddenly born it would die, no matter where the fetus happened to be and no matter what kind of devoted and sophisticated medical care we would then give it. It is not due to the pre-viable fetus' "bad luck" that it is not already a person; it has not yet reached the stage at which it could be a person.

Against this the Objection goes as follows: if this particular pre-viable fetus were conceived in the year 2079 rather than 1979 it would already be viable. So it *is* a matter of "bad luck" that by your (the liberal's) standards this pre-viable fetus is not already a person, for it is a matter of "bad luck" that this pre-viable fetus is not capable of surviving without its mother's help in some incubator of the future. It is at any rate a matter of bad luck for this pre-viable fetus that current medical technology is not already as sophisticated as it will someday be. *If geographical and socioeconomic handicaps play no role in determining viability (and thus personhood), why should historical fortuities be admitted as legitimate?*

The foregoing is the essence of the Objection, but there is an ancillary motif which should be mentioned before we continue any further. For one could also urge against the liberal a related challenge. Viability is, by its very nature, a changing criterion. A liberal who rests his "liberal" pronouncements in favor of abortion throughout early pregnancy upon the viability criterion will, in time, find himself saddled with a very (ultimately, *extremely*) conservative stand, forbidding (or at any rate denying a woman's right to) abortions, from the earliest stages of pregnancy on. (Mutatis mutandis, the conservative proponent of the viability criterion will soon find himself defending what is today the arch-conservative stand.) It may be thought that this alone should make the liberal wary of the viability criterion.

I believe that this "ancillary objection" can be rebutted in one of two ways. The first is obvious; the ancillary objection has force only if directed against a liberal more committed to allowing abortions throughout early pregnancy than to the viability criterion itself. For if the liberal is *genuinely* committed to the viability criterion he will respond quite adequately by promising to someday accept the "conservative" consequences of the viability criterion.

The second possibility is vastly more complex. Surely the liberal will not see a fertilized ovum as a person, no matter what viability it may someday enjoy. And so one expects the liberal to avoid the ancillary objection by modifying his use of the viability notion: viability is a necessary condition for personhood but is not, on its own, a sufficient condition. Just what, according to the liberal, the other conditions are which, together with viability, might constitute a set of necessary *and* sufficient conditions is a question of the utmost difficulty. I shall soon have some suggestions to make on the liberal's behalf, but we must first return to the core of the Objection and see why historical contingencies can be held to differ from geographical and socioeconomic fortuities.

It has often been noted that participants in the abortion controversy do not really *infer* the personhood or non-personhood of the fetus (at this or that stage of its development) from a general thesis concerning necessary and sufficient conditions for personhood. Rather they react by *seeing* the fetus (at some stage of its development) *as* a person (or non-person).[4] The visual idiom should not mislead us; we are dealing with more than a conceptual classification prompted by visual stimuli. What the liberal is reacting *to* in "seeing" the viable fetus as a person is a complex set of possible interactions between ourselves and the fetus, and what he is reacting *to* in "not seeing" the pre-viable fetus as a person is the absence of these interactions, or rather their impossibility.

Consider the prematurely born baby. We know what it is to fondle it, to feed it, to change its diapers, to get up in the middle of the night to see why it is crying, to invite relatives and friends to visit it, and so on. These interactions are not plausibly recast as a set of logically necessary or sufficient conditions (a *criterion*) for personhood. But it is clearly not "arbitrary" or a matter of "caprice" that, given these interactions between ourselves and the prematurely born baby, we see it as "one of us," as a member of the human community, as a person.

Now the liberal is reacting to the viable fetus in much the same way. He *imagines* the viable fetus having been a bit luckier than it was in fact, having escaped from its mother's womb and found refuge in a sophisticated incubator before its mother got a doctor to destroy it. The liberal imagines the very same interactions as mentioned above occurring between us and what is still in fact a viable fetus rather than a prematurely born baby; after all, imagines the liberal, we could at this very moment be fondling it, feeding it, changing its diapers, visiting it, and so on, rather than deliberating over its destruction. And so the liberal's response is a response to possible interactions that, if the fetus were but a little more fortunate, could already be occurring between us and it.

The Objection threatens the liberal with a trivialization of the notion of "possible interactions" which we "can imagine" as occurring. For isn't it *possible,* can't one *imagine,* that this currently pre-viable fetus should exist at some later date at which it would be sustainable (capable of being fondled, fed, changed, visited) in an incubator? Isn't is *possible,* can't one *imagine,* that current medical technology should be sophisticated enough to make possible these interactions? If what is "possible" or "imaginable" is insensitive to geography, socioeconomics, and the fact that even the viable fetus is in actuality still trapped in its mother's body, why should the limits of the "possible" or the "imaginable" be determined by historical accident?

The liberal should reply in the following way. Clearly enough one *can* imagine all sorts of things, from owning the Brooklyn Bridge to teaching philosophy to

---

[4]Wertheimer is not alone in making this point, pp. 51–54.

a pet chimpanzee. All sorts of things are logically possible, too—Lichtenstein's someday being a world power, creatures from Pluto teaching us how to perform brain transplants, and so on. The issue, however, is not the limits of imagination or possibility but rather the moral relevance or moral significance of certain possibilities and of certain imaginable states of affairs. And it is a fact about the way we generally make our moral judgments that only certain possibilities and only certain imaginable states of affairs are allowed to prompt our moral responses. It is important to note that only those possibilities and imaginable alternatives which we either occasionally witness or which we can actually manipulate are usually admitted as relevant.

Two examples will suffice to show what I mean. For all we know it may someday be possible to revive a person hours after all brain and heart activity has "ceased" by today's standards of detection. We do not on that account refuse *today* to see a person as dead immediately upon the "cessation" (as far we can *today* tell) of brain or heart activity or both. For all we know, someday we shall learn to communicate with porpoises and discover that we can interact with them in many of the ways we interact with each other but with no other species; we may be able to enter into promissory or fiduciary relationships with porpoises. As long as these imaginable possibilities remain nothing more than *logically* imaginable or *logically* possible states of affairs, however, we do not on their account see porpoises as anything more than highly intelligent animals, or see corpses (by our standards) as temporarily incapacitated persons. For we have no experience of the sort imagined; there is nothing we can *do* to realize these logical possibilities in any given actual instance. They are too remote from our actual experience to elicit the conceptual response we would have were they "real possibilities."

Now we do see premature births, and we do know what it is to transport oneself in space; expectant parents often rush off to the hospital in early morning cabs. And we know exactly what we would have to do in order to deliver health services to someone too poor to buy them on his own. All these possibilities are real possibilities for us; we witness them often and can even manipulate them.

But we have no idea how to secure for a twentieth-century fetus the fruits of twenty-first century medical technology. (And we certainly cannot imagine *this* fetus of 1979 being conceived in 2079, for in that case it would have to be some *other* fetus.) The logical possibilities here are as irrelevant to our moral responses, to "how we see things as," as are our logically possible discoveries about porpoises or our logically imaginable ability to "revive the dead."

Is this an "arbitrary" fact? Yes and no. It is "arbitrary" in the way that all of our *basic* moral responses are *"arbitrary,"* that is, it is a non-inferred and non-justifiable general feature of our moral perspectives. But it is *not* an arbitrary judgment (in the genuine sense of "arbitrary") to the effect that some particular type of unfortunate should be excluded from the human community, as would be, for example, the decision to count a black slave as a nonperson.

Historical contingencies, we might say, shape the general framework of "really possible" alternatives that prompt our moral responses, but they do not appear *in* that framework as factors to be manipulated by imagination. The kinds of interactions we may someday see as real possibilities vis-à-vis a fertilized ovum are, like "radically different" scientific theories of years to come, locked away in the future. It may be part of the "arbitrary" natural history of mankind that we shall someday experience them and make our moral responses accordingly, but it is equally part of the natural history of mankind that we dismiss them as incomprehensible and irrelevant in the present.

We can now better see why the "ancillary objection" mentioned above, namely that the liberal surely does not want to *now* commit himself to *someday* seeing the fertilized ovum as a person, is also beside the point. Of course the liberal refuses to commit himself. But he doesn't have to. For viability belongs to a family of features that together determine the response, "That is a person." These considerations include handling, feeding, caring for, talking to, and so on, and it is the supercession of this entire family that is contemplated in the ancillary objection. One may as well ask whether Tooley, who sees personhood as resting upon the possession of a concept of self and of concerns for one's future,[5] would count as a person a creature who had lucid, self-conscious episodes for thirty seconds every 10,000 years but who was as impassive as a rock during the intervals. The experience and praxis which give rise to our conceptual and moral organization of the world around us are simply *too* different from the logically imaginable possibility described to prompt any answer to the question asked. The best we can do is reply that if and when our experience is like that, if and when we interact with such creatures, then we shall know what to say, and what to do.

It turns out, then, that viability is not morally arbitrary just because it is a shifting standard. For relative to the real possibilities we currently have for interacting with a fetus in those ways *generally* used to determine that something is a person, viability guarantees that only *happenstance* has intervened to prevent that judgment. And setting aside happenstance is not morally arbitrary in the least.[6]

---

[5]Michael Tooley, "Abortion and Infanticide," *Philosophy & Public Affairs,* vol. 2, no. 1 (Fall 1972), reprinted in abridged form in *Problem of Abortion.*

[6]This setting aside of happenstance bears obvious relations to a "possible worlds" analysis of Kant's notion of universalizability. For further discussion see S. Lappin, "Moral Judgments and Identity Across Possible Worlds," *Ratio* 20 (1978), and Y. Freundlich, "Who Cares about Identity Across Possible Worlds in Moral Deliberation," *Ratio* (forthcoming). I thank Professor Freundlich for letting me read the article in manuscript.

I want to thank students and colleagues for helpful criticism of an earlier draft read to the Beersheva Forum for Philosophy and Public Policy in November 1979.

Justifying "Wholesale Slaughter"

Donald VanDeVeer

. . . Can one find a nonarbitrary cutoff point in the stages of fetal development from the zygote to the infant such that one can say prior to that point that only a fetus exists and after that point a human being exists? Or is there some point in fetal development such that the stages prior to that point and after that point are so different as to justify radically different treatment? Wertheimer characterizes those who give affirmative answers as "liberals" and those who give negative answers as "conservatives." The gist of the conservative's challenge to the liberal is identified by Wertheimer:

> That is, he can ask liberals to name the earliest stage at which they are willing to call the organism a human being, something which may not be killed for any reason short of saving some other human life. The conservative will then take the stage of development immediately preceding the one the liberals choose and challenge them to point to a difference between the two stages, a difference that is a morally relevant difference.[1]

The possibility of finding differences between successive stages is not excluded a priori; more specifically, Wertheimer's view is:

> But I am inclined to suppose that the conservative is right, that going back stage by stage from the infant to the zygote one will not find any differences between successive stages significant enough to bear the enormous moral burden of allowing wholesale slaughter at the earlier stage while categorically denying that permission at the next stage.[2]

Excerpted from Donald VanDeVeer, "Justifying 'Wholesale Slaughter,'" *Canadian Journal of Philosophy,* vol. 5, no. 2 (October 1975). Reprinted by permission of the Canadian Association for Publishing in Philosphy.

[1]Roger Wertheimer, "Understanding the Abortion Argument," *Philosophy and Public Affairs,* vol. 1, no. 1 (Fall 1971), [*supra,* p. 43.]

[2]*Loc. cit.* This passage and numerous others strongly indicate that Wertheimer's position is roughly that of the conservative, in spite of much detached third-person language about

What is of logical, and not merely psychological, importance is the claim that one will not find features in fetal development which both (a) constitute differences between successive stages and (b) are significant enough to bear the enormous moral burden of allowing wholesale slaughter at the earlier stage while categorically denying that permission at the next stage.

My main concern is an examination of aspects of the argument(s) in which the above claim functions as a premise. . . .

The expression 'morally relevant difference' provokes questions. The conservative need not deny the existence of any morally relevant difference between, say, a neonate and a fetus. He denies that there are any differences between successive stages *significant enough* to bear the enormous moral burden. If someone proposes that the kind of dependence that a late stage fetus has on its mother is relevantly different from a moral standpoint from the kind of dependence that a neonate has on its mother, the conservative may simply deny that the difference is *both* morally relevant *and* also significant enough to do the desired justificatory job. A proposed difference might be rejected by saying, e.g., "well, surely, *mere* geographical relocation won't do." We either accept his rejection as reasonable or we do not. If we do not, we have only a juxtaposition of competing claims. Ideally we need some criterion for what counts as a morally relevant difference of the sort the liberal is demanded to produce. It is a defect of the conservative's use of the strategy of a challenge to the liberal that none is provided or even sketched. The liberal is issued a challenge: here is what you must do to justify differential treatment of, e.g., the neonate and a prior, fetal, stage. However, the possibility of meeting the challenge is, or may be, an ethereal one. If the conservative continues as he begins, by simply rejecting all candidates, it begins to look like no proposal can satisfy his demand. If the challenge is to be taken seriously, one must know what conditions must be satisfied in order to meet the challenge; yet we are not told. If it is assumed *a priori* that no empirical difference between stages could be a morally relevant difference of the requisite sort, then the conservative position is rendered, in a familiar way, immune to refutation. It may be unfair to demand a detailed analysis or criterion for what counts as a morally relevant difference of the requisite sort. The question is a most basic and difficult one of ethical theory. Still, we need not rest content with the conservative's intuitions as to whether proposed differences do the justificatory job. The possibility of *arbitrary* rejection of proposed differences as inadequate is not excluded.

The liberal may reasonably balk, then, at accepting the conservative's demand. We have just seen one reason to do so; another is related to his demanding that the morally relevant difference be one *between successive stages*. Is it reasonable

---

what "the conservative" stresses, and so on. He speaks of the "full power and persuasiveness of the conservative argument" (p. 51), and, generally, waxes most eloquent when describing it, while, in contrast, stopping to concede that the liberal does have a few arrows in his "meager quiver" (p. 50).

to build such a restrictive condition into the challenge to the liberal? More to the point, why think that the condition as stated needs to be satisfied to justify differential treatment of, e.g., the neonate and the fetus? Consider the following schema of development from the zygote to the neonate; successive stages are labeled S_1, S_2, and so on:

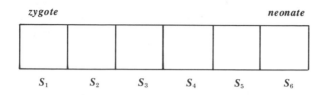

The conservative concedes, we may presume, the logical possibility of there being morally relevant differences of the requisite sort between successive stages. Suppose it to be correct that no such differences between any pair of successive stages exist. However, it remains possible (compatible with the previous supposition) that the requisite differences *do* exist between *non-successive* stages, say between S_3 and S_6, or S_2 and S_6. If so, there would be a justification for, say, permitting elimination of fetuses at stage S_2 or S_3 while regarding as morally impermissible the elimination of neonates, other things being equal. In this view a reason probably insufficient to justify destroying a newborn (e.g., the mother could thereby earn a decent livelihood) may justify the elimination of the fetus at stage S_2 or S_3. The basic point is that if one is going to regard as decisive in a justification the discovery of empirical differences of a morally relevant sort, why must the search for such differences be restricted to an examination and comparison of *successive* stages? The fact, if it is a fact, that the requisite differences do not exist between successive stages does not show they do not exist between non-successive stages.

Analogously, consider an example of a non-moral sort where the reasoning is formally similar. We can imagine various stages in the growth of an animal, e.g., a giraffe, where at each stage the animal is an inch taller than in the previous stage. So, with respect to height the animal at any stage is similar to the stage just preceding; there is no notable difference. Yet it does not follow that there is no notable difference in height between very early and very late stages. Similar remarks can be made with regard to gradual changes of shape, color, hairiness, linguistic competence, and so on. If one restricts one's comparisons vis-à-vis a certain respect to successive stages (where the taxonomy is rather fine or discriminating) of an entity undergoing gradual change, one will simply fail to attend to notable dissimilarities in that respect between widely separate non-adjacent stages. If one's principle for detecting differences precludes at the outset the finding of impressive empirical ones, it will almost certainly prevent one from finding *morally relevant* empirical differences. Thus, the conservative seems to offer a "meetable" challenge to the liberal with one hand, and then removes the possibility of successfully meeting it with the other. His restriction that one must attend only to *successive* fetal stages must be regarded as arbitrary.

More concretely, what impresses many persons who are neither abortionists nor uncomfortably pregnant is that there are substantial differences between the early fetal stages (sometimes called "embryonic" during the first eight weeks) and the neonate. Early on, the embryo is quite indeterminately formed, comparatively speaking; in the early fetal stages there is no heart or brain function and no movement of limbs. The empirical differences between what we may loosely designate as S_2 or S_3 and the neonate are striking. If those impressive empirical differences do not constitute a morally relevant difference, what could? It is one thing to reject implantation of the zygote in the uterus, the presence of all organs, initial heart functioning, "quickening," initial brain functioning, viability, or birth as *the* moment of transition from non-human to human or as marking a sudden and singular alteration of moral status; it is another matter to wink at the imposing difference between an organism that has undergone most or all of these developments and one which has undergone very few or none of them. The result of focusing only on successive stages is to ignore such great differences; more positively, if we must resort to intuitions about what a morally relevant difference of the requisite sort would be, it is clear that just the sorts of differences mentioned above *are* thought by many to constitute a morally relevant difference significant enough to bear the moral burden of radically differential treatment of the entities in question. The approach considered disallows in *a priori* fashion the taking into account, then, of pretheoretical convictions which are of presumptive importance.

It should be observed that the principle of attending to differences between non-successive stages and allowing or requiring radically differential treatment of the stages when the differences are substantial is a consideration implicit or explicit in many common moral judgments, and, for that reason, ought not be dismissed lightly. It is commonly held that insane persons ought not to be held morally responsible for their acts (if insane at the time of the act) or at least not in the same way that sane persons should (where no other exculpating conditions are satisfied). Imagine a person who gradually progresses through various stages (say S_1 to S_6 from being sane to being insane. It is not an uncommon view today to think that there is no "categorical difference" between sanity and insanity, and that such gradual transformations occasionally occur. In such a case, there may be no point where we can confidently say "prior to this point the person was sane, and after, insane." Surely such a fact is not a good reason to conclude that sane persons are really insane or that there is no morally relevant difference which would justify differential treatment for the person at S_1 and the person at S_6. With regard, for example, to being fearful, being stimulus-bound, or exhibiting disordered thought processes, emotional blunting, loss of memory, withdrawal, curious posturing, such features are symptomatic of psychosis when present in extreme forms but more or less common in a token fashion in those thought to be "normal," "sane," and even "healthy." The presence of the extreme forms at, say, S_6 and their absence at S_1 constitutes a morally relevant difference on our ordinary way of thinking (even among many who oppose society's paternalism toward persons at S_6). We may not, to emphasize a point, be able to point to a pair of successive stages and say: "sane here; insane there."

That the differences between adjacent stages in an organism's development are morally negligible or insufficient to justify such differential treatment of those stages is simply not a reason to judge as unjustifiable the radically different treatment of certain non-adjacent stages. If this is one of the liberal's convictions it introduces no new principle of moral consideration; rather it appeals to a principle implicit in common judgments as to when morally relevant differences obtain. From that standpoint the "liberal's" position is, in a familiar sense, conservative (in one meaning, "conservative" describes one who believes that there is a presumption against adopting new policies which require a surrendering of "tried and true" principles), and the approach which fixates only on successive stages to detect morally relevant differences is quite anti-conservative since, if it were consistently applied in analogous cases, it would require a radical revision of certain moral beliefs and, presumably, practice as well. When confronted by the suggestion that their view violates a principle of the Western tradition, those who morally approve abortion need not, then, be cowed into saying "so much the worse for Western values" for not only are "not being innocent" and "not being human" recognized as morally relevant traits but also "inability to think," "inability to decide," and "inability to form intentions." Certain traditional values are, it is arguable, embedded in the liberal position. . . .

Consider an   objection that might be raised. Wertheimer might claim to have anticipated and undermined much of my argument. He recognizes that

> While the liberal stresses the differences between disparate stages, the conservative stresses the resemblances between consecutive stages.[3]

Further, in unpacking his notion that the liberal's argument is the conservative one turned "inside out" he maintains

> The arguments are equally strong and equally weak, for they are the same argument, an argument that can be pointed in either of two directions. The argument does not itself point in either direction: it is we who must point it, and we who are led by it.[4]

These remarks are more misleading than not. The liberal surely has no objection to noting the similarities between consecutive stages; he says, in effect, attend to that comparison as well if you will. The conservative is restrictive; he permits attention only to consecutive stages. There *is* an asymmetry in these two modes

---

[3] Ibid., p. 52.

[4] Loc. cit.

of argument. There is genuine disagreement over the moral relevance of the considerable differences of the disparate stages; hence, the liberal's view on this point is not a turning "inside out" of the conservative's argument, unless turning inside out is tantamount to rejection or denial. Wertheimer argues as if the issue is analogous to different interpretations of an ambiguous drawing: if you start here it looks like a rabbit; start there and it looks like a duck. He implies that you can start where you want. This suggestion tends to render the problem as merely subjective. However, the liberal maintains that the conservative search for requisite morally relevant differences between consecutive stages is arbitrary and myopic, blinding him to impressive differences which are relevant and of considerable moral import; the conservative, at least implicitly, denies that. The arguments of the liberal and the conservative are simply different arguments, not just "one that can be pointed in two directions." The conservative and liberal get to different conclusions because they start with different premises. . . .

A Third Way

L. W. Sumner

T he practice of abortion confronts us with two different sets of moral questions belonging to two different decision contexts. The primary context is that in which a woman chooses whether to have an abortion and a physician chooses whether to perform it; here the focus is on the moral quality of abortion itself. Because this context is one of individual decision we will call the set of moral questions which it contains the *personal* problem of abortion. The secondary context is that in which a society chooses how, or whether, to regulate abortions; here the focus is on the merits of alternative abortion policies. Because this context is one of social decision we will call the set of moral questions which it contains the *political* problem of abortion.

Although the two kinds of problem raised by abortion are distinct, they are also connected. A complete view of the morality of abortion will therefore offer connected solutions to them. In most countries in the West, public discussion of abortion has been distorted by the dominance of two such views. The liberal view, espoused by "pro-choice" groups, holds that (voluntary) abortion is always morally innocuous and (therefore) that the only acceptable abortion policy is one which treats abortion as another variety of minor elective surgery. The conservative view, espoused by "pro-life" groups, holds that abortion is always morally serious and (therefore) that the only acceptable abortion policy is one which treats abortion as another variety of homicide.

Because they define the extremities of the continuum of possible positions, and because each is sufficiently simple and forceful to be advocated by a powerful movement, these established views constitute the familiar reference points in our abortion landscape. Yet neither has managed to command the allegiance of more than a small minority of the public. For the rest of us who are unwilling to embrace either of the extreme options the problem has been the lack of a well-defined

This is a revised version of L. W. Sumner, *Abortion and Moral Theory* (Copyright © 1981 by Princeton University Press), Chapter 4, pp. 124–160. Reprinted by permission of Princeton University Press.

middle ground between them. In contrast to the power of the established views more moderate alternatives may appear both indistinct and indecisive.

Public distrust of the established views is well grounded: neither stands up under critical scrutiny.[1] If their demise is not to leave us without any credible view of abortion three tasks must be successfully completed. The first is to define a third way with abortion and to distinguish it from both of the views which it will supersede. The second is to give it an intuitive defense by showing that it coheres better than either of its predecessors with our considered moral judgments both on abortion itself and on closely related issues. Then, finally, the third way must be grounded in a moral theory. The first two of these tasks will be undertaken here; the more daunting theoretical challenge is confronted elsewhere.[2]

1. Specifications

Despite their opposition, the two established views suffer from similar defects. Collating their failures will provide us with some positive guidelines to follow in building a more satisfactory alternative. The central issue in the morality of abortion is the moral status of the fetus. Let us say that a creature has *moral standing* if, for the purpose of moral decisionmaking, it must be counted for something in its own right. To count for nothing is to have no moral standing; to count for as much as possible (as much, that is, as any creature does) is to have full moral standing. We may, for the purpose of the present discussion, make this rather vague notion more precise by adopting the rights vocabulary favored by both of the established views. We will suppose that having (some) moral standing is equivalent to having (some) right to life. The central issue in the morality of abortion is then whether fetuses have moral standing in this sense.[3]

The conservative view, and also the more naive versions of the liberal view, select a precise point (conception, birth, etc.) as the threshold of moral standing, implying that the transition from no standing to full standing occurs abruptly. In doing so they rest more weight on these sudden events than they are capable of bearing. A view that avoids this defect will allow full moral standing to be

---

[1] I will not be defending this assessment in the present paper. For the arguments see *Abortion and Moral Theory*, chs. 2 and 3.

[2] *Abortion and Moral Theory*, chs. 5 and 6.

[3] The adoption of this working definition of moral standing should not be construed as a concession that rights are the appropriate category for dealing with the moral issues posed by abortion. But since both of the established views employ the rhetoric of rights, there is some point to showing how that rhetoric is equally available to a moderate view. For a generalized notion of moral standing freed from all connection with rights, see *Abortion and Moral Theory*, Section 23.

acquired gradually. It will therefore attempt to locate not a threshold point, but a threshold period or stage.

Both of the established views attribute a uniform moral status to all fetuses, regardless of their dissimilarities. Each, for example, counts a newly conceived zygote for precisely as much (or as little) as a full-term fetus, despite the enormous differences between them. A view that avoids this defect will assign moral status differentially, so that the threshold stage occurs sometime during pregnancy.

A consequence of the uniform approach adopted by both of the established views is that neither can attach any significance to the development of the fetus during gestation. Yet this development is the most obvious feature of gestation. A view that avoids this defect will base the (differential) moral standing of the fetus at least in part on its level of development. It will thus assign undeveloped fetuses a moral status akin to that of ova and spermatozoa, whereas it will assign developed fetuses a moral status akin to that of infants.

So far, then, an adequate view of the fetus must be gradual, differential, and developmental. It must also be derived from a satisfactory criterion of moral standing. Such a criterion must be general (applicable to beings other than fetuses), it must connect moral standing with the empirical properties of such beings, and it must be morally relevant. Its moral relevance is partly testable by appeal to intuition, for arbitrary or shallow criteria will be vulnerable to counterexamples. But the final test of moral relevance is grounding in a moral theory.

An adequate view of the fetus promises a morally significant division between early abortions (before the threshold stage) and late abortions (after the threshold stage). It also promises borderline cases (during the threshold stage). Wherever that stage is located, abortions that precede it will be private matters, since the fetus will at that stage lack moral standing. Thus the provisions of the liberal view will apply to early abortions: they will be morally innocent (as long as the usual conditions of maternal consent, etc., are satisfied) and ought to be legally unregulated (except for rules equally applicable to all other medical procedures). Early abortion will have the same moral status as contraception.

Abortions that follow the threshold stage will be interpersonal matters, since the fetus will at that stage possess moral standing. Thus the provisions of the conservative view will apply to late abortions: they must be assessed on a case-by-case basis and they ought to be legally permitted only on appropriate grounds Late abortions will have the same moral status as infanticide, except for the difference made by the physical connection between fetus and mother.

A third way with abortion is thus a moderate and differential view, combining elements of the liberal view for early abortions with elements of (a weakened version of) the conservative view for late abortions. The policy that a moderate view will support is a moderate policy, permissive in the early stages of pregnancy and more restrictive (though not as restrictive as conservatives think appropriate) in the later stages. So far as the personal question of the moral evaluation of particular abortions is concerned, there is no pressing need to resolve the borderline cases around the threshold stage. But a workable abortion policy cannot tolerate this vagueness and will need to establish a definite time limit beyond which the stipulated grounds will come into play. Although the precise location of the time limit will unavoidably be somewhat arbitrary, it will be defensible as long as it falls somewhere within the threshold stage. Abortion on request up to the time limit and only for cause thereafter: these are the elements of a satisfactory abortion policy.

A number of moderate views may be possible, each of them satisfying all of the foregoing constraints. A particular view will be defined by selecting (a) a criterion of moral standing, (b) the natural characteristics whose gradual acquisition during normal fetal development carries with it the acquisition of moral standing, and (c) a threshold stage. Of these three steps, the first is the crucial one, since it determines both of the others.

2. A Criterion of Moral Standing

We are assuming that for a creature to have moral standing is for it to have a right to life. Any such right imposes duties on moral agents; these duties may be either negative (not to deprive the creature of life) or positive (to support the creature's life). Possession of a right to life implies at least some immunity against attack by others, and possibly also some entitlement to the aid of others. As the duties may vary in strength, so may the corresponding rights. To have some moral standing is to have some right to life, whether or not it may be overridden by the rights of others. To have full moral standing is to have the strongest right to life possessed by anyone, the right to life of the paradigm person. Depending on one's moral theory, this right may or may not be inviolable and indefeasible and thus may or may not impose absolute duties on others.

To which creatures should we distribute (some degree of) moral standing? On which criterion should we base this distribution? It may be easier to answer these questions if we begin with the clear case and work outward to the unclear ones. If we can determine why we ascribe full standing to the paradigm case, we may learn what to look for in other creatures when deciding whether or not to include them in the moral sphere.

The paradigm bearer of moral standing is an adult human being with normal capacities of intellect, emotion, perception, sensation, decision, action, and the like. If we think of such a person as a complex bundle of natural properties, then in principle we could employ as a criterion any of the properties common to all normal and mature members of our species. Selecting a particular property or set of properties will define a class of creatures with moral standing, namely, all (and only) those who share that property. The extension of that class will depend on how widely the property in question is distributed. Some putative criteria will be obviously frivolous and will immediately fail the tests of generality or moral relevance. But even after excluding the silly candidates, we are left with a number of serious ones. There are four that appear to be the most serious: we might attribute full moral standing to the paradigm person on the ground that he/she is (a) intrinsically valuable, (b) alive, (c) sentient, or (d) rational. An intuitive test of the adequacy of any of these candidates will involve first enumerating the class of beings to whom it will distribute moral standing and then determining whether that class either excludes creatures that upon careful reflection we believe ought to be included or includes creatures that we believe ought to be excluded. In the former case the criterion draws the boundary of the moral sphere too narrowly and fails as a necessary condition of moral standing. In the latter case the criterion draws the boundary too broadly and fails as a sufficient condition. (A given criterion may, of course, be defective in both respects.)

Beings may depart from the paradigm along several different dimensions, each of which presents us with unclear cases that a criterion must resolve. These cases may be divided into seven categories: (1) inanimate objects (natural and artificial); (2) non-human terrestrial species of living things (animals and plants); (3) nonhuman extraterrestrial species of living things (should there be any); (4) artificial "life forms" (androids, robots, computers); (5) grossly defective human beings (the severely and permanently retarded or deranged); (6) human beings at the end of life (especially the severely and permanently senile or comatose); (7) human beings at the beginning of life (fetuses, infants, children). Since the last context is the one in which we wish to apply a criterion, it will here be set aside. This will enable us to settle on a criterion without tailoring it specially for the problem of abortion. Once a criterion has established its credentials in other domains, we will be able to trace out its implications for the case of the fetus.

The first candidate for a criterion takes a direction rather different from that of the remaining three. It is a commonplace in moral philosophy to attribute to (normal adult) human beings a special worth or value or dignity in virtue of which they possess (among other rights) a full right to life. This position implies that (some degree of) moral standing extends just as far as (some degree of) this intrinsic value, a higher degree of the latter entailing a higher degree of the former. We cannot know which things have moral standing without being told which things have intrinsic worth (and why)—without, that is, being offered a theory of intrinsic value. What is unique about this criterion, however, is that it is quite capable in principle of extending moral standing beyond the class of living beings, thus embracing such inanimate objects as rocks and lakes, entire landscapes (or indeed worlds), and artifacts. Of course, nonliving things cannot literally have a right to *life*, but it would be simple enough to generalize to a right to (continued) *existence*, where this might include both a right not to be destroyed and a right to such support as is necessary for that existence. A criterion that invokes intrinsic value is thus able to define a much more capacious moral sphere than is any of the other candidates.

Such a criterion is undeniably attractive in certain respects: how else are we to explain why it is wrong to destroy priceless icons or litter the moon even when doing so will never affect any living, sentient, or rational being? But it is clear that it cannot serve our present purpose. A criterion must connect moral standing with some property of things whose presence or absence can be confirmed by a settled, objective, and public method of investigation. The property of being intrinsically valuable is not subject to such verification. A criterion based on intrinsic value cannot be applied without a theory of intrinsic value. Such a theory will supply a criterion of intrinsic value by specifying the natural properties of things in virtue of which they possess such value. But if things have moral standing in virtue of having intrinsic value, and if they have intrinsic value in virtue of having some natural property, then it is that natural property which is serving as the real criterion of moral standing, and the middle term of intrinsic value is eliminable without loss. A theory of intrinsic value may thus entail a criterion of moral standing, but intrinsic value cannot itself serve as that criterion.

There is a further problem confronting any attempt to ground moral rights in the intrinsic worth of creatures. One must first be certain that this is not merely a verbal exercise in which attributing intrinsic value to things is just another way of attributing intrinsic moral standing to them. Assuming that the relationship between value and rights is synthetic, there are then two possibilities: the value in question is moral or it is nonmoral. If it is moral, the criterion plainly fails to break out of the circle of moral properties to connect them with the nonmoral properties of things. But if it is nonmoral, it is unclear what it has to do with moral rights. If there are realms of value, some case must be made for deriving moral duties toward things from the nonmoral value of these things.

The remaining three candidates for a criterion of moral standing (life, sentience, rationality) all satisfy the verification requirement since they all rest standing on empirical properties of things. They may be ordered in terms of the breadth of the moral spheres they define. Since rational beings are a proper subset of sentient beings, which are a proper subset of living beings, the first candidate is the weakest and will define the broadest sphere, whereas the third is the strongest and will define the narrowest sphere. [4] In an interesting recent discussion, Kenneth Goodpaster has urged that moral standing be accorded to all living beings, simply in virtue of the fact that they are alive. [5] Although much of his argument is negative, being directed against more restrictive criteria, he does provide a positive case for including all forms of life within the moral sphere. [6]

---

[4] Or so we shall assume, though it is certainly possible that some (natural or artificial) entity might display signs of intelligence but no signs of either sentience or life. We might, for instance, create forms of artificial intelligence before creating forms of artificial life.

[5] Kenneth E. Goodpaster, "On Being Morally Considerable," *Journal of Philosophy* 75, 6 (June 1978). Goodpaster speaks of "moral considerability" where we are speaking of moral standing. The notions are identical, except for the fact that Goodpaster explicitly refrains from restricting moral considerability to possession of rights, let alone the right to life. Nothing in my assessment of Goodpaster's view will hang on this issue of rights.

[6] In the paragraph to follow I have stated that case in my own words.

Let us assume that the usual signs of life—nutrition, metabolism, spontaneous growth, reproduction—enable us to draw a tolerably sharp distinction between animate and inanimate beings, so that all plant and animal species, however primitive, are collected together in the former category. All such creatures share the property of being *teleological systems:* they have functions, ends, directions, natural tendencies, and so forth. In virtue of their teleology such creatures have needs, in a nonmetaphorical sense—conditions that must be satisfied if they are to thrive or flourish. Creatures with needs can be benefited or harmed; they are benefited when their essential needs are satisfied and harmed when they are not. It also makes sense to say that such creatures have a good: the conditions that promote their life and health are good for them, whereas those that impair their normal functioning are bad for them. But it is common to construe morality as having essentially to do with benefits and harms or with the good of creatures. So doing will lead us to extend moral standing to all creatures capable of being benefited and harmed, that is, all creatures with a good. But this condition will include all organisms (and systems of organisms), and so life is the only reasonable criterion of moral standing.

This extension of moral standing to plants and to the simpler animals is of course highly counterintuitive, since most of us accord the lives of such creatures no weight whatever in our practical deliberations. How could we conduct our affairs if we were to grant protection of life to every plant and animal species? Some of the more extreme implications of this view are, however, forestalled by Goodpaster's distinction between a criterion of inclusion and a criterion of comparison. [7] The former determines which creatures have (some) moral standing and thus locates the boundary of the moral sphere; it is Goodpaster's contention that life is the proper inclusion criterion. The latter is operative entirely within the moral sphere and enables us to assign different grades of moral standing to different creatures in virtue of some natural property that they may possess in different degrees. Since all living beings are (it seems) equally alive, life cannot serve as a comparison criterion. Goodpaster does not provide such a criterion, though he recognizes its necessity. Thus his view enables him to affirm that all living creatures have (some) moral standing but to deny that all such creatures have equal standing. Though the lives of all animate beings deserve consideration, some deserve more than others. Thus, for instance, higher animals might count for more than lower ones, and all animals might count for more than plants.

---

[7] These are my terms; Goodpaster distinguishes between a criterion of moral considerability and a criterion of moral significance (p. 311). It is odd that when Goodpaster addresses the practical problems created by treating life as an inclusion criterion (p. 324) he does not appeal to the inclusion/comparison distinction. Instead he invokes the quite different distinction between its being reasonable to attribute standing to a creature and its being (psychologically and causally) possible to act on that attribution. One would have thought the question is not what we *can* bring ourselves to do but what we *ought* to bring ourselves to do, and that the inclusion/comparison distinction is precisely designed to help us answer this question.

In the absence of a criterion of comparison, it is difficult to ascertain just what reforms Goodpaster's view would require in our moral practice. How much weight must human beings accord to the lives of lichen or grass or bacteria or insects? When are such lives more important than some benefit for a higher form of life? How should we modify our eating habits, for example? There is a problem here that extends beyond the incompleteness and indeterminacy of Goodpaster's position. Suppose that we have settled on a comparison criterion; let it be sentience (assuming that sentience admits of degrees in some relevant respect). Then a creature's ranking in the hierarchy of moral standing will be determined by the extent of its sentience: nonsentient (living) beings will have minimal standing, whereas the most sentient beings (human beings, perhaps) will have maximal standing. But then we are faced with the obvious question: if sentience is to serve as the comparison criterion, why should it not also serve as the inclusion criterion? Conversely, if life is the inclusion criterion, does it not follow that nothing else can serve as the comparison criterion, in which case all living beings have equal standing? It is difficult to imagine an argument in favor of sentience as a comparison criterion that would not also be an argument in favor of it as an inclusion criterion.[8] Since the same will hold for any other comparison criterion, Goodpaster's view can avoid its extreme implications only at the price of inconsistency.

Goodpaster's view also faces consistency problems in its claim that life is necessary for moral standing. Beings need not be organisms in order to be teleological systems, and therefore to have needs, a good, and the capacity to be benefited and harmed. If these conditions are satisfied by a tree (as they surely are), then they are equally satisfied by a car. In order to function properly most machines need periodic maintenance; such maintenance is good for them, they are benefited by it, and they are harmed by its neglect. Why then is being alive a necessary condition of moral standing? Life is but an (imperfect) indicator of teleology and the capacity to be benefited and harmed. But Goodpaster's argument then commits him to treating these deeper characteristics as the criterion of moral standing, and thus to according standing to many (perhaps most) inanimate objects.

This inclusion of (at least some) nonliving things should incline us to reexamine Goodpaster's argument—if the inclusion of all living things has not already done

---

[8] Goodpaster does not defend separating the two criteria but merely says "we should not expect that the criterion for having 'moral standing' at all will be the same as the criterion for adjudicating competing claims to priority among beings that merit that standing" (p. 311). Certainly inclusion and comparison criteria can be different, as in Mill's celebrated evaluation of pleasures. For Mill every pleasure has some value simply in virtue of being a pleasure (inclusion), but its relative value is partly determined by its quality or kind (comparison). All of this is quite consistent (despite claims to the contrary by some critics) because every pleasure has some quality or other. Goodpaster's comparison criterion threatens to be narrower than his inclusion criterion; it certainly will be if degrees of standing are based on sentience, since many living things have no sentience at all. It is inconsistent to base degrees of standing on (variations) in a property and also to extend (some) standing to beings who lack that property entirely.

so. The connection between morality and the capacity to be benefited and harmed appears plausible, so what has gone wrong? We may form a conjecture if we again consider our paradigm bearer of moral standing. In the case of a fully normal adult human being, it does appear that moral questions are pertinent whenever the actions of another agent promise to benefit or threaten to harm such a being. Both duties and rights are intimately connected with benefits and harms. The kinds of acts that we have a (strict) duty not to do are those that typically cause harm, whereas positive duties are duties to confer benefits. Liberty-rights protect autonomy, which is usually thought of as one of the chief goods for human beings, and the connection between welfare-rights and benefits is obvious. But if we ask what counts as a benefit or a harm for a human being, the usual answers take one or both of the following directions:

(1) *The desire model.* Human beings are benefited to the extent that their desires (or perhaps their considered and informed desires) are satisfied; they are harmed to the extent that these desires are frustrated.

(2) *The experience model.* Human beings (are) benefited to the extent that they are brought to have experiences that they like or find agreeable; they are harmed to the extent that they are brought to have experiences that they dislike or find disagreeable.

We need not worry at this stage whether one of these models is more satisfactory than the other. On both models benefits and harms for particular persons are interpreted in terms of the psychological states of those persons, in terms, that is, of their interests or welfare. Such states are possible only for beings who are conscious or sentient. Thus, if morality has to do with the promotion and protection of interests or welfare, morality can concern itself only with beings who are conscious or sentient.[9] No other beings can be beneficiaries or victims *in the morally relevant way.* Goodpaster is not mistaken in suggesting that nonsentient beings can be benefited and harmed. But he is mistaken in suggesting that morality has to do with benefits and harms as such, rather than with a particular category of them. And that can be seen the more clearly when we realize that the broadest capacity to be benefited and harmed extends not only out to but beyond the frontier of life. Leaving my lawn mower out in the rain is bad for the mower, pulling weeds is bad for the weeds, and swatting mosquitoes is bad for the mosquitoes; but there are no moral dimensions to any of these acts unless the interests

---

[9] Goodpaster does not shrink from attributing interests to nonsentient organisms since he assumes that if a being has needs, a good, and a capacity to be benefited and harmed, then that being has interests. There is much support for this assumption in the dictionary definitions of both "interest" and "welfare," though talk of protecting the interests or welfare of plants seems contrived and strained. But philosophers and economists have evolved technical definitions of "interest" and "welfare" that clearly tie these notions to the psychological states of sentient beings. It is the existence of beings with interests or welfare *in this sense* that is a necessary condition of the existence of moral issues.

or welfare of some sentient creature is at stake. Morality requires the existence of sentience in order to obtain a purchase on our actions.

The failure of Goodpaster's view has thus given us some reason to look to sentience as a criterion of moral standing. Before considering this possibility directly, it will be helpful to turn to the much narrower criterion of rationality. The rational/nonrational boundary is more difficult to locate with certainty than the animate/inanimate boundary, since rationality (or intelligence) embraces a number of distinct but related capacities for thought, memory, foresight, language, self-consciousness, objectivity, planning, reasoning, judgment, deliberation, and the like.[10] It is perhaps possible for a being to possess some of these capacities and entirely lack others, but for simplicity we will assume that the higher-order cognitive processes are typically owned as a bundle.[11] The bundle is possessed to one extent or another by normal adult human beings, by adolescents and older children, by persons suffering from the milder cognitive disorders, and by some other animal species (some primates and cetaceans for example). It is not possessed to any appreciable extent by fetuses and infants, by the severely retarded or disordered, by the irreversibly comatose, and by most other animal species. To base moral standing on rationality is thus to deny it alike to most nonhuman beings and to many human beings. Since the implications for fetuses and infants have already been examined, they will be ignored in the present discussion. Instead we will focus on why one might settle on rationality as a criterion in the first place.

That rationality is sufficient for moral standing is not controversial (though there are some interesting questions to be explored here about forms of artificial intelligence). As a necessary condition, however, rationality will exclude a good many sentient beings—just how many, and which ones, to be determined by the kind and the stringency of the standards employed. Many will find objectionable this constriction of the sphere of moral concern. Because moral standing has been defined in terms of the right to life, to lack moral standing is not necessarily to lack all rights. Thus one could hold that, although we have no duty to (nonrational) animals to respect their lives, we do have a duty to them not to cause them suffering. For the right not to suffer, one might choose a different (and broader)

---

[10] Possession of a capacity at a given time does not entail that the capacity is being manifested or displayed at that time. A person does not lose the capacity to use language, for instance, in virtue of remaining silent or being asleep. The capacity remains as long as the appropriate performance could be elicited by the appropriate stimuli. It is lost only when this performance can no longer be evoked (as when the person has become catatonic or comatose). Basing moral standing on the possession of some capacity or set of capacities does not therefore entail silly results, such as that persons lose their rights when they fall asleep. This applies, of course, not only to rationality but also to other capacities, such as sentience.

[11] The practical impact of basing moral standing on rationality will, however, depend on which particular capacities are treated as central. Practical rationality (the ability to adjust means to ends, and vice versa) is, for instance, much more widely distributed through the animal kingdom than is the use of language.

criterion—sentience, for example. (However, if this is the criterion appropriate for that right, why is it not also the criterion appropriate for the right to life?) But even if we focus strictly on the (painless) killing of animals, the implications of the criterion are harsh. Certainly we regularly kill nonhuman animals to satisfy our own needs or desires. But the justification usually offered for these practices is either that the satisfaction of those needs and desires outweighs the costs to the animals (livestock farming, hunting, fishing, trapping, experimentation) or that no decent life would have been available for them anyway (the killing of stray dogs and cats). Although some of these arguments doubtless are rationalizations, their common theme is that the lives of animals do have some weight (however slight) in the moral scales, which is why the practice of killing animals is one that requires moral justification (raises moral issues). If rationality is the criterion of moral standing, and if (most) nonhuman animals are nonrational, killing such creatures could be morally questionable only when it impinges on the interests of rational beings (as where animals are items of property). In no case could killing an animal be a wrong against it. However callous and chauvinistic the common run of our treatment of animals may be, still the view that killing a dog or a horse is morally no more serious (ceteris paribus) than weeding a garden can be the considered judgment of only a small minority.

The standard that we apply to other species we must in consistency apply to our own. The greater the number of animals who are excluded by that standard, the greater the number of human beings who will also be excluded. In the absence of a determinate criterion it is unclear just where the moral line will be drawn on the normal/abnormal spectrum: will a right to life be withheld from mongoloids, psychotics, the autistic, the senile, the profoundly retarded? If so, killing such persons will again be no wrong *to them*. Needless to say, most such persons (in company with many animals) are sentient and capable to some extent of enjoyable and satisfying lives. To kill them is to deprive them of lives that are of value to them. If such creatures are denied standing, this loss will be entirely discounted in our moral reasoning. Their lack of rationality may ensure that their lives are less full and rich than ours, that they consist of simpler pleasures and more basic enjoyments. But what could be the justification for treating their deaths as though they cost them nothing at all?

There is a tradition, extending back at least to Kant, that attempts just such a justification. One of its modern spokesmen is A. I. Melden, who treats the capacity for moral agency as the criterion of moral standing.[12] This capacity is manifested by participation in a moral community—a set of beings sharing allegiance to moral rules and recognition of one another's integrity. Rights can be attributed only to beings with whom we can have such moral intercourse, thus only to beings who have interests similar to ours, who show concern for the well-

---

[12] A. I. Melden, *Rights and Persons* (Oxford: Basil Blackwell, 1977).

being of others, who are capable of uniting in cooperative endeavors, who regulate their activities by a sense of right and wrong, and who display the characteristically moral emotions of indignation, remorse, and guilt. [13] Rationality is a necessary condition (though not a sufficient one) for possessing this bundle of capacities. Melden believes that of all living creatures known to us only human beings are capable of moral agency. [14] Natural rights, including the right to life, are thus human rights.

We may pass over the obvious difficulty of extending moral standing to all human beings on this basis (including the immature and abnormal) and focus on the question of why the capacity for moral agency should be thought necessary for possession of a right to life. The notion of a moral community to which Melden appeals contains a crucial ambiguity. On the one hand it can be thought of as a community of moral agents—the bearers of moral duties. Clearly to be a member of such a community one must be capable of moral agency. On the other hand a moral community can be thought of as embracing all beings to whom moral agents owe duties—the bearers of moral rights. It cannot simply be assumed that the class of moral agents (duty-bearers) is coextensive with the class of moral patients (right-bearers). It is quite conceivable that some beings (infants, nonhuman animals) might have rights though they lack duties (because incapable of moral agency). The capacity for moral agency is (trivially) a condition of having moral duties. It is not obviously also a condition of having moral rights. The claim that the criterion for rights is the same as the criterion for duties is substantive and controversial. The necessity of defending this claim is merely concealed by equivocating on the notion of a moral community.

Beings who acknowledge one another as moral agents can also acknowledge that (some) creatures who are not themselves capable of moral agency nonetheless merit (some) protection of life. The more we reflect on the function of rights, the stronger becomes the inclination to extend them to such creatures. Rights are securities for beings who are sufficiently autonomous to conduct their own lives but who are also vulnerable to the aggression of others and dependent upon these others for some of the necessaries of life. Rights protect the goods of their owners and shield them from evils. We ascribe rights to one another because we all alike satisfy these minimal conditions of autonomy, vulnerability, and dependence. In order to satisfy these conditions a creature need not itself be capable of morality:

---

[13] Melden rejects rationality as a criterion of standing (p. 187), but only on the ground that a being's rationality does not ensure its possessing a sense of morality. Clearly rationality is a necessary condition of moral agency. Thus a criterion of moral agency will not extend standing beyond the class of rational beings.

[14] Whether or not this is so will depend on how strong the conditions of moral agency are. Certainly many nonhuman species display altruism, if we mean by this a concern for the well-being of conspecifics and a willingness to accept personal sacrifices for their good. On p. 199 Melden enumerates a number of features of our lives that are to serve as the basis of our possession of rights; virtually all mammals display all of these features.

it need only possess interests that can be protected by rights. A higher standard thus seems appropriate for possession of moral duties than for possession of moral rights. Rationality appears to be the right sort of criterion for the former, but something less demanding (such as sentience) is better suited to the latter.

A criterion of life (or teleology) is too weak, admitting classes of beings (animate and inanimate) who are not suitable loci for moral rights; being alive is necessary for having standing, but it is not sufficient. A criterion of rationality (or moral agency) is too strong, excluding classes of beings (human and nonhuman) who are suitable loci for rights; being rational is sufficient for having standing, but it is not necessary. A criterion of sentience (or consciousness) is a promising middle path between these extremes. Sentience is the capacity for feeling or affect. In its most primitive form it is the ability to experience sensations of pleasure and pain, and thus the ability to enjoy and suffer. Its more developed forms include wants, aims, and desires (and thus the ability to be satisfied and frustrated); attitudes, tastes, and values; and moods, emotions, sentiments, and passions. Consciousness is a necessary condition of sentience, for feelings are states of mind of which their owner is aware. But it is not sufficient; it is at least possible in principle for beings to be conscious (percipient, for instance, or even rational) while utterly lacking feelings. If rationality embraces a set of cognitive capacities, then sentience is rooted in a being's affective and conative life. It is in virtue of being sentient that creatures have interests, which are compounded either out of their desires or out of the experiences they find agreeable (or both). If morality has to do with the protection and promotion of interests, it is a plausible conjecture that we owe moral duties to all those beings capable of having interests. But this will include all sentient creatures.

Like rationality, and unlike life, it makes sense to think of sentience as admitting of degrees. Within any given mode, such as the perception of pain, one creature may be more or less sensitive than another. But there is a further sense in which more developed (more rational) creatures possess a higher degree of sentience. The expansion of consciousness and of intelligence opens up new ways of experiencing the world, and therefore new ways of being affected by the world. More rational beings are capable of finding either fulfillment or frustration in activities and states of affairs to which less developed creatures are, both cognitively and affectively, blind. It is in this sense of a broader and deeper sensibility that a higher being is capable of a richer, fuller, and more varied existence. The fact that sentience admits of degrees (whether of sensitivity or sensibility) enables us to employ it both as an inclusion criterion and as a comparison criterion of moral standing. The animal kingdom presents us with a hierarchy of sentience. Nonsentient beings have no moral standing; among sentient beings the more developed have greater standing than the less developed, the upper limit being occupied by the paradigm of a normal adult human being. Although sentience is the criterion of moral standing, it is also possible to explain the relevance of rationality. The evolutionary order is one of ascending intelligence. Since rationality expands a creature's interests, it is a reliable indicator of the degree of moral standing which that creature possesses. Creatures less rational than human beings do not altogether lack standing, but they do lack full standing.

An analysis of degrees of standing would require a graded right to life, in which the strength of the right varied inversely with the range of considerations capable of overriding it. The details of any such analysis will be complex and need not be worked out here. However, it seems that we are committed to extending (some) moral standing at least to all vertebrate animals, and also to counting higher animals for more than lower.[15] Thus we should expect the higher vertebrates (mammals) to merit greater protection of life than the lower (fish, reptiles, amphibia, birds) and we should also expect the higher mammals (primates, cetaceans) to merit greater protection of life than the lower (canines, felines, etc.). Crude as this division may be, it seems to accord reasonably well with most people's intuitions that in our moral reasoning paramecia and horseflies count for nothing, dogs and cats count for something, chimpanzees and dolphins count for more, and human beings count for most of all.

A criterion of sentience can thus allow for the gradual emergence of moral standing in the order of nature. It can explain why no moral issues arise (directly) in our dealings with inanimate objects, plants, and the simpler forms of animal life. It can also function as a moral guideline in our encounters with novel life forms on other planets. If the creatures we meet have interests and are capable of enjoyment and suffering, we must grant them some moral standing. We thereby constrain ourselves not to exploit them ruthlessly for our own advantage. The kind of standing that they deserve may be determined by the range and depth of their sensibility, and in ordinary circumstances this will vary with their intelligence. We should therefore recognize as equals beings who are as rational and sensitive as ourselves. The criterion also implies that if we encounter creatures who are rational but nonsentient—who utterly lack affect and desire—nothing we can do will adversely affect such creatures (in morally relevant ways). We would be entitled, for instance, to treat them as a species of organic computer. The same obviously holds for forms of artificial intelligence; in deciding whether to extend moral standing to sophisticated machines, the question (as Bentham put it) is not whether they can reason but whether they can suffer.

A criterion of sentience also requires gentle usage of the severely abnormal. Cognitive disabilities and disorders may impair a person's range of sensibility, but they do not generally reduce that person to the level of a nonsentient being. Even the grossly retarded or deranged will still be capable of some forms of enjoyment and suffering and thus will still possess (some) moral standing in their own right. This standing diminishes to the vanishing point only when sentience is entirely

---

[15] It is unclear at present whether invertebrates are capable of feeling pain, though the discovery of endorphins (opiates manufactured by the body) even in very simple organisms suggests that they may be. If so, then we are committed to extending (some) moral standing to invertebrates as well.

lost or never gained in the first place. If all affect and responsivity are absent, and if they cannot be engendered, then (but only then) are we no longer dealing with a sentient creature. This verdict accords well with the contemporary trend toward defining death in terms of the permanent loss of cerebral functioning. Although such patients are in one obvious sense still alive (their blood circulates and is oxygenated), in the morally relevant sense they are now beyond our reach, for we can cause them neither good nor ill. A criterion of life would require us to continue treating them as beings with (full?) moral standing, whereas a criterion of rationality would withdraw that standing when reason was lost even though sensibility should remain. Again a criterion of sentience enables us to find a middle way.

Fastening upon sentience as the criterion for possession of a right to life thus opens up the possibility of a reasonable and moderate treatment of moral problems other than abortion, problems pertaining to the treatment of nonhuman animals, extraterrestrial life, artificial intelligence, "defective" human beings, and persons at the end of life. We need now to trace out its implications for the fetus.

3. The Morality
of Abortion

The adoption of sentience as a criterion determines the location of a threshold of moral standing. Since sentience admits of degrees, we can in principle construct a continuum ranging from fully sentient creatures at one extreme to completely nonsentient creatures at the other. The threshold of moral standing is that area of the continuum through which sentience fades into nonsentience. In phylogenesis the continuum extends from homo sapiens to the simple animals and plants, and the threshold area is the boundary between vertebrates and invertebrates. In pathology the continuum extends from the fully normal to the totally incapacitated, and the threshold area is the transition from consciousness to unconsciousness. Human ontogenesis also presents us with a continuum from adult to zygote. The threshold area will be the stage at which sentience first emerges, but where is that to be located?

A mental life is built upon a physical base. The capacity for sentience is present only when the necessary physiological structures are present. Physiology, and in particular neurophysiology, is our principal guide in locating a threshold in the phylogenetic continuum. Like a stereo system, the brain of our paradigm sentient being is a set of connected components. These components may be roughly sorted into three groups: forebrain (cerebral hemispheres, thalamus, hypothalamus, amygdala), midbrain (cerebellum), and brainstem (upper part of the spinal cord, pineal and pituitary glands). The brainstem and midbrain play no direct role in the individual's conscious life; their various parts regulate homeostasis (temperature, respiration, heartbeat, etc.), secrete hormones, make reflex connections, route nerves, coordinate motor activities, and so on. All of these functions can be carried on in the total absence of consciousness. Cognitive, perceptual, and voluntary motor functions are all localized in the forebrain, more particularly in the cerebral cortex. Sensation (pleasure/pain), emotion, and basic drives (hunger, thirst, sex, etc.) are controlled by subcortical areas in the forebrain. Although the nerves that transmit pleasure/pain impulses are routed through the cortex, their ultimate destination is the limbic system (amygdala, hypothalamus). The most primitive forms of sentience are thus possible in the absence of cortical activity.

Possession of particular neural structures cannot serve as a criterion of moral standing, for we cannot rule out encounters with sentient beings whose structures are quite different from ours. But in all of the species with which we are familiar, the components of the forebrain (or some analogues) are the minimal conditions of sentience. Thus the evolution of the forebrain serves as an indicator of the kind and degree of sentience possessed by a particular animal species. When we turn to human ontogenesis we may rely on the same indicator.

The normal gestation period for our species is 280 days from the onset of the last menstrual period to birth. This duration is usually divided into three equal trimesters of approximately thirteen weeks each. A zygote has no central nervous system of any sort. The spinal cord makes its first appearance early in the embryonic period (third week), and the major divisions between forebrain, midbrain, and brainstem are evident by the end of the eighth week. At the conclusion of the first trimester virtually all of the major neural components can be clearly differentiated and EEG activity is detectable. The months to follow are marked chiefly by the growth and elaboration of the cerebral hemispheres, especially the cortex. The brain of a seven-month fetus is indistinguishable, at least in its gross anatomy, from that of a newborn infant. Furthermore, by the seventh month most of the neurons that the individual's brain will contain during its entire lifetime are already in existence. In the newborn the brain is closer than any other organ to its mature level of development.

There is no doubt that a newborn infant is sentient—that it feels hunger, thirst, physical pain, the pleasure of sucking, and other agreeable and disagreeable sensations. There is also no doubt that a zygote, and also an embryo, are presentient. It is difficult to locate with accuracy the stage during which feeling first emerges in fetal development. The structure of the fetal brain, including the cortex, is well laid down by the end of the second trimester. But there is reason to expect the more primitive and ancient parts of that brain to function before the rest. The needs of the fetus dictate the order of appearance of neural functions. Thus the brainstem is established and functioning first, since it is required for the regulation of heartbeat and other metabolic processes. Since the mammalian fetus develops in an enclosed and protected environment, cognition and perception are not essential for survival and their advent is delayed. It is therefore not surprising that the cortex, the most complex part of the brain and the least important to the fetus, is the last to develop to an operational level.

Simple pleasure/pain sensations would seem to occupy a medial position in this priority ranking. They are localized in a part of the brain that is more primitive than the cortex, but they could have little practical role for a being that is by and large unable either to seek pleasurable stimuli or to avoid painful ones. Behavioral evidence is by its very nature ambiguous. Before the end of the first trimester, the fetus will react to unpleasant stimuli by flinching and withdrawing. However, this reaction is probably a reflex that is entirely automatic. How are we to tell when mere reflex has crossed over into consciousness? The information we now possess does not enable us to date with accuracy the emergence of fetal sentience. Of some judgments, however, we can be reasonably confident. First-trimester fetuses are clearly not yet sentient. Third-trimester fetuses probably possess some degree of sentience, however minimal. The threshold of sentience thus appears to fall in the second trimester. More ancient and primitive than cognition, the ability to discriminate simple sensations of pleasure and pain is probably the first form of consciousness to appear in the ontogenetic order. Further, when sentience emerges it does not do so suddenly. The best we can hope for is to locate a threshold stage or period in the second trimester. It is at present unclear just how far into that trimester this stage occurs.

The phylogenetic and pathological continua yield us clear cases at the extremes and unclear cases in the middle. The ontogenetic continuum does the same. Because there is no quantum leap into consciousness during fetal development, there is no clean and sharp boundary between sentient and nonsentient fetuses. There is therefore no precise point at which a fetus acquires moral standing. More and better information may enable us to locate the threshold stage ever more accurately, but it will never collapse that stage into a point. We are therefore inevitably confronted with a class of fetuses around the threshold stage whose sentience, and therefore whose moral status, is indeterminate.

A criterion based on sentience enables us to explain the status of other putative thresholds. Neither conception nor birth marks the transition from a presentient to a sentient being. A zygote has not one whit more consciousness than the gametes out of which it is formed. Likewise, although a neonate has more opportunity to employ its powers, it also has no greater capacity for sensation than a full-term fetus. Of thresholds located during gestation, quickening is the perception of fetal movement that is probably reflex and therefore preconscious. Only viability has some relevance, though at one remove. A fetus is viable when it is equipped to survive in the outside world. A being that is aware of, and can respond to, its own inner states is able to communicate its needs to others. This ability is of no use in utero but may aid survival in an extrauterine environment. A fetus is therefore probably sentient by the conventional stage of viability (around the end of the second trimester). Viability can therefore serve as a (rough) indicator of moral standing.

Our common moral consciousness locates contraception and infanticide in quite different moral categories. This fact suggests implicit recognition of a basic asymmetry between choosing not to create a new life in the first place and choosing to destroy a new life once it has been created. The boundary between the two kinds of act is the threshold at which that life gains moral protection. Since gametes lack moral standing, contraception (however it is carried out) merely prevents the creation of a new person. Since an infant has moral standing, infanticide (however it is carried out) destroys a new person. A second-trimester threshold of moral standing introduces this asymmetry into the moral assessment of abortion. We may define an early abortion as one performed sometime during the first trimester or early in the second, and a late abortion as one performed sometime late in the second trimester or during the third. An early abortion belongs in the same moral category as contraception: it prevents the emergence of a new being with moral standing. A late abortion belongs in the same moral category as infanticide: it terminates the life of a new being with moral standing. The threshold of sentience thus extends the morality of contraception forward to cover early abortion and extends the morality of infanticide backward to cover late abortion. One of the sentiments voiced by many people who contemplate the problem of abortion is that early abortions are importantly different from late ones. The abortion techniques of the first trimester (the IUD, menstrual extraction, vacuum aspiration) are not to be treated as cases of homicide. Those employed later in pregnancy (saline induction, hysterotomy) may, however, have a moral quality approaching that of infanticide. For most people, qualms about abortion are qualms about late abortion. It is a virtue of the sentience criterion that it explains and supports this differential approach.

The moral issues raised by early abortion are precisely those raised by contraception. It is for early abortions that the liberal view is appropriate. Since the fetus at this stage has no right to life, early abortion (like contraception) cannot violate its rights. But if it violates no one's rights, early abortion (like contraception) is a private act. There are of course significant differences between contraception and early abortion, since the former is generally less hazardous, less arduous, and less expensive. A woman has, therefore, good prudential reasons for relying on contraception as her primary means of birth control. But if she elects an early abortion, then, whatever the circumstances and whatever her reasons, she does nothing immoral.[16]

The moral issues raised by late abortion are similar to those raised by infanticide. It is for late abortions that (a weakened form of) the conservative view is appropriate. Since the fetus at this stage has a right to life, late abortion (like infanticide) may violate its rights. But if it may violate the fetus' rights, then late abortion (like infanticide) is a public act. There is, however, a morally significant difference between late abortion and infanticide. A fetus is parasitic upon a unique individual in a manner in which a newborn infant is not. That parasitic relation will justify

---

[16] Unless there are circumstances (such as extreme underpopulation) in which contraception would also be immoral.

late abortion more liberally than infanticide, for they do not occur under the same circumstances.

Since we have already explored the morality of abortion for those cases in which the fetus has moral standing, the general approach to late abortions is clear enough. Unlike the simple and uniform treatment of early abortion, only a case-by-case analysis will here suffice. We should expect a serious threat to the woman's life or health (physical or mental) to justify abortion, especially if that threat becomes apparent only late in pregnancy. We should also expect a risk of serious fetal deformity to justify abortion, again especially if that risk becomes apparent (as it usually does) only late in pregnancy. On the other hand, it should not be necessary to justify abortion on the ground that pregnancy was not consented to, since a woman will have ample opportunity to seek an abortion before the threshold stage. If a woman freely elects to continue a pregnancy past that stage, she will thereafter need a serious reason to end it.

A differential view of abortion is therefore liberal concerning early abortion and conservative (in an extended sense) concerning late abortion. The status of the borderline cases in the middle weeks of the second trimester is simply indeterminate. We cannot say of them with certainty either that the fetus has a right to life or that it does not. Therefore we also cannot say either that a liberal approach to these abortions is suitable or that a conservative treatment of them is required. What we can say is that, from the moral point of view, the earlier an abortion is performed the better. There are thus good moral reasons, as well as good prudential ones, for women not to delay their abortions.

A liberal view of early abortion in effect extends a woman's deadline for deciding whether to have a child. If all abortion is immoral, her sovereignty over that decision ends at conception. Given the vicissitudes of contraception, a deadline drawn that early is an enormous practical burden. A deadline in the second trimester allows a woman enough time to discover that she is pregnant and to decide whether to continue the pregnancy. If she chooses not to continue it, her decision violates neither her duties nor any other being's rights. From the point of view of the fetus, the upshot of this treatment of early abortion is that its life is for a period merely probationary; only when it has passed the threshold will that life be accorded protection. If an abortion is elected before the threshold, it is as though from the moral point of view that individual had never existed.

Settling on sentience as a criterion of moral standing thus leads us to a view of the moral status of the fetus, and of the morality of abortion, which satisfies the constraints set out in Section 1. It is gradual, since it locates a threshold stage rather than a point and allows moral standing to be acquired incrementally. It is differential, since it locates the threshold stage during gestation and thus distinguishes the moral status of newly conceived and full-term fetuses. It is developmental, since it grounds the acquisition of moral standing in one aspect of the normal development of the fetus. And it is moderate, since it distinguishes the moral status of early and late abortions and applies each of the established views to that range of cases for which it is appropriate.

4. An Abortion Policy

A differential view of the morality of abortion leads to a differential abortion policy—one that draws a legal distinction between early and late abortions. If we work within the framework of a liberal social theory, then it is understood that the state has no right to interfere in the private activities of individuals. An early abortion is a private act—or, rather, a private transaction between a woman and her physician. No regulation of this transaction will be legitimate unless it is also legitimate for other contractual arrangements between patients and physicians. It might be quite in place for the state to require that abortions be performed by qualified (perhaps licensed) personnel in properly equipped (perhaps licensed) facilities: whether or not this is so will depend on whether the state is in general competent to regulate trade in medical skills. Both the decision to abort and the decision to use contraceptives are private ones on which a woman ought to seek medical advice and medical assistance. There is no justification in either case for restricting access to that advice or that assistance.

An abortion policy must therefore be permissive for early abortions. There is at this stage no question of inquiring into a woman's reason for seeking an abortion. Her autonomy here is absolute; the simple desire not to have a child (or not to have one now) is sufficient. Grounds for abortion become pertinent only when we turn to late abortions. Since virtually all such abortions will result in the death of a being that has a right to life (though not all will violate that right), the state has a legitimate role to play in governing trade in abortion at this stage. Legal grounds for late abortion are a special case of conditions for justifiable homicide. As much as possible (allowing for the unique relation between mother and fetus) these grounds should authorize abortion when killing would also be justified in relevantly similar cases not involving fetuses. Two general conditions for justifiable homicide will be applicable to abortions: self-defense and euthanasia.

The usual legal grounds for abortion provided by moderate policies may be divided into four categories: (a) therapeutic (threat to maternal life or health); (b) eugenic (risk of fetal abnormality); (c) humanitarian (pregnancy due to the commision of a crime, such as rape or incest); (d) socioeconomic (poverty, family size, etc.). If a moderate treatment of late abortion is coupled (as it should be) with a permissive treatment of early ones, only the first two categories are necessary. Therapeutic grounds for abortion follow from a woman's right of self-defense. The threat, however, must be serious in two different respects: the injury in prospect must be more than trivial and the probability of its occurrence must be greater than normal. The risks generally associated with pregnancy will not here suffice. Further, there must be good medical reason not to delay until the fetus has a better chance of survival, and every effort must be made to save the fetus' life if this is possible. Thus late abortion for therapeutic reasons ought to be reserved for genuine medical emergencies in which no other course of action would qualify as proper care of the mother. In many putatively moderate policies therapeutic grounds for abortion (especially mental health clauses) are interpreted so liberally as to cover large numbers of cases that are not by any stretch of the imagination medical emergencies. This is the standard device whereby a policy moderate in principle becomes permissive in practice. Since the policy here advanced is permissive in principle (for early abortions), a strict interpretation of the therapeutic grounds for late abortions will be mandatory.

The same strictures will apply to eugenic grounds. Where there is a substantial risk of some severe anomaly (rubella, spina bifida, Tay-Sachs disease, etc.), abortion may be the best course of action for the fetus. This is not obviously the case for less severe defects (Down's syndrome, dwarfism, etc.). Again there will be no justification for an interpretation of eugenic grounds so elastic that it permits abortion whenever the child is unwanted (because, say, it is the "wrong" sex). A rough rule of thumb is that late abortion for reasons of fetal abnormality is permissible only in those cases in which euthanasia for defective newborns would also be permissible. Probability will play a different role in the two kinds of case, since prenatal diagnosis of these conditions is often less certain than postnatal. But against this reason for delay we must balance the anguish of a woman carrying a fetus who may turn out at birth to be grossly deformed. Since diagnostic techniques such as ultrasound and amniocentesis cannot be employed until the second trimester, a permissive treatment of early abortions will not eliminate the need for late abortions on eugenic grounds.

Both therapeutic and eugenic grounds can be alleged for a wide range of abortions. Some of these cases will be clearly justified, others will be just as clearly unjustified, and the remainder will just be hard cases. There is no formula that can be applied mechanically to decide the hard cases. We should look to a statute for only the most perfunctory statement of justifying grounds for abortion. Particular decisions (the analogue of case law) are best undertaken by persons with the relevant medical expertise. This might be a hospital or clinic committee established especially to monitor late abortions or an "ethics committee" with broader responsibilities. In either case, establishing the right sort of screening mechanism is the best means of ensuring that the justifying grounds are given a reasonable application.

There is no need for any special notice of humanitarian grounds. It is doubtful indeed whether incest ought to be a crime, except in those cases in which someone is being exploited. In any case, any woman who has become pregnant due to incestuous intercourse will have ready access to an early abortion. If she declines this opportunity and if there is no evidence of genetic abnormality, she may not simply change her mind later. The same obviously applies to pregnancy due to rape, including statutory rape. The practical problems should be approached by providing suitable counseling.

A permissive policy for early abortions will also render socioeconomic grounds redundant. Since social constraints do not normally create an emergency for which abortion is the only solution, and since women will be able to terminate pregnancies at will in the early stages, there is no need for separate recognition of social or economic justifications for abortion.

An adequate abortion policy is thus a conjunction of a permissive policy for early abortions and a moderate policy for late abortions. The obvious remaining question is where to draw the boundary between the two classes of cases. When we are dealing with the morality of abortion, borderline fuzziness is both inevitable and tolerable. Many moral problems turn on factors that are matters of degree. Where such factors are present, we cannot avoid borderline cases whose status is unclear or indeterminate. It is a defect in a moral theory to draw sharp lines where there are none, or to treat hard cases as though they were easy. But what makes for good morals may also make for bad law. An abortion policy must be enforceable and so must divide cases as clearly as possible. A threshold stage separating early from late abortions must here give way to a cutoff point.

Since there is no threshold point in fetal development, any precise upper limit on the application of a permissive policy will be to some extent arbitrary. Clearly it must be located within the threshold period, thus sometime in the second trimester. Beyond this constraint the choice of a time limit may be made on pragmatic grounds. If a permissive policy for early abortions is to promote their autonomy, women must have time to discover that they are pregnant and to decide on a course of action. This factor will tend to push the cutoff point toward the end of the second trimester. On the other hand, earlier abortions are substantially safer and more economical of scarce medical resources than later ones. This factor will tend to pull the cutoff point toward the beginning of the second trimester. Balancing these considerations would incline one toward a time limit located sometime around the midpoint of pregnancy. But it should not be pretended that there is a unique solution to this policy problem. Differential policies may legitimately vary (within constraints) in their choice of a boundary between permissiveness and moderation.

Since abortion is a controversial matter, a society's abortion policy ought to include a "conscience clause" that allows medical personnel with conscientious objections to avoid involvement in abortions. It is in general preferable not to require doctors and nurses to perform tasks that deeply offend their moral principles, at least as long as others are willing to meet patients' needs. But it should be stated plainly that dissenting scruples are here being honored, not because they are correct (for they are not), but because a pluralistic society thrives when it promotes as much mutual respect of values as is compatible with the common good. The position of hospitals may be quite different. Any institution that is publicly funded is obliged to provide a suitably wide range of public services. Individual persons may opt out of performing abortions without thereby rendering abortions unavailable, but if entire hospitals do so, substantial numbers of women may have no meaningful access to this service. Whether abortions ought to be subsidized by government medical insurance plans is a question of social justice that cannot be answered without investigating the moral basis of compulsory social welfare programs in general. However, once a s[...] installed such a plan, there is no justification for omitting abortions from [...] of services covered by it.[17]

The abortion policy here proposed is not novel: a differential policy with a time limit in the second trimester is already in operation in a number of countries.[18] But these policies seem usually to have been settled on as compromises between the opposed demands of liberals and conservatives rather than as matters of principle. Such compromises are attractive to politicians, who do not seek any deeper justification for the policies they devise. But there is a deeper justification for this policy. Although it does define a middle ground between the established views, it has not been defended here as the outcome of a bargaining procedure. Instead it has been advanced as the only policy congruent with an adequate criterion of moral standing and proper recognition of both a woman's right to autonomy and a fetus' right to life. A differential policy does not mediate between alternatives both of which are rationally defensible; instead it supersedes alternatives both of which have been discredited.

There is, therefore, a third way with the abortion issue. Its superiority over the established views lies largely in its sensitivity to a factor which both of them are committed to ignoring: the manifest differences between a fetus at the beginning and at the end of its prenatal existence. Views which deny the relevance of this factor deserve to command no more than minority support. Those who, for this reason, can embrace neither of the established views need feel no diffidence about seeking a middle ground between them. A moderate and differential view of abortion is capable of drawing the common-sense distinction between early and late abortions, and of showing that such a distinction is neither shallow nor arbitrary. The view from the middle lacks of course the simplicity which has made it so easy to market its more extreme counterparts. But then why should we think that the moral problems raised by abortion are simple?

---

[17] If abortion should be omitted on the ground that most pregnancies can be easily avoided, then treatment for lung cancer must also be omitted since most cases of lung cancer can be even more easily avoided. There is no justification for restricting a woman's access to abortion by requiring the consent of the father. Until men learn to become pregnant, if a man wishes to father a child he must find a woman willing to carry and bear it. Parental consent is a slightly more complicated issue, since it raises questions about the competence of minors. In most cases a girl who is mature enough to be sexually active is also mature enough to decide on an abortion; in any case no parental consent regulation is justified for abortion that is not also justified for all comparable forms of minor surgery.

[18] Notably the United States, Great Britain, France, Italy, Sweden, the Soviet Union, China, India, Japan, and most of the countries of Eastern Europe. The cutoff points in these jurisdictions vary from the beginning to the end of the second trimester.

nd Human Rights

Norman C. Gillespie

Philosophical and popular thinking about abortion is influenced by the belief that the fundamental issue in settling the morality of abortion is whether a fetus is a person (is a human being, has a right to life, or has passed the point at which "life begins"). Despite widespread disagreement over "where to draw the line," many people believe (a) that there is a point somewhere between conception and adulthood that is morally significant, and (b) that the morality of a particular abortion depends upon whether it occurs before or after that point. These assumptions are widely shared: ardent antiabortionists insist that the significant point is conception; at least one philosopher thinks that the Supreme Court, in permitting abortions during the first two trimesters of pregnancy, has " . . . for all practical purposes . . . resolve[d] the difficult question of when life begins;"[1] and more than one philosopher has searched for criteria for determining whether or not a being is a person in order to settle the morality of abortion—the basic idea being that if a fetus is not a person, then abortion is morally permissible. All of these ideas, I shall argue, rest upon mistaken assumptions, and after explicating briefly some of the principles that determine the distribution of human rights, I shall argue on the basis of those principles that (a) and (b) are false.

I

In many philosophic discussions of abortion, the problem arises: if an early abortion is morally permissible, why not a late abortion or even, as one philos-

Reprinted by permission of the publisher, from *Ethics*, vol. 87, no. 3 (April 1977; © 1977 by the University of Chicago), pp. 237–43.

[1] Daniel Callahan, "Remarks on the Supreme Court's Ruling on Abortion," in *The Problem of Abortion* [first ed.], ed. Joel Feinberg (Belmont, Calif., 1973), p. 194.

opher has suggested, infanticide?[2] What is the *morally relevant difference* between them? These questions rely upon some standard principles of moral reasoning; yet, as we shall see, their full implications have not been recognized by most participants in such discussions. According to the principle of universalizability (U), if an act is morally right for one person, then it is morally right for all relevantly similar persons, and this principle can be restated as: (R) If one person has a right to *x*, then all relevantly similar persons have the same right to *x*. In analyzing these principles and the role of relevant similarities and relevant differences in moral reasoning, one finds, as Alan Gewirth puts it, that "according to the universalizability thesis, a singular moral judgment, which says that some individual subject S has some moral predicate P, is based on a reason according to which *(a)* S has some nonmoral property Q and *(b)* having Q is a sufficient justifying condition for having P, so that if one accepts the judgment and the reason then one must accept the generalization that every subject that has Q has P."[3] In short, moral properties are supervenient upon nonmoral ones; individuals are relevantly similar or relevantly different in virtue of their nonmoral properties; and whatever moral properties one has, all relevantly similar individuals share the same moral properties.

In the abortion dispute, the relevant nonmoral properties are thought to be viability, brain activity, independence, memory, and desires; and on that basis it is argued that human beings have rights.

Some philosophers have argued that universalizability is trivial in that there can be unique nonmoral properties in virtue of which only one individual, or only one class of individuals, has certain moral properties. In responding to this criticism, Gewirth points out that "in all these cases, . . . the justifying [nonmoral] properties in question [may] involve an important *comparative* element. . . . The point is that even when a reason for a right or duty directly applies only to one person, where that reason logically involves a comparative element it applies in a comparative or proportional way to other persons. The logical form of that proportionality is [L] if *x* units of some property Q justify that one have *x* units of some right or duty E, then *y* units of Q justify that one have *y* units of E. Such proportionality is a pervasive feature of traditional doctrines of distributive justice."[4]

Now, whatever nonmoral properties one selects as a basis for determining human rights, it seems likely that those properties will be comparative and thus involve (L) in any assessment of whether a being has any rights. Indeed, as is true of most people, even if someone does not know on what basis we say that adult human beings have rights, he can appreciate that children are sufficiently

---

[2] Michael Tooley, "In Defense of Abortion and Infanticide," in *The Problem of Abortion,* ed. Joel Feinberg [*infra,* pp. 120–134].

[3] Alan Gewirth, "The Non-Trivializability of Universalizability," *Australasian Journal of Philosophy* 47, no. 2 (1969): 123, n. 2.

[4] Ibid., p. 126 (cf. Aristotle *Nichomachean Ethics* 5. 3. 1131a. 18 ff).

like adults to have some rights, that the same is true of small children, that about-to-be-born babies are comparatively like infants, and that fetuses are comparatively similar to about-to-be-born babies.

This line of reasoning is familiar. When it is used with 'bald' and the number of hairs on one's head (or 'poor' and the number of pennies one has), it is called "the Sorites paradox." Yet, on the basis of (L) it is not paradoxical at all; it is, instead, what reason would demand in dealing with such continuums. That 'bald,' 'poor,' and 'person' are vague is widely recognized; what is not so widely appreciated is how to deal with such terms, especially in moral argument. Insisting upon "drawing the line" in applying such terms is irrational; it only produces such paradoxical remarks as "it is not true that the fetus is a human being—but it is not false either," and "the indeterminateness of the fetus' humanity . . . means that, whatever you believe, it's not true—but neither is it false."[5]

The rational thing to do is to treat such cases on a *comparative* basis: to say that A is poorer (balder) than B, and, in the abortion dispute, that small children are not full-fledged, responsible adults, that infants are further from adulthood than small children, and fetuses further still removed from adulthood than infants. Given our awareness of the spectrum from poverty to riches, from baldness to a full head of hair, and from conception to adulthood, we can specify quite precisely where an individual falls along any of those spectrums. So precision is possible without drawing any lines; and in determining the rights of a being we can proceed in exactly the same fashion. Thus, when an adult requests an abortion, if it is seen as a conflict of rights case, the comparative strength of the rights of the being to be aborted is determined by its stage of development. A conceptus would have a minimal right to live (supposing that an unfertilized ovum has none), whereas an almost full term fetus would have considerably more of a right, but still less than its mother. So that one morally relevant difference between an early and a late abortion is the degree of development of the fetus.

It is this reasoning, I find, that influences our moral thinking about abortion. It explains (1) why no one favors infanticide, since with infants there is no comparable *conflict* of rights, (2) why we think one should save the life of the mother if it is necessary to choose between her life and that of the unborn, (3) why we find it impossible to draw a line (say, at six months of fetal development) and insist that abortions a few minutes earlier are significantly morally different, (4) why "we are more and more reluctant [as we go back in the life of a fetus] to say that this is a human being and must be treated as such,"[6] and (5) why the use of the "morning-after pill" seems to so many people to be morally unobjectionable. On this reasoning, a fetus has a right to life, but that right is less than that of its

---

[5] Roger Wertheimer, "Understanding the Abortion Argument," *Philosophy and Public Affairs* 1, no. 1 (1971) [*supra*, pp. 43–57].

[6] Phillipa Foot, "The Problem of Abortion and the Doctrine of Double Effect," *Oxford Review*, no. 5 (1967); reprinted in *Moral Problems*, ed. James Rachels (New York, 1971), p. 29.

mother. A fetus is, as the Supreme Court put it, "less than a full person," which implies that its rights are less than full—*not that it has no rights at all.* Thus, given the facts of human development, (L) explains why abortion *is* a genuine moral problem, why it is the sort of problem it is, and why it troubles us in the way it does. An abortion cannot be dismissed as simply "elective surgery," but neither is an early abortion equivalent to murder. Furthermore, (L) renders consistent the assignment of fetal rights (as some courts have done) with the Supreme Court decision that a fetus is not a person in the full legal sense of that term: one does not have to be a full-fledged person in order to have rights, or to be treated immorally.

II

The most serious distortion that affects moral discussions of abortion is the idea that abortion presents a "line-drawing problem." In introducing a series of essays on abortion, Joel Feinberg characterizes the views implicit in many of those essays when he writes, "I do not wish to suggest that 'the status of the unborn' problem is insoluble, but only that it *is* a problem, and a difficult one, for liberal, moderate and conservative alike, insofar as they seek principled, and not merely arbitrary solutions to line drawing problems."[7] If one thinks he must be able to "draw a line" in order to defend early abortions, no wonder the "status of the unborn problem" seems insoluble. Yet, Feinberg's remarks overlook entirely, as do many philosophic essays on abortion, the *principled* solution provided by (L) to that problem and the question of whether the unborn have any rights.

In his remarks, Feinberg embraces an assumption that is at the heart of the antiabortionist position, namely, *(c)* if a being has a right to life, it is the same right to life that an adult human being has. In accepting *(c)*, Feinberg considerably increases the burden which any liberal or moderate on abortion must bear. For an antiabortionist can argue: *(d)* an infant has a right to life, *(e)* there is no reasonable place to "draw the line" between conception and birth, therefore, *(f)* a conceptus has the same right to life as an infant. The inference from *(d)* and *(e)* to *(f)* is common; yet it depends crucially upon *(c)*. If *(c)* is false, *(f)* does not follow from *(d)* and *(e)*, and the antiabortionist must argue for *(c)* in order to defend his position. Too often, this requirement is overlooked—as Feinberg overlooks it— and liberals and moderates are left with the impression that their respective positions are unreasonable because they are unable to reasonably "draw the line." Yet, anyone who favors early abortions can emphasize the very facts about human development that are crucial for the antiabortionist position, and, in doing so, maintain that the right to life of a conceptus or zygote are minimal, while those of infants and about-to-be-born babies are considerable. Once one sees this

---

[7] Feinberg [first ed.], p. 4.

possibility, the "line-drawing problem" and the intellectual burden it imposes disappear.

In other philosophical discussions of abortion, one finds such remarks as, "What properties must something have to be a person, i.e., to have a serious right to life?"[8] Here, the mistake is: *(g)* If something is not a person, it does not have a serious right to life. And, in another discussion, the claim is made that "to stabilize his position [on abortion] the moderate would have to *invent* a new set of moral categories and principles . . . because our principles of justice apply solely to the relations between persons."[9] Here the fallacy is: *(h)* If something is not a person, our principles of justice do not apply to it. Position *(g)* is fallacious because being a person is a sufficient, but not a necessary condition, for having rights; and *(h)* is false because, as (L), which is a principle of justice, makes plain, less than full persons can have rights, and these rights can be unjustly violated.

III

More than any other position on abortion, it is the moderate position—that early abortions generally, and some late abortions, are morally justified—that has been misunderstood by failing to appreciate the role of (L) in our moral reasoning. Roger Wertheimer finds the moderate position popular, but problematic.[10] What are its problems? First, it complicates specific moral decisions: there is a great variety of possible cases, and a difference in details—especially for mid-term abortions—often requires a difference in moral judgment. Second, Wertheimer claims that a moderate, to support his position, must *invent* new categories and moral principles. Any moderate would grant the first point, perhaps even insist upon it as a true account of the nature of the problem, but the second criticism is simply bizarre. After all, if the moderate position is popular, are all its adherents simply relying upon their own invented moral categories and moral principles? A much more likely explanation of its popularity is that it relies upon such standard moral principles as (U), (R), and (L).

Wertheimer notes that most liberals and conservatives on abortion are really only extreme moderates, since they agree that while abortion is not simply elective surgery, a fetus is not a fellow adult who must be treated as such. In short, the fetus occupies a special, intermediate place in our moral thinking. In Wertheimer's words, "it has a separate moral status, just as animals do," and he apparently infers from that claim that if the fetus has a separate status, our ordinary principles

---

[8] Tooley [*infra*, p. 120].

[9] Wertheimer [*supra*, p. 55].

[10] Ibid. [p. 55].

of justice do not apply to it. He argues that "our principles of justice apply solely to relations between persons," hence they do not apply to a fetus, and that argument is simply fallacious. For (L) is a principle of justice (which Wertheimer ignores), and it makes it plain that fetuses as well as animals can be treated unjustly. (Indeed, in trying to understand our moral thinking about animals, (L) would seem to be indispensable, since they, like fetuses, are like persons in some ways, but not in others. To treat them as sticks or stones would be to ignore that fact and to violate (L).)

If one adopts a moderate position on abortion, then one requires a reason to abort a fetus, and the strength of the requisite reason is proportional to the facts of the situation and the comparative rights of the parties involved. In "A Defense of Abortion," [11] Judith Thomson supposes, for the sake of argument, that the right to life of a fetus is the same as that of its mother, and then examines several analogous conflict of rights cases in order to determine whether it is always morally wrong to kill, or let die, an innocent person. Many women would reject the supposition that their rights are on a par with those of a fetus and resent antiabortionists who make that supposition the cornerstone of their position. Since that supposition is mistaken, according to (L), their rejection of it is well founded. Yet, in Thomson's cases, the conclusion that the rights of a fetus are less than those of a normal adult only strengthens her conclusion that some abortions are morally permissible. For if it is sometimes morally permissible to let an innocent person die, or to cause his death, then the reasons required to do so with a being that is less than a full person are proportionally less. Hence the moral principles (U), (R), and (L), the supervenience analysis of the attribution of human rights, and the categories 'person' and 'less than a full person' provide the basis for the moderate position on abortion.

IV

Two important criticisms might be made of the position I have argued. The first is that while (L) requires a proportionality in our moral assessments based on claims of human rights, unless one knows for certain what the nonmoral or natural characteristics are for determining human rights, one cannot be certain that fetuses and infants possess such characteristics in any proportional or comparative degree. This criticism seems accurate. We do not know for certain that a fetus is less than a full person in a morally significant sense unless we know those characteristics upon which we base the attribution of human rights. Yet, how would one establish what those natural characteristics are? Only, it seems, by analyzing our moral thinking about human beings and why *we think* that persons

---

[11] Judith Jarvis Thomson, "A Defense of Abortion," *Philosophy and Public Affairs* 1, no. 1 (1971): 47–66 [*infra,* pp. 173–87].

have rights. If one so proceeds, I think it is evident, or at least extremely likely, that fetuses will be found to occupy the "in-between" status I have attributed to them. That intuition, after all, is one datum that any analysis of 'person' or 'has rights' would have to take into account. So if not certain, the moderate position on abortion is reasonably secure.

The second criticism objects to the idea of "partial rights" or "less than full rights."[12] A right, one might insist, is not something that grows or diminishes, or something you can have more or less of. You either have it or you do not, in the way that a statement is either true or false. But one has only to substitute 'person' for 'right' in that claim to argue against it. If there is a certain symmetry between being a person and having rights, then if persons can grow and develop, why should their rights not do the same? The idea that a child acquires more rights as it develops is not incoherent; it is, instead, the way most parents raise their children. And it is not simply that a child acquires more rights of different kinds as it develops; it also acquires more of the same right, such as the right to self-determination. One reply to this argument might be that, while a *child* grows and develops, a *person* does not—that is, a child becomes a person at some point and remains so from then on. So "personhood" is not elastic in the way that my position requires.

The trouble with that reply is that, if it is granted, it loses its force. Any "line-drawing" definition of 'person' which insists that only those beings who satisfy the definition have any rights is simply unrealistic. For once so defined, 'person' and 'has rights' would be inadequate to handle the moral problems we confront in dealing with abortion. It is not the definition of 'person,' but the reality to which that term applies, that is crucial for moral assessments. So if someone defines 'person' in such a way that a fetus, an infant, and even a small child is not a person, the continuum of human development and the moral problems it presents are still before us. It is not as if a "line-drawing" definition of 'person' makes those problems disappear. So even if my use of 'person' and 'has rights' is revisionary, the facts of the situation require it, if those terms are to be adequate for discussing the morality of abortion. The alternative "line-drawing" approach only produces intellectual confusion and paradox.

V

Two assumptions, *(a)* there is a point somewhere between conception and adulthood that is morally significant, and *(b)* the morality of particular abortions depends on whether they occur before or after that point, underlie many discussions of the morality of abortion. In this paper, I have pointed out that if the properties

---

[12] Editor's note: See "Potentiality, Development, and Rights," by Joel Feinberg, *infra,* pp. 145–50.

in virtue of which persons have rights are comparative, then *(b)* is false and there is no reason to think that *(a)* is true. There are morally significant differences between early and late abortions, but these do not entail the conclusion that there is a point somewhere between the two at which one can draw a line and demarcate the morally right from the morally wrong abortions. Instead, mid-term and late abortions are morally complicated. Their correct resolution depends upon numerous factors, some peculiar to the individual case, and not the discovery of that point at which "life begins." There are many biological reasons for doubting that there is such a point, and I have argued that it is not morally necessary that we find or create it.

On the Moral and Legal Status of Abortion

Mary Anne Warren

W e will be concerned with both the moral status of abortion, which for our purposes we may define as the act which a woman performs in voluntarily terminating, or allowing another person to terminate, her pregnancy, and the legal status which is appropriate for this act. I will argue that, while it is not possible to produce a satisfactory defense of a woman's right to obtain an abortion without showing that a fetus is not a human being, in the morally relevant sense of that term, we ought not to conclude that the difficulties involved in determining whether or not a fetus is human make it impossible to produce any satisfactory solution to the problem of the moral status of abortion. For it is possible to show that, on the basis of intuitions which we may expect even the opponents of abortion to share, a fetus is not a person, and hence not the sort of entity to which it is proper to ascribe full moral rights.

Of course, while some philosophers would deny the possibility of any such proof,[1] others will deny that there is any need for it, since the moral permissibility of abortion appears to them to be too obvious to require proof. But the inadequacy of this attitude should be evident from the fact that both the friends and the foes of abortion consider their position to be morally self-evident. Because pro-abortionists have never adequately come to grips with the conceptual issues surrounding abortion, most, if not all, of the arguments which they advance in opposition to laws restricting access to abortion fail to refute or even weaken the traditional antiabortion argument, i.e., that a fetus is a human being, and therefore abortion is murder.

[1] For example, Roger Wertheimer, who in "Understanding the Abortion Argument," *Philosophy and Public Affairs,* 1, no. 1 (Fall, 1971), [*supra,* pp. 43–57], argues that the problem of the moral status of abortion is insoluble, in that the dispute over the status of the fetus is not a question of fact at all, but only a question of how one responds to the facts.

These arguments are typically of one of two sorts. Either they point to the terrible side effects of the restrictive laws, e.g., the deaths due to illegal abortions, and the fact that it is poor women who suffer the most as a result of these laws, or else they state that to deny a woman access to abortion is to deprive her of her right to control her own body. Unfortunately, however, the fact that restricting access to abortion has tragic side effects does not, in itself, show that the restrictions are unjustified, since murder is wrong regardless of the consequences of prohibiting it; and the appeal to the right to control one's body, which is generally construed as a property right, is at best a rather feeble argument for the permissibility of abortion. Mere ownership does not give me the right to kill innocent people whom I find on my property, and indeed I am apt to be held responsible if such people injure themselves while on my property. It is equally unclear that I have any moral right to expel an innocent person from my property when I know that doing so will result in his death.

Furthermore, it is probably inappropriate to describe a woman's body as her property, since it seems natural to hold that a person is something distinct from her property, but not from her body. Even those who would object to the identification of a person with his body, or with the conjunction of his body and his mind, must admit that it would be very odd to describe, say, breaking a leg, as damaging one's property, and much more appropriate to describe it as injuring one*self*. Thus it is probably a mistake to argue that the right to obtain an abortion is in any way derived from the right to own and regulate property.

But however we wish to construe the right to abortion, we cannot hope to convince those who consider abortion a form of murder of the existence of any such right unless we are able to produce a clear and convincing refutation of the traditional antiabortion argument, and this has not, to my knowledge, been done. With respect to the two most vital issues which that argument involves, i.e., the humanity of the fetus and its implication for the moral status of abortion, confusion has prevailed on both sides of the dispute.

Thus, both proabortionists and antiabortionists have tended to abstract the question of whether abortion is wrong to that of whether it is wrong to destroy a fetus, just as though the rights of another person were not necessarily involved. This mistaken abstraction has led to the almost universal assumption that if a fetus is a human being, with a right to life, then it follows immediately that abortion is wrong (except perhaps when necessary to save the woman's life), and that it ought to be prohibited. It has also been generally assumed that unless the question about the status of the fetus is answered, the moral status of abortion cannot possibly be determined.

Two recent papers, one by B. A. Brody,[2] and one by Judith Thomson,[3] have

---

[2] B. A. Brody, "Abortion and the Law," *The Journal of Philosophy*, 68, no. 12 (June 17, 1971), 357–69.

[3] Judith Thomson, "A Defense of Abortion," *Philosophy and Public Affairs*, 1, no. 1 (Fall, 1971), [*infra*, pp. 173–87].

attempted to settle the question of whether abortion ought to be prohibited apart from the question of whether or not the fetus is human. Brody examines the possibility that the following two statements are compatible: (1) that abortion is the taking of innocent human life, and therefore wrong; and (2) that nevertheless it ought not to be prohibited by law, at least under the present circumstances.[4] Not surprisingly, Brody finds it impossible to reconcile these two statements, since, as he rightly argues, none of the unfortunate side effects of the prohibition of abortion is bad enough to justify legalizing the *wrongful* taking of human life. He is mistaken, however, in concluding that the incompatibility of (1) and (2), in itself, shows that "the legal problem about abortion cannot be resolved independently of the status of the fetus problem" [p. 369].

What Brody fails to realize is that (1) embodies the questionable assumption that if a fetus is a human being, then of course abortion is morally wrong, and that an attack on *this* assumption is more promising, as a way of reconciling the humanity of the fetus with the claim that laws prohibiting abortion are unjustified, than is an attack on the assumption that if abortion is the wrongful killing of innocent human beings then it ought to be prohibited. He thus overlooks the possibility that a fetus may have a right to life and abortion still be morally permissible, in that the right of a woman to terminate an unwanted pregnancy might override the right of the fetus to be kept alive. The immorality of abortion is no more demonstrated by the humanity of the fetus, in itself, than the immorality of killing in self-defense is demonstrated by the fact that the assailant is a human being. Neither is it demonstrated by the *innocence* of the fetus, since there may be situations in which the killing of innocent human beings is justified.

It is perhaps not surprising that Brody fails to spot this assumption, since it has been accepted with little or no argument by nearly everyone who has written on the morality of abortion. John Noonan is correct in saying that "the fundamental question in the long history of abortion is, How do you determine the humanity of a being?"[5] He summarizes his own antiabortion argument, which is a version of the official position of the Catholic Church, as follows:

> . . . it is wrong to kill humans, however poor, weak, defenseless, and lacking in opportunity to develop their potential they may be. It is therefore morally wrong to kill Biafrans. Similarly, it is morally wrong to kill embryos.[6]

Noonan bases his claim that fetuses are human upon what he calls the theologians' criterion of humanity: that whoever is conceived of human beings is human. But although he argues at length for the appropriateness of this criterion, he never

---

[4] I have abbreviated these statements somewhat, but not in a way which affects the argument.

[5] John Noonan, "Abortion and the Catholic Church: A Summary History," *Natural Law Forum,* 12 (1967), 125.

[6] John Noonan, "Deciding Who Is Human," *Natural Law Forum,* 13 (1968), 134.

questions the assumption that if a fetus is human then abortion is wrong for exactly the same reason that murder is wrong.

Judith Thomson is, in fact, the only writer I am aware of who has seriously questioned this assumption; she has argued that, even if we grant the antiabortionist his claim that a fetus is a human being, with the same right to life as any other human being, we can still demonstrate that, in at least some and perhaps most cases, a woman is under no moral obligation to complete an unwanted pregnancy.[7] Her argument is worth examining, since if it holds up it may enable us to establish the moral permissibility of abortion without becoming involved in problems about what entitles an entity to be considered human, and accorded full moral rights. To be able to do this would be a great gain in the power and simplicity of the proabortion position, since, although I will argue that these problems can be solved at least as decisively as can any other moral problem, we should certainly be pleased to be able to avoid having to solve them as part of the justification of abortion.

On the other hand, even if Thomson's argument does not hold up, her insight, i.e., that it requires *argument* to show that if fetuses are human then abortion is properly classified as murder, is an extremely valuable one. The assumption she attacks is particularly invidious, for it amounts to the decision that it is appropriate, in deciding the moral status of abortion, to leave the rights of the pregnant woman out of consideration entirely, except possibly when her life is threatened. Obviously, this will not do; determining what moral rights, if any, a fetus possesses is only the first step in determining the moral status of abortion. Step two, which is at least equally essential, is finding a just solution to the conflict between whatever rights the fetus may have, and the rights of the woman who is unwillingly pregnant. While the historical error has been to pay far too little attention to the second step, Ms. Thomson's suggestion is that if we look at the second step first we may find that a woman has a right to obtain an abortion *regardless* of what rights the fetus has.

Our own inquiry will also have two stages. In Section I, we will consider whether or not it is possible to establish that abortion is morally permissible even on the assumption that a fetus is an entity with a full-fledged right to life. I will argue that in fact this cannot be established, at least not with the conclusiveness which is essential to our hopes of convincing those who are skeptical about the morality of abortion, and that we therefore cannot avoid dealing with the question of whether or not a fetus really does have the same right to life as a (more fully developed) human being.

In Section II, I will propose an answer to this question, namely, that a fetus cannot be considered a member of the moral community, the set of beings with full and equal moral rights, for the simple reason that it is not a person, and that it is personhood, and not genetic humanity, i.e., humanity as defined by Noonan,

---

[7] "A Defense of Abortion."

which is the basis for membership in this community. I will argue that a fetus, whatever its stage of development, satisfies none of the basic criteria of personhood, and is not even enough *like* a person to be accorded even some of the same rights on the basis of this resemblance. Nor, as we will see, is a fetus's *potential* personhood a threat to the morality of abortion, since, whatever the rights of potential people may be, they are invariably overridden in any conflict with the moral rights of actual people.

I

We turn now to Professor Thomson's case for the claim that even if a fetus has full moral rights, abortion is still morally permissible, at least sometimes, and for some reasons other than to save the woman's life. Her argument is based upon a clever, but I think faulty, analogy. She asks us to picture ourselves waking up one day, in bed with a famous violinist. Imagine that you have been kidnapped, and your bloodstream hooked up to that of the violinist, who happens to have an ailment which will certainly kill him unless he is permitted to share your kidneys for a period of nine months. No one else can save him, since you alone have the right type of blood. He will be unconscious all that time, and you will have to stay in bed with him, but after the nine months are over he may be unplugged, completely cured, that is provided that you have cooperated.

Now then, she continues, what are your obligations in this situation? The antiabortionist, if he is consistent, will have to say that you are obligated to stay in bed with the violinist: for all people have a right to life, and violinists are people, and therefore it would be murder for you to disconnect yourself from him and let him die [p. 174]. But this is outrageous, and so there must be something wrong with the same argument when it is applied to abortion. It would certainly be commendable of you to agree to save the violinist, but it is absurd to suggest that your refusal to do so would be murder. His right to life does not obligate you to do whatever is required to keep him alive; not does it justify anyone else in forcing you to do so. A law which required you to stay in bed with the violinist would clearly be an unjust law, since it is no proper function of the law to force unwilling people to make huge sacrifices for the sake of other people toward whom they have no such prior obligation.

Thomson concludes that, if this analogy is an apt one, then we can grant the antiabortionist his claim that a fetus is a human being, and still hold that it is at least sometimes the case that a pregnant woman has the right to refuse to be a Good Samaritan towards the fetus, i.e., to obtain an abortion. For there is a great gap between the claim that x has a right to life, and the claim that y is obligated to do whatever is necessary to keep x alive, let alone that he ought to be forced to do so. It is y's duty to keep x alive only if he has somehow contracted a *special* obligation to do so; and a woman who is unwillingly pregnant, e.g., who was raped, has done nothing which obligates her to make the enormous sacrifice which is necessary to preserve the conceptus.

This argument is initially quite plausible, and in the extreme case of pregnancy due to rape It Is probably conclusive. Difficulties aiise, howevei, when we try to specify more exactly the range of cases in which abortion is clearly justifiable even on the assumption that the fetus is human. Professor Thomson considers it a virtue of her argument that it does not enable us to conclude that abortion is *always* permissible. It would, she says, be "indecent" for a woman in her seventh month to obtain an abortion just to avoid having to postpone a trip to Europe. On the other hand, her argument enables us to see that "a sick and desperately frightened schoolgirl pregnant due to rape may *of course* choose abortion, and that any law which rules this out is an insane law" [p. 187]. So far, so good; but what are we to say about the woman who becomes pregnant not through rape but as a result of her own carelessness, or because of contraceptive failure, or who gets pregnant intentionally and then changes her mind about wanting a child? With respect to such cases, the violinist analogy is of much less use to the defender of the woman's right to obtain an abortion.

Indeed, the choice of a pregnancy due to rape, as an example of a case in which abortion is permissible even if a fetus is considered a human being, is extremely significant; for it is only in the case of pregnancy due to rape that the woman's situation is adequately analogous to the violinist case for our intuitions about the latter to transfer convincingly. The crucial difference between a pregnancy due to rape and the *normal* case of an unwanted pregnancy is that in the normal case we cannot claim that the woman is in no way responsible for her predicament; she could have remained chaste, or taken her pills more faithfully, or abstained on dangerous days, and so on. If, on the other hand, you are kidnapped by strangers, and hooked up to a strange violinist, then you are free of any shred of responsibility for the situation, on the basis of which it could be argued that you are obligated to keep the violinist alive. Only when her pregnancy is due to rape is a woman clearly just as nonresponsible. [8]

Consequently, there is room for the antiabortionist to argue that in the normal case of unwanted pregnancy a woman has, by her own actions, assumed responsibility for the fetus. For if x behaves in a way which he could have avoided, and which he knows involves, let us say, a 1 percent chance of bringing into existence a human being, with a right to life, and does so knowing that if this should happen then that human being will perish unless x does certain things to keep him alive, then it is by no means clear that when it does happen x is free of

---

[8] We may safely ignore the fact that she might have avoided getting raped, e.g., by carrying a gun, since by similar means you might likewise have avoided getting kidnapped, and in neither case does the victim's failure to take all possible precautions against a highly unlikely event (as opposed to reasonable precautions against a rather likely event) mean that she is morally responsible for what happens.

any obligation to what he knew in advance would be required to keep that human being alive.

The plausibility of such an argument is enough to show that the Thomson analogy can provide a clear and persuasive defense of a woman's right to obtain an abortion only with respect to those cases in which the woman is in no way responsible for her pregnancy, e.g., where it is due to rape. In all other cases, we would almost certainly conclude that it was necessary to look carefully at the particular circumstances in order to determine the extent of the woman's responsibility, and hence the extent of her obligation. This is an extremely unsatisfactory outcome, from the viewpoint of the opponents of restrictive abortion laws, most of whom are convinced that a woman has a right to obtain an abortion regardless of how and why she got pregnant.

Of course a supporter of the violinist analogy might point out that it is absurd to suggest that forgetting her pill one day might be sufficient to obligate a woman to complete an unwanted pregnancy. And indeed it *is* absurd to suggest this. As we will see, the moral right to obtain an abortion is not in the least dependent upon the extent to which the woman is responsible for her pregnancy. But unfortunately, once we allow the assumption that a fetus has full moral rights, we cannot avoid taking this absurd suggestion seriously. Perhaps we can make this point more clear by altering the violinist story just enough to make it more analogous to a normal unwanted pregnancy and less to a pregnancy due to rape, and then seeing whether it is still obvious that you are not obligated to stay in bed with the fellow.

Suppose, then, that violinists are peculiarly prone to the sort of illness the only cure for which is the use of someone else's bloodstream for nine months, and that because of this there has been formed a society of music lovers who agree that whenever a violinist is stricken they will draw lots and the loser will, by some means, be made the one and only person capable of saving him. Now then, would you be obligated to cooperate in curing the violinist if you had voluntarily joined this society, knowing the possible consequences, and then your name had been drawn and you had been kidnapped? Admittedly, you did not promise ahead of time that you would, but you did deliberately place yourself in a position in which it might happen that a human life would be lost if you did not. Surely this is at least a prima facie reason for supposing that you have an obligation to stay in bed with the violinist. Suppose that you had gotten your name drawn deliberately; surely *that* would be quite a strong reason for thinking that you had such an obligation.

It might be suggested that there is one important disanalogy between the modified violinist case and the case of an unwanted pregnancy, which makes the woman's responsibility significantly less, namely, the fact that the fetus *comes into existence* as the result of the result of the woman's actions. This fact might give her a right to refuse to keep it alive, whereas she would not have had this right had it existed previously, independently, and then as a result of her actions become dependent upon her for its survival.

My own intuition, however, is that *x* has no more right to bring into existence, either deliberately or as a foreseeable result of actions he could have avoided, a being with full moral rights *(y),* and then refuse to do what he knew beforehand would be required to keep that being alive, than he has to enter into an agreement with an existing person, whereby he may be called upon to save that person's life, and then refuse to do so when so called upon. Thus, *x*'s responsibility for *y*'s existence does not seem to lessen his obligation to keep *y* alive, if he is also responsible for *y*'s being in a situation in which only he can save him.

Whether or not this intuition is entirely correct, it brings us back once again to the conclusion that once we allow the assumption that a fetus has full moral rights it becomes an extremely complex and difficult question whether and when abortion is justifiable. Thus the Thomson analogy cannot help us produce a clear and persuasive proof of the moral permissibility of abortion. Nor will the opponents of the restrictive laws thank us for anything less; for their conviction (for the most part) is that abortion is obviously *not* a morally serious and extremely unfortunate, even though sometimes justified act, comparable to killing in self-defense or to letting the violinist die, but rather is closer to being a morally neutral act, like cutting one's hair.

The basis of this conviction, I believe, is the realization that a fetus is not a person, and thus does not have a full-fledged right to life. Perhaps the reason why this claim has been so inadequately defended is that it seems self-evident to those who accept it. And so it is, insofar as it follows from what I take to be perfectly obvious claims about the nature of personhood, and about the proper grounds for ascribing moral rights, claims which ought, indeed, to be obvious to both the friends and foes of abortion. Nevertheless, it is worth examining these claims, and showing how they demonstrate the moral innocuousness of abortion, since this apparently has not been adequately done before.

II

The question which we must answer in order to produce a satisfactory solution to the problem of the moral status of abortion is this: How are we to define the moral community, the set of beings with full and equal moral rights, such that we can decide whether a human fetus is a member of this community or not? What sort of entity, exactly, has the inalienable rights to life, liberty, and the pursuit of happiness? Jefferson attributed these rights to all *men*, and it may or may not be fair to suggest that he intended to attribute them *only* to men. Perhaps he ought to have attributed them to all human beings. If so, then we arrive, first, at Noonan's problem of defining what makes a being human, and second, at the equally vital question which Noonan does not consider, namely, What reason is there for identifying the moral community with the set of all human beings, in whatever way we have chosen to define that term?

1. On the Definition of 'Human'

One reason why this vital second question is so frequently overlooked in the debate over the moral status of abortion is that the term 'human' has two distinct, but not often distinguished, senses. This fact results in a slide of meaning, which serves to conceal the fallaciousness of the traditional argument that since (1) it is wrong to kill innocent human beings, and (2) fetuses are innocent human beings, then (3) it is wrong to kill fetuses. For if 'human' is used in the same sense in both (1) and (2) then, whichever of the two senses is meant, one of these premises is question-begging. And if it is used in two different senses then of course the conclusion doesn't follow.

Thus, (1) is a self-evident moral truth,[9] and avoids begging the question about abortion, only if 'human being' is used to mean something like "a full-fledged member of the moral community." (It may or may not also be meant to refer exclusively to members of the species *Homo sapiens*.) We may call this the *moral* sense of 'human'. It is not to be confused with what we will call the *genetic* sense, i.e., the sense in which *any* member of the species is a human being, and no member of any other species could be. If (1) is acceptable only if the moral sense is intended, (2) is non-question-begging only if what is intended is the genetic sense.

In "Deciding Who Is Human," Noonan argues for the classification of fetuses with human beings by pointing to the presence of the full genetic code, and the potential capacity for rational thought (p. 135). It is clear that what he needs to show, for his version of the traditional argument to be valid, is that fetuses are human in the moral sense, the sense in which it is analytically true that all human beings have full moral rights. But, in the absence of any argument showing that whatever is genetically human is also morally human, and he gives none, nothing more than genetic humanity can be demonstrated by the presence of the human genetic code. And, as we will see, the *potential* capacity for rational thought can at most show that an entity has the potential for *becoming* human in the moral sense.

2. Defining the Moral Community

Can it be established that genetic humanity is sufficient for moral humanity? I think that there are very good reasons for not defining the moral community in this way. I would like to suggest an alternative way of defining the moral community, which I will argue for only to the extent of explaining why it

---

[9] Of course, the principle that it is (always) wrong to kill innocent human beings is in need of many other modifications, e.g., that it may be permissible to do so to save a greater number of other innocent human beings, but we may safely ignore these complications here.

is, or should be, self-evident. The suggestion is simply that the moral community consists of all and only *people*, rather than all and only human beings;[10] and probably the best way of demonstrating its self-evidence is by considering the concept of personhood, to see what sorts of entity are and are not persons, and what the decision that a being is or is not a person implies about its moral rights.

What characteristics entitle an entity to be considered a person? This is obviously not the place to attempt a complete analysis of the concept of personhood, but we do not need such a fully adequate analysis just to determine whether and why a fetus is or isn't a person. All we need is a rough and approximate list of the most basic criteria of personhood, and some idea of which, or how many, of these an entity must satisfy in order to properly be considered a person.

In searching for such criteria, it is useful to look beyond the set of people with whom we are acquainted, and ask how we would decide whether a totally alien being was a person or not. (For we have no right to assume that genetic humanity is necessary for personhood.) Imagine a space traveler who lands on an unknown planet and encounters a race of beings utterly unlike any he has ever seen or heard of. If he wants to be sure of behaving morally toward these beings, he has to somehow decide whether they are people, and hence have full moral rights, or whether they are the sort of thing which he need not feel guilty about treating as, for example, a source of food.

How should he go about making this decision? If he has some anthropological background, he might look for such things as religion, art, and the manufacturing of tools, weapons, or shelters, since these factors have been used to distinguish our human from our prehuman ancestors, in what seems to be closer to the moral than the genetic sense of 'human'. And no doubt he would be right to consider the presence of such factors as good evidence that the alien beings were people, and morally human. It would, however, be overly anthropocentric of him to take the absence of these things as adequate evidence that they were not, since we can imagine people who have progressed beyond, or evolved without ever developing, these cultural characteristics.

I suggest that the traits which are most central to the concept of personhood, or humanity in the moral sense, are, very roughly, the following:

1.   consciousness (of objects and events external and/or internal to the being), and in particular the capacity to feel pain;

2.   reasoning (the *developed* capacity to solve new and relatively complex problems);

---

[10] From here on, we will use 'human' to mean genetically human, since the moral sense seems closely connected to, and perhaps derived from, the assumption that genetic humanity is sufficient for membership in the moral community.

3. self-motivated activity (activity which is relatively independent of either genetic or direct external control);

4. the capacity to communicate, by whatever means, messages of an indefinite variety of types, that is, not just with an indefinite number of possible contents, but on indefinitely many possible topics;

5. the presence of self-concepts, and self-awareness, either individual or racial, or both.

Admittedly, there are apt to be a great many problems involved in formulating precise definitions of these criteria, let alone in developing universally valid behavioral criteria for deciding when they apply. But I will assume that both we and our explorer know approximately what (1)–(5) mean, and that he is also able to determine whether or not they apply. How, then, should he use his findings to decide whether or not the alien beings are people? We needn't suppose that an entity must have *all* of these attributes to be properly considered a person; (1) and (2) alone may well be sufficient for personhood, and quite probably (1)–(3) are sufficient. Neither do we need to insist that any one of these criteria is *necessary* for personhood, although once again (1) and (2) look like fairly good candidates for necessary conditions, as does (3), if 'activity' is construed so as to include the activity of reasoning.

All we need to claim, to demonstrate that a fetus is not a person, is that any being which satisfies *none* of (1)–(5) is certainly not a person. I consider this claim to be so obvious that I think anyone who denied it, and claimed that a being which satisfied none of (1)–(5) was a person all the same, would thereby demonstrate that he had no notion at all of what a person is—perhaps because he had confused the concept of a person with that of genetic humanity. If the opponents of abortion were to deny the appropriateness of these five criteria, I do not know what further arguments would convince them. We would probably have to admit that our conceptual schemes were indeed irreconcilably different, and that our dispute could not be settled objectively.

I do not expect this to happen, however, since I think that the concept of a person is one which is very nearly universal (to people), and that it is common to both proabortionists and antiabortionists, even though neither group has fully realized the relevance of this concept to the resolution of their dispute. Furthermore, I think that on reflection even antiabortionists ought to agree not only that (1)–(5) are central to the concept of personhood, but also that it is a part of this concept that all and only people have full moral rights. The concept of a person is in part a moral concept; once we have admitted that x is a person we have recognized, even if we have not agreed to respect, x's right to be treated as a member of the moral community. It is true that the claim that x is a *human being* is more commonly voiced as part of an appeal to treat x decently than is the claim that x is a person, but this is either because 'human being' is here used in the sense which implies personhood, or because the genetic and moral senses of 'human' have been confused.

Now if (1)–(5) are indeed the primary criteria of personhood, then it is clear that genetic humanity is neither necessary nor sufficient for establishing that an entity is a person. Some human beings are not people, and there may well be people who are not human beings. A man or woman whose consciousness has been permanently obliterated but who remains alive is a human being which is no longer a person; defective human beings, with no appreciable mental capacity, are not and presumably never will be people; and a fetus is a human being which is not yet a person, and which therefore cannot coherently be said to have full moral rights. Citizens of the next century should be prepared to recognize highly advanced, self-aware robots or computers, should such be developed, and intelligent inhabitants of other worlds, should such be found, as people in the fullest sense, and to respect their moral rights. But to ascribe full moral rights to an entity which is not a person is as absurd as to ascribe moral obligations and responsibilities to such an entity.

3. Fetal Development and the Right to Life

Two problems arise in the application of these suggestions for the definition of the moral community to the determination of the precise moral status of a human fetus. Given that the paradigm example of a person is a normal adult human being, then (1) How like this paradigm, in particular how far advanced since conception, does a human being need to be before it begins to have a right to life by virtue, not of being fully a person as of yet, but of being *like* a person? and (2) To what extent, if any, does the fact that a fetus has the *potential* for becoming a person endow it with some of the same rights? Each of these questions requires some comment.

In answering the first question, we need not attempt a detailed consideration of the moral rights of organisms which are not developed enough, aware enough, intelligent enough, etc., to be considered people, but which resemble people in some respects. It does seem reasonable to suggest that the more like a person, in the relevant respects, a being is, the stronger is the case for regarding it as having a right to life, and indeed the stronger its right to life is. Thus we ought to take seriously the suggestion that, insofar as "the human individual develops biologically in a continuous fashion . . . the rights of a human person might develop in the same way."[11] But we must keep in mind that the attributes which are relevant in determining whether or not an entity is enough like a person to be regarded as having some of the same moral rights are no different from those which are relevant to determining whether or not it is fully a person—i.e., are

---

[11] Thomas L. Hayes, "A Biological View," *Commonweal, 85* (March 17, 1967), 677–78; quoted by Daniel Callahan, in *Abortion, Law, Choice, and Morality* (London: Macmillan & Co., 1970).

no different from (1)–(5)—and that being genetically human, or having recognizably human facial and other physical features, or detectable brain activity, or the capacity to survive outside the uterus, are simply not among these relevant attributes.

Thus it is clear that even though a seven- or eight-month fetus has features which make it apt to arouse in us almost the same powerful protective instinct as is commonly aroused by a small infant, nevertheless it is not significantly more personlike than is a very small embryo. It is *somewhat* more personlike; it can apparently feel and respond to pain, and it may even have a rudimentary form of consciousness, insofar as its brain is quite active. Nevertheless, it seems safe to say that it is not fully conscious, in the way that an infant of a few months is, and that it cannot reason, or communicate messages of indefinitely many sorts, does not engage in self-motivated activity, and has no self-awareness. Thus, in the *relevant* respects, a fetus, even a fully developed one, is considerably less personlike than is the average mature mammal, indeed the average fish. And I think that a rational person must conclude that if the right to life of a fetus is to be based upon its resemblance to a person, then it cannot be said to have any more right to life than, let us say, a newborn guppy (which also seems to be capable of feeling pain), and that a right of that magnitude could never override a woman's right to obtain an abortion, at any stage of her pregnancy.

There may, of course, be other arguments in favor of placing legal limits upon the stage of pregnancy in which an abortion may be performed. Given the relative safety of the new techniques of artificially inducing labor during the third trimester, the danger to the woman's life or health is no longer such an argument. Neither is the fact that people tend to respond to the thought of abortion in the later stages of pregnancy with emotional repulsion, since mere emotional responses cannot take the place of moral reasoning in determining what ought to be permitted. Nor, finally, is the frequently heard argument that legalizing abortion, especially late in the pregnancy, may erode the level of respect for human life, leading, perhaps, to an increase in unjustified euthanasia and other crimes. For this threat, if it is a threat, can be better met by educating people to the kinds of moral distinctions which we are making here than by limiting access to abortion (which limitation may, in its disregard for the rights of women, be just as damaging to the level of respect for human rights).

Thus, since the fact that even a fully developed fetus is not personlike enough to have any significant right to life on the basis of its personlikeness shows that no legal restrictions upon the stage of pregnancy in which an abortion may be performed can be justified on the grounds that we should protect the rights of the older fetus; and since there is no other apparent justification for such restrictions, we may conclude that they are entirely unjustified. Whether or not it would be *indecent* (whatever that means) for a woman in her seventh month to obtain an abortion just to avoid having to postpone a trip to Europe, it would not, in itself, be *immoral,* and therefore it ought to be permitted.

4. Potential Personhood and the Right to Life

We have seen that a fetus does not resemble a person in ~~any way that~~ can support the claim that it has even some of the same rights. But ~~what of~~ its *potential*, the fact that if nurtured and allowed to develop naturally it will probably become a person? Doesn't that alone give it at least some right ~~to life?~~ It is hard to deny that the fact that an entity is a potential person is a strong prima facie reason for not destroying it; but we need not conclude from this that a potential person has a right to life, by virtue of that potential. It may be that our feeling that it is better, other things being equal, not to destroy a potential person is better explained by the fact that potential people are still (felt to be) an invaluable resource, not to be lightly squandered. Surely, if every speck of dust were a potential person, we would be much less apt to conclude that every potential person has a right to become actual.

Still, we do not need to insist that a potential person has no right to life whatever. There may well be something immoral, and not just imprudent, about wantonly destroying potential people, when doing so isn't necessary to protect anyone's rights. But even if a potential person does have some prima facie right to life, such a right could not possibly outweigh the right of a woman to obtain an abortion, since the rights of any actual person invariably outweigh those of any potential person, whenever the two conflict. Since this may not be immediately obvious in the case of a human fetus, let us look at another case.

Suppose that our space explorer falls into the hands of an alien culture, whose scientists decide to create a few hundred thousand or more human beings, by breaking his body into its component cells, and using these to create fully developed human beings, with, of course, his genetic code. We may imagine that each of these newly created men will have all of the original man's abilities, skills, knowledge, and so on, and also have an individual self-concept, in short that each of them will be a bona fide (though hardly unique) person. Imagine that the whole project will take only seconds, and that its chances of success are extremely high, and that our explorer knows all of this, and also knows that these people will be treated fairly. I maintain that in such a situation he would have every right to escape if he could, and thus to deprive all of these potential people of their potential lives; for his right to life outweighs all of theirs together, in spite of the fact that they are all genetically human, all innocent, and all have a very high probability of becoming people very soon, if only he refrains from acting.

Indeed, I think he would have a right to escape even if it were not his life which the alien scientists planned to take, but only a year of his freedom, or, indeed, only a day. Nor would he be obligated to stay if he had gotten captured (thus bringing all these people-potentials into existence) because of his own carelessness, or even if he had done so deliberately, knowing the consequences. Regardless of how he got captured, he is not morally obligated to remain in captivity for *any* period of time for the sake of permitting any number of potential people to come

actuality, so great is the margin by which one actual person's right to liberty
outweighs whatever right to life even a hundred thousand potential people have.
And it seems reasonable to conclude that the rights of a woman will outweigh by
a similar margin whatever right to life a fetus may have by virtue of its potential
personhood.

Thus, neither a fetus's resemblance to a person, nor its potential for becoming
a person provides any basis whatever for the claim that it has any significant right
to life. Consequently, a woman's right to protect her health, happiness, freedom,
and even her life,[12] by terminating an unwanted pregnancy, will always override
whatever right to life it may be appropriate to ascribe to a fetus, even a fully
developed one. And thus, in the absence of any overwhelming social need for
every possible child, the laws which restrict the right to obtain an abortion, or
limit the period of pregnancy during which an abortion may be performed, are
a wholly unjustified violation of a woman's most basic moral and constitutional
rights.[13]

Postscript on Infanticide, February 26, 1982

One of the most troubling objections to the argument presented in this
article is that it may appear to justify not only abortion but infanticide
as well. A newborn infant is not a great deal more personlike than a
nine-month fetus, and thus it might seem that if late-term abortion is
sometimes justified, then infanticide must also be sometimes justified.
Yet most people consider that infanticide is a form of murder, and thus
never justified.

While it is important to appreciate the emotional force of this
objection, its logical force is far less than it may seem at first glance.
There are many reasons why infanticide is much more difficult to justify
than abortion, even though if my argument is correct neither constitutes
the killing of a person. In this country, and in this period of history, the
deliberate killing of viable newborns is virtually never justified. This is
in part because neonates are so very *close* to being persons that to kill
them requires a very strong moral justification—as does the killing of
dolphins, whales, chimpanzees, and other highly personlike creatures. It
is certainly wrong to kill such beings just for the sake of convenience, or
financial profit, or "sport."

---

[12] That is, insofar as the death rate, for the woman, is higher for childbirth than for early
abortion.

[13] My thanks to the following people, who were kind enough to read and criticize an earlier
version of this paper: Herbert Gold, Gene Glass, Anne Lauterbach, Judith Thomson, Mary
Mohersill, and Timothy Binkley.

116   Mary Anne Warren

Another reason why infanticide is usually wrong, in our society, is that if the newborn's parents do not want it, or are unable to care for it, there are (in most cases) people who are able and eager to adopt it and to provide a good home for it. Many people wait years for the opportunity to adopt a child, and some are unable to do so even though there is every reason to believe that they would be good parents. The needless destruction of a viable infant inevitably deprives some person or persons of a source of great pleasure and satisfaction, perhaps severely impoverishing their lives. Furthermore, even if an infant is considered to be unadoptable (e.g., because of some extremely severe mental or physical handicap) it is still wrong in most cases to kill it. For most of us value the lives of infants, and would prefer to pay taxes to support orphanages and state institutions for the handicapped rather than to allow unwanted infants to be killed. So long as most people feel this way, and so long as our society can afford to provide care for infants which are unwanted or which have special needs that preclude home care, it is wrong to destroy any infant which has a chance of living a reasonably satisfactory life.

If these arguments show that infanticide is wrong, at least in this society, then why don't they also show that late-term abortion is wrong? After all, third trimester fetuses are also highly personlike, and many people value them and would much prefer that they be preserved, even at some cost to themselves. As a potential source of pleasure to some family, a viable fetus is just as valuable as a viable infant. But there is an obvious and crucial difference between the two cases: once the infant is born, its continued life cannot (except, perhaps, in very exceptional cases) pose any serious threat to the woman's life or health, since she is free to put it up for adoption, or, where this is impossible, to place it in a state-supported institution. While she might prefer that it die, rather than being raised by others, it is not clear that such a preference would constitute a right on her part. True, she may suffer greatly from the knowledge that her child will be thrown into the lottery of the adoption system, and that she will be unable to ensure its well-being, or even to know whether it is healthy, happy, doing well in school, etc.; for the law generally does not permit natural parents to remain in contact with their children, once they are adopted by another family. But there are surely better ways of dealing with these problems than by permitting infanticide in such cases. (It might help, for instance, if the natural parents of adopted children could at least receive some information about their progress, without necessarily being informed of the identity of the adopting family.)

In contrast, a pregnant woman's right to protect her own life and health clearly outweighs other people's desire that the fetus be preserved—just as, when a person's life or limb is threatened by some wild animal, and when the threat cannot be removed without killing the animal, the person's right to self-protection outweighs the desires of those who would prefer that the animal not be harmed. Thus, while the moment of birth may not mark any sharp discontinuity in the degree to which an infant possesses a right to life, it does mark the end of the mother's absolute right to determine its fate. Indeed, if and when a late-term abortion could be safely performed without killing the fetus, she would have no absolute right to insist on its death (e.g., if others wish to adopt it or to pay for its care), for the same reason that she does not have a right to insist that a viable infant be killed.

It remains true that according to my argument neither abortion nor the killing of neonates is properly considered a form of murder. Perhaps it is understandable that the law should classify infanticide as murder or homicide, since there is no other existing legal category which adequately or conveniently expresses the force of our society's disapproval of this action. But the moral distinction remains, and it has several important consequences.

In the first place, it implies that when an infant is born into a society which—unlike ours—is so impoverished that it simply cannot care for it adequately without endangering the survival of existing persons, killing it or allowing it to die is not necessarily wrong—provided that there is no *other* society which is willing and able to provide such care. Most human societies, from those at the hunting and gathering stage of economic development to the highly civilized Greeks and Romans, have permitted the practice of infanticide under such unfortunate circumstances, and I would argue that it shows a serious lack of understanding to condemn them as morally backward for this reason alone.

In the second place, the argument implies that when an infant is born with such severe physical anomalies that its life would predictably be a very short and/or very miserable one, even with the most heroic of medical treatment, and where its parents do not choose to bear the often crushing emotional, financial and other burdens attendant upon the artificial prolongation of such a tragic life, it is not morally wrong to cease or withhold treatment, thus allowing the infant a painless death. It is wrong (and sometimes a form of murder) to practice involuntary euthanasia on persons, since they have the right to decide for themselves whether or not they wish to continue to live. But terminally ill neonates cannot make this decision for themselves, and thus it is incumbent upon responsible persons to make the decision for them, as best they can. The mistaken belief that infanticide is always tantamount to murder is responsible for a great deal of unnecessary suffering, not just on the part of infants which are made to endure needlessly prolonged and painful deaths, but also on the part of parents, nurses, and other involved persons, who must watch infants suffering needlessly, helpless to end that suffering in the most humane way.

I am well aware that these conclusions, however modest and reasonable they may seem to some people, strike other people as morally monstrous, and that some people might even prefer to abandon their previous support for women's right to abortion rather than accept a theory which leads to such conclusions about infanticide. But all that these facts show is that abortion is not an isolated moral issue; to fully understand the moral status of abortion we may have to reconsider other moral issues as well, issues not just about infanticide and euthanasia, but also about the moral rights of women and of nonhuman animals. It is a philosopher's task to criticize mistaken beliefs which stand in the way of moral understanding, even when—perhaps especially when—those beliefs are popular and widespread. The belief that moral strictures against killing should apply equally to *all* genetically human entities, and *only* to genetically human entities, is such an error. The overcoming of this error will undoubtedly require long and often painful struggle; but it must be done.

In Defense of Abortion and Infanticide

Michael Tooley

T his essay deals with the question of the morality of abortion and infanticide. The fundamental ethical objection traditionally advanced against these practices rests on the contention that human fetuses and infants have a right to life. It is this claim which will be the focus of attention here. The basic issue to be discussed, then, is what properties a thing must possess in order to have a right to life. My approach will be to set out and defend a basic moral principle specifying a condition an organism must satisfy if it is to have a right to life. It will be seen that this condition is not satisfied by human fetuses and infants, and thus that they do not have a right to life. So unless there are other objections to abortion and infanticide which are sound, one is forced to conclude that these practices are morally acceptable ones.[1] In contrast, it may turn out that our treatment of adult members of some other species is morally indefensible. For it is quite possible that some nonhuman animals do possess properties that endow them with a right to life.

I. Abortion and Infanticide

What reason is there for raising the question of the morality of infanticide? One reason is that it seems very difficult to formulate a completely satisfactory pro-abortion position without coming to grips with the infanticide issue. For the problem that the liberal on abortion encounters here is that of specifying a cutoff point which is not arbitrary: at what stage in the development of a human being does it cease to be morally permissible to destroy it, and why?

---

[1] My forthcoming book, *Abortion and Infanticide,* contains a detailed examination of other important objections.

It is important to be clear about the difficulty here. The problem is not, as some have thought, that since there is a continuous line of development from a zygote to a newborn baby, one cannot hold that it is seriously wrong to destroy a newborn baby without also holding that it is seriously wrong to destroy a zygote, or any intermediate stage in the development of a human being. The problem is rather that if one says that it is wrong to destroy a newborn baby but not a zygote or some intermediate stage, one should be prepared to point to a *morally relevant* difference between a newborn baby and the earlier stage in the development of a human being.

Precisely the same difficulty can, of course, be raised for a person who holds that infanticide is morally permissible, since one can ask what morally relevant difference there is between an adult human being and a newborn baby. What makes it morally permissible to destroy a baby, but wrong to kill an adult? So the challenge remains. But I shall argue that in the latter case there is an extremely plausible answer.

Reflecting on the morality of infanticide forces one to face up to this challenge. In the case of abortion a number of events—quickening or viability, for instance— might be taken as cutoff points, and it is easy to overlook the fact that none of these events involves any morally significant change in the developing human. In contrast, if one is going to defend infanticide, one has to get very clear about what it is that gives something a right to life.

One of the interesting ways in which the abortion issue differs from most other moral issues is that the plausible positions on abortion appear to be extreme ones. For if a human fetus has a right to life, one is inclined to say that, in general, one would be justified in killing it only to save the life of the mother, and perhaps not even in that case.[2] Such is the extreme anti-abortion position. On the other hand, if the fetus does not have a right to life, why should it be seriously wrong to destroy it? Why would one need to point to special circumstances—such as the presence of genetic disease, or a threat to the woman's health—in order to justify such action? The upshot is that there does not appear to be any room for a moderate position on abortion such as one finds, for example, in the Model Penal Code recommendations.[3]

Aside from the light it may shed on the abortion question, the issue of infanticide is both interesting and important in its own right. The theoretical interest has been mentioned above: it forces one to face up to the question of what it is that gives something a right to life. The practical importance need not be labored. Most people would prefer to raise children who do not suffer from gross deformities or from severe physical, emotional, or intellectual handicaps. If it could be shown

---

[2] Judith Jarvis Thomson, in her article "A Defense of Abortion," *Philosophy & Public Affairs,* vol. 1, no. 1, 1971, pp. 47–66, argues very forcefully for the view that this conclusion is incorrect. For a critical discussion of her argument, see chapter 3 of *Abortion and Infanticide.*

[3] Section 230.3 of the American Law Institute's *Model Penal Code* (Philadelphia, 1962).

that there is no moral objection to infanticide, the happiness of society could be significantly and justifiably increased.

The suggestion that infanticide may be morally permissible is not an idea that many people are able to consider dispassionately. Even philosophers tend to react in a way which seems primarily visceral—offering no arguments, and dismissing infanticide out of hand.

Some philosophers have argued, however, that such a reaction is not inappropriate, on the ground that, first, moral principles must, in the final analysis, be justified by reference to our moral feelings, or intuitions, and secondly, infanticide is one practice that is judged wrong by virtually everyone's moral intuition. I believe, however, that this line of thought is unsound, and I have argued elsewhere that even if [one] grants, at least for the sake of argument, that moral intuitions are the final court of appeal regarding the acceptability of moral principles, the question of the morality of infanticide is not one that can be settled by an appeal to our intuitions concerning it.[4] If infanticide is to be rejected, an argument is needed, and I believe that the considerations advanced in this essay show that it is unlikely that such an argument is forthcoming.

II. What Sort of Being Can Possess a Right to Life?

The issues of the morality of abortion and of infanticide seem to turn primarily upon the answers to the following four questions:

(1) What properties, other than potentialities, give something a right to life?
(2) Do the corresponding potentialities also endow something with a right to life?
(3) If not, do they at least make it seriously wrong to destroy it?
(4) At what point in its development does a member of the biologically defined species Homo sapiens first possess those nonpotential properties that give something a right to liife? The argument to be developed in the present section bears upon the answers to the first two questions.

How can one determine what properties endow a being with a right to life? An approach that I believe is very promising starts out from the observation that there appear to be two radically different sorts of reasons why an entity may lack a certain right. Compare, for example, the following two claims:

(1) A child does not have a right to smoke.
(2) A newspaper does not have a right not to be torn up.

---

[4]*Abortion and Infanticide,* chapter 10.

The first claim raises a substantive moral issue. People might well disagree about it, and support their conflicting views by appealing to different moral theories. The second dispute, in contrast, seems an unlikely candidate for moral dispute. It is natural to say that newspapers just are not the sort of thing that can have any rights at all, including a right not to be torn up. So there is no need to appeal to a substantive moral theory to resolve the question whether a newspaper has a right not to be torn up.

One way of characterizing this difference, albeit one that will not especially commend itself to philosophers of a Quinean[5] bent, is to say that the second claim, unlike the first, is true in virtue of a certain *conceptual* connection, and that is why no moral theory is needed in order to see that it is true. The explanation, then, of why it is that a newspaper does not have a right not to be torn up, is that there is some property P such that, first, newspapers lack property P, and secondly, it is a conceptual truth that only things with property P can be possessors of rights.

What might property P be? A plausible answer, I believe, is set out and defended by Joel Feinberg in his paper, "The Rights of Animals and Unborn Generations."[6] It takes the form of what Feinberg refers to as the *interest principle:* ". . . the sorts of beings who *can* have rights are precisely those who have (or can have) interests."[7] And then, since "interests must be compounded somehow out of conations,"[8] it follows that things devoid of desires, such as newspapers, can have neither interests nor rights. Here, then, is one account of the difference in status between judgments such as (1) and (2) above.

Let us now consider the right to life. The interest principle tells us that an entity cannot have any rights at all, and *a fortiori,* cannot have a right to life, unless it is capable of having interests. This in itself may be a conclusion of considerable importance. Consider, for example, a fertilized human egg cell. Someday it will come to have desires and interests. As a zygote, however, it does not have desires, nor even the *capacity* for having desires. What about interests? This depends upon the account one offers of the relationship between desires and interests. It seems to me that a zygote cannot properly be spoken of as a subject of interests. My reason is roughly this. What is in a thing's interest is a function of its present and future desires, both those it will actually have and those it could have. In the case of an entity that is not presently capable of any desires, its interest must be based entirely upon the satisfaction of future desires. Then, since the satisfaction of future desires presupposes the continued existence of the entity in question, anything which has an interest which is based upon the satisfaction of future desires

---

[5] Editor's note: That is, followers of the Harvard philosopher Willard van Orman Quine.

[6] In *Philosophy and Environmental Crisis,* edited by William T. Blackstone (Athens, Georgia, 1974), pp. 43–68.

[7] Op. cit., p. 51.

[8] Ibid., pp. 49–50.

must also have an interest in its own continued existence. Therefore something which is not presently capable of having any desires at all—like a zygote—cannot have any interests at all unless it has an interest in its own continued existence. I shall argue shortly, however, that a zygote cannot have such an interest. From this it will follow that it cannot have any interests at all, and this conclusion, together with the interest principle, entails that not all members of the species *Homo sapiens* have a right to life.

The interest principle involves, then, a thesis concerning a necessary condition which something must satisfy if it is to have a right to life, and it is a thesis which has important moral implications. It implies, for example, that abortions, if performed sufficiently early, do not involve any violation of a right to life. But on the other hand, the interest principle provides no help with the question of the moral status of human organisms once they have developed to the point where they do have desires, and thus are capable of having interests. The interest principle states that they *can* have rights. It does not state whether they *do* have rights—including, in particular, a right not to be destroyed.

It is possible, however, that the interest principle does not exhaust the conceptual connections between rights and interests. It formulates only a very general connection: a thing cannot have any rights at all unless it is capable of having at least some interest. May there not be more specific connections, between particular rights and particular sorts of interests? The following line of thought lends plausibility to this suggestion. Consider animals such as cats. Some philosophers are inclined to hold that animals such as cats do not have any rights at all. But let us assume, for the purpose of the present discussion, that cats do have some rights, such as a right not to be tortured, and consider the following claim:

(3) A cat does not have a right to a university education.

How is this statement to be regarded? In particular, is it comparable in status to the claim that children do not have a right to smoke, or, instead, to the claim that newspapers do not have a right not to be torn up? To the latter, surely. Just as a newspaper is not the sort of thing that can have any rights at all, including a right not to be destroyed, so one is inclined to say that a cat, though it may have some rights, such as a right not to be tortured, is not the sort of thing that can possibly have a right to a university education.

This intuitive judgment about the status of claims such as (3) is reinforced, moreover, if one turns to the question of the grounds of the interest principle. Consider, for example, the account offered by Feinberg, which he summarizes as follows:

> Now we can extract from our discussion of animal rights a crucial principle for tentative use in the resolution of the other riddles about the applicability of the concept of a right, namely, that the sorts of beings who *can* have rights are precisely those who have (or can have) interests. I have come to this tentative

conclusion for two reasons: (1) because a right holder must be capable of being represented and it is impossible to represent a being that has no interests, and (2) because a right holder must be capable of being a beneficiary in his own person, and a being without interests is a being that is incapable of being harmed or benefited, having no good or 'sake' of its own. Thus a being without interests has no 'behalf' to act in, and no 'sake' to act for.[9]

If this justification of the interest principle is sound, it can also be employed to support principles connecting particular rights with specific sorts of interests. Just as one cannot represent a being that has no interests at all, so one cannot, in demanding a university education for a cat, be representing the cat unless one is thereby representing some interest that the cat has, and that would be served by its receiving a university education. Similarly, one cannot be acting for the sake of a cat in arguing that it should receive a university education unless the cat has some interest that will thereby be furthered. The conclusion, therefore, is that if Feinberg's defense of the interest principle is sound, other more specific principles must also be correct. These more specific principles can be summed up, albeit somewhat vaguely, by the following, *particular-interests principle:*

> It is a conceptual truth that an entity cannot have a particular right, R, unless it is at least capable of having some interest, I, which is furthered by its having right R.

Given this particular-interests principle, certain familiar facts, whose importance has not often been appreciated, become comprehensible. Compare an act of killing a normal adult human being with an act of torturing one for five minutes. Though both acts are seriously wrong, they are not equally so. Here, as in most cases, to violate an individual's right to life is more seriously wrong than to violate his right not to have pain inflicted upon him. Consider, however, the corresponding actions in the case of a newborn kitten. Most people feel that it is seriously wrong to torture a kitten for five minutes, but not to kill it painlessly. How is this difference in the moral ordering of the two types of acts, between the human case and the kitten case, to be explained? One answer is that while normal adult human beings have both a right to life and a right not to be tortured, a kitten has only the latter. But why should this be so? The particular-interests principle suggests a possible explanation. Though kittens have some interests, including, in particular, an interest in not being tortured, which derives from their capacity to feel pain, they do not have an interest in their own continued existence, and hence do not have a right not to be destroyed. This answer contains, of course, a large promissory element. One needs a defense of the view that kittens have no interest in continued existence. But the point here is simply that there is an important question about the rationale underlying the moral ordering of certain sorts of acts, and that the particular-interests principle points to a possible answer.

---

[9] Ibid., p. 51.

This fact lends further plausibility, I believe, to the particular-interests principle. What one would ultimately like to do, of course, is to set out an analysis of the concept of a right, show that the analysis is indeed satisfactory, and then show that the particular-interests principle is entailed by the analysis. Unfortunately, it will not be possible to pursue such an approach here, since formulating an acceptable analysis of the concept of a right is a far from trivial matter. What I should like to do, however, is to touch briefly upon the problem of providing such an analysis, and then to indicate the account that seems to me most satisfactory— an account which does entail the particular-interests principle.

It would be widely agreed, I believe, both that rights impose obligations, and that the obligations they impose upon others are *conditional* upon certain factors. The difficulty arises when one attempts to specify what the obligations are conditional upon. There seem to be two main views in this area. According to the one, rights impose obligations that are conditional upon the interests of the possessor of the right. To say that Sandra has a right to something is thus to say, roughly, that if it is in Sandra's interest to have that thing, then others are under an obligation not to deprive her of it. According to the second view, rights impose obligations that are conditional upon the right's not having been waived. To say that Sandra has a right to something is to say, roughly, that if Sandra has not given others permission to take the thing, then they are under an obligation not to deprive her of it.

Both views encounter serious difficulties. On the one hand, in the case of minors, and nonhuman animals, it would seem that the obligations that rights impose must be taken as conditional upon the interests of those individuals, rather than upon whether they have given one permission to do certain things. On the other, in the case of individuals who are capable of making informed and rational decisions, if that person has not given one permission to take something that belongs to him, it would seem that one is, in general, still under an obligation not to deprive him of it, even if having that thing is no longer in his interest.

As a result, it seems that a more complex account is needed of the factors upon which the obligations imposed by rights are conditional. The account which I now prefer, and which I have defended elsewhere,[10] is this:

> A has a right to X

means the same as

> A is such that it can be in A's interest to have X, and *either* (1) A is not capable of making an informed and rational choice whether to grant others permission to deprive him of X, in which case, if it is in A's interest not to be deprived of X, then, by that fact alone, others are under a prima facie obligation not to deprive

---

[10] Op. cit., section 5.2.

A of X, *or* (2) A is capable of making an informed and rational choice whether to grant others permission to deprive him of X, in which case others are under a prima facie obligation not to deprive A of X if and only if A has not granted them permission to do so.

And if this account, or something rather similar is correct, then so is the particular-interests principle.

What I now want to do is to apply the particular-interests principle to the case of the right to life. First, however, one needs to notice that the expression, "right to life," is not entirely happy, since it suggests that the right in question concerns the continued existence of a biological organism. That this is incorrect can be brought out by considering possible ways of violating an individual's right to life. Suppose, for example, that future technological developments make it possible to change completely the neural networks in a brain, and that the brain of some normal adult human being is thus completely reprogrammed, so that the organism in question winds up with memories (or rather, apparent memories), beliefs, attitudes, and personality traits totally different from those associated with it before it was subjected to reprogramming. (The pope is reprogrammed, say, on the model of Bertrand Russell.) In such a case, however beneficial the change might be, one would surely want to say that *someone* had been destroyed, that an adult human being's right to life had been violated, even though no biological organism had been killed. This shows that the expression, "right to life," is misleading, since what one is concerned about is not just the continued existence of a biological organism.

How, then, might the right in question be more accurately described? A natural suggestion is that the expression "right to life" refers to the right of a subject of experiences and other mental states to continue to exist. It might be contended, however, that this interpretation begs the question against certain possible views. For someone might hold—and surely some people in fact do—that while continuing subjects of experiences and other mental states certainly have a right to life, so do some other organisms that are only potentially such continuing subjects, such as human fetuses. A right to life, on this view, is *either* the right of a subject of experiences to continue to exist, *or* the right of something that is only potentially a continuing subject of experiences to become such an entity.

This view is, I believe, to be rejected, for at least two reasons. In the first place, this view appears to be clearly incompatible with the interest principle, as well as with the particular-interests principle. Secondly, this position entails that the destruction of potential persons is, in general, prima facie seriously wrong, and I shall argue, in the next section, that the latter view is incorrect.

Let us consider, then, the right of a subject of experiences and other mental states to continue to exist. The particular-interests principle implies that something cannot possibly have such a right unless its continued existence can be in its interest. We need to ask, then, what must be the case if the continued existence of something is to be in its interest.

It will help to focus our thinking, I believe, if we consider a crucial case, stressed by Derek Parfit. Imagine a human baby that has developed to the point of being sentient, and of having simple desires, but that is not yet capable of having any desire for continued existence. Suppose, further, that the baby will enjoy a happy life, and will be glad that it was not destroyed. Can we or can we not say that it is in the baby's interest not to be destroyed?

To approach this case, let us consider a closely related one, namely, that of a human embryo that has not developed sufficiently far to have any desires, or even any states of consciousness at all, but that will develop into an individual who will enjoy a happy life, and who will be glad that his mother did not have an abortion. Can we or can we not say that it is the embryo's interest not to be destroyed?

Why might someone be tempted to say that it is in the embryo's interest that it not be destroyed? One line of thought which, I believe, tempts some people, is this. Let Mary be an individual who enjoys a happy life. Then, though some philosophers have expressed serious doubts about this, it might very well be said that it was certainly in Mary's interest that a certain embryo was not destroyed several years earlier. And this claim, together with the tendency to use expressions such as "Mary before she was born" to refer to the embryo in question, may lead one to think that it was in the embryo's interest not to be destroyed. But this way of thinking involves conceptual confusion. A subject of interests, in the relevant sense of "interest," must necessarily be a subject of conscious states, including experiences and desires. This means that in identifying Mary with the embryo, and attributing to it her interest in its earlier nondestruction, one is treating the embryo as if it were itself a subject of consciousness. But by hypothesis, the embryo being considered has not developed to the point where there is any subject of consciousness associated with it. It cannot, therefore, have any interests at all, and *a fortiori,* it cannot have any interest in its own continued existence.

Let us now return to the first case—that of a human baby that is sentient, and which has simple desires, but which is not yet capable of having more complex desires, such as a desire for its own continued existence. Given that it will develop into an individual who will lead a happy life, and who will be glad that the baby was not destroyed, does one want to say that the baby's not being destroyed is in the baby's own interest?

Again, the following line of thought may seem initially tempting. If Mary is the resulting individual, then it was in Mary's interest that the baby not have been destroyed. But the baby just *is* Mary when she was young. So it must have been in the baby's interest that it not have been destroyed.

Indeed, this argument is considerably more tempting in the present case than in the former, since here there is something that is a subject of consciousness, and which it is natural to identify with Mary. I suggest, however, that when one reflects upon the case, it becomes clear that such an identification is justified only if certain further things are the case. Thus, on the one hand, suppose that Mary is able to remember quite clearly some of the experiences that the baby enjoyed. Given that sort of causal and psychological connection, it would seem perfectly reasonable to hold that Mary and the baby are one and the same subject of consciousness, and thus, that if it is in Mary's interest that the baby not have been destroyed, then this must also have been in the baby's interest. On the other hand, suppose that not only does Mary, at a much later time, not remember any of the baby's experiences, but the experiences in question are not psychologically linked, either via memory or in any other way, to mental states enjoyed by the human organism in question at *any* later time. Here it seems to me clearly incorrect to say that Mary and the baby are one and the same subject of consciousness, and therefore it cannot be correct to transfer, from Mary to the baby, Mary's interest in the baby's not having been destroyed.

Let us now return to the question of what must be the case if the continued existence of something is to be in [its] own interest. The picture that emerges from the two cases just discussed is this. In the first place, nothing at all can be in an entity's interest unless it has desires at some time or other. But more than this is required if the continued existence of the entity is to be in its own interest. One possibility, which will generally be sufficient, is that the individual have, at the time in question, a desire for its own continued existence. Yet it also seems clear that an individual's continued existence can be in its own interest even when such a desire is not present. What is needed, apparently, is that the continued existence of the individual will make possible the satisfaction of some desires existing at other times. But not just any desires existing at other times will do. Indeed, as is illustrated both by the case of the baby just discussed, and by the deprogramming/ reprogramming example, it is not even sufficient that they be desires associated with the same physical organism. It is crucial that they be desires that belong to one and the same subject of consciousness.

The critical question, then, concerns the conditions under which desires existing at different times can be correctly attributed to a single, continuing subject of consciousness. This question raises a number of difficult issues which cannot be considered here. Part of the rationale underlying the view I wish to advance will be clear, however, if one considers the role played by memory in the psychological unity of an individual over time. When I remember a past experience, what I know is not merely that there was a certain experience which someone or other had, but that there was an experience that belonged to the *same* individual as the present memory beliefs, and it seems clear that this feature of one's memories is, in general, a crucial part of what it is that makes one a continuing subject of experiences, rather than merely a series of psychologically isolated, momentary subjects of consciousness. This suggests something like the following principle.

> Desires existing at different times can belong to a single, continuing subject of consciousness only if that subject of consciousness possesses, at some time, the concept of a continuing self or mental substance.[11]

---

[11] For a fuller discussion, and defense of this principle, see op. cit., section 5.3.

Given this principle, together with the particular-rights principle, one can set out the following argument in support of a claim concerning a necessary condition which an entity must satisfy if it is to have a right to life:

(1) The concept of a right is such that an individual cannot have a right at time t to continued existence unless the individual is such that it can be in its interest at time t that it continue to exist.

(2) The continued existence of a given subject of consciousness cannot be in that individual's interest at time t unless *either* that individual has a desire, at time t, to continue to exist as a subject of consciousness, *or* that individual can have desires at other times.

(3) An individual cannot have a desire to continue to exist as a subject of consciousness unless it possesses the concept of a continuing self or mental substance.

(4) An individual existing at one time cannot have desires at other times unless there is at least one time at which it possesses the concept of a continuing self or mental substance.

Therefore:

(5) An individual cannot have a right to continued existence unless there is at least one time at which it possesses the concept of a continuing self or mental substance.

This conclusion is obviously significant. But precisely what implications does it have with respect to the morality of abortion and infanticide? The answer will depend upon what relationship there is between, on the one hand, the behavioral and neurophysiological development of a human being, and, on the other, the development of that individual's mind. Some people believe that there is no relationship at all. They believe that a human mind, with all its mature capacities, is present in a human from conception onward, and so is there before the brain has even begun to develop, and before the individual has begun to exhibit behavior expressive of higher mental functioning. Most philosophers, however, reject this view. They believe, on the one hand, that there is, in general, a rather close relation between an individual's behavioral capacities and its mental functioning, and, on the other, that there is a very intimate relationship between the mind and the brain. As regards the latter, some philosophers hold that the mind is in fact identical with the brain. Others maintain that the mind is distinct from the brain, but causally dependent upon it. In either case, the result is a view according to which the development of the mind and the brain are necessarily closely tied to one another.

If one does adopt the view that there is a close relation between the behavioral and neurophysiological development of a human being, and the development of its mind, then the above conclusion has a very important, and possibly decisive implication with respect to the morality of abortion and infanticide. For when human development, both behavioral and neurophysiological, is closely examined, it is seen to be most unlikely that human fetuses, or even newborn babies, possess any concept of a continuing self.[12] And in the light of the above conclusion, this means that such individuals do not possess a right to life.

But is it reasonable to hold that there is a close relation between human behavioral and neurophysiological development, and the development of the human mind? Approached from a scientific perspective, I believe that there is excellent reason for doing so. Consider, for example, what is known about how, at later stages, human mental capacities proceed in step with brain development, or what is known about how damage to different parts of the brain can affect, in different ways, an individual's intellectual capacities.

Why, then, do some people reject the view that there is a close relationship between the development of the human mind, and the behavioral and neurophysiological development of human beings? There are, I think, two main reasons. First, some philosophers believe that the scientific evidence is irrelevant, because they believe that it is possible to establish, by means of a purely metaphysical argument, that a human mind, with its mature capacities, is present in a human from conception onward. I have argued elsewhere that the argument in question is unsound.[13]

Secondly, and more commonly, some people appeal to the idea that it is a divinely revealed truth that human beings have minds from conception onward. There are a number of points to be made about such an appeal. In the first place, the belief that a mind, or soul, is infused into a human body at conception by God is not an essential belief within many of the world religions. Secondly, even within religious traditions, such as Roman Catholicism, where that belief is a very common one, it is by no means universally accepted. Thus, for example, the well-known Catholic philosopher, Joseph Donceel, has argued very strongly for the claim that the correct position on the question of ensoulment is that the soul enters the body only when the human brain has undergone a sufficient process of development.[14] Thirdly, there is the question of whether it is reasonable to accept the religious outlook which is being appealed to in support of the contention that humans have minds which are capable of higher intellectual activities from conception onward. This question raises very large issues in philosophy of religion which cannot be pursued here. But it should at least be said that many contemporary philosophers who have reflected upon religious beliefs have come to the view that there is not sufficient reason even for believing in the existence of God, let alone for accepting the much more detailed religious claims which are

---

[12] For a detailed survey of the scientific evidence concerning human development, see op. cit., section 11.5.

[13] Op. cit., section 11.42.

[14] For a brief discussion, see Joseph F. Donceel, "A Liberal Catholic's View," in *Abortion in a Changing World,* Volume I, edited by R. E. Hall, New York, 1970 [*supra,* pp. 15–20]. A more detailed philosophical discussion can be found in Donceel's "Immediate Animation and Delayed Hominization," *Theological Studies,* Volume 31, 1970, pp. 76–105.

part of a religion such as Christianity. Finally, suppose that one nonetheless decides to accept the contention that it is a divinely revealed truth that humans have, from conception onward, minds that are capable of higher mental activities, and that one appeals to this purported revelation in order to support the claim that all humans have a right to life. One needs to notice that if one then goes on to argue, not merely that abortion is morally wrong, but that there should be a law against it, one will encounter a very serious objection. For it is surely true that it is inappropriate, at least in a pluralistic society, to appeal to specific religious beliefs of a nonmoral sort—such as the belief that God infuses souls into human bodies at conception—in support of legislation that will be binding upon everyone, including those who either accept different religious beliefs, or none at all.

III. Summary and Conclusions

In this paper I have advanced three main philosophical contentions:

> (1) An entity cannot have a right to life unless it is capable of having an interest in its own continued existence.
> (2) An entity is not capable of having an interest in its own continued existence unless it possesses, at some time, the concept of a continuing self, or subject of experiences and other mental states.
> (3) The fact that an entity will, if not destroyed, come to have properties that would give it a right to life does not in itself make it seriously wrong to destroy it.[15]

If these philosophical contentions are correct, the crucial question is a factual one: At what point does a developing human being acquire the concept of a continuing self, and at what point is it capable of having an interest in its own continued existence? I have not examined this issue in detail here, but I have suggested that careful scientific studies of human development, both behavioral and neurophysiological, strongly support the view that even newborn humans do not have the capacities in question. If this is right, then it would seem that infanticide during a time interval shortly after birth must be viewed as morally acceptable.

But where is the line to be drawn? What is the precise cutoff point? If one maintained, as some philosophers do, that an individual can possess a concept

---

[15] Editor's note: I have very reluctantly deleted Tooley's important arguments against the potentiality principle. The interested reader is referred to Tooley's original article in *Philosophy & Public Affairs,* vol. 2, no. 1 (Fall 1972), and his forthcoming book.

only if it is capable of expressing that concept linguistically, then it would be a relatively simple matter to determine whether a given organism possessed the concept of a continuing subject of experiences and other mental states. It is far from clear, however, that this claim about the necessary connection between the possession of concepts and the having of linguistic capabilities is correct. I would argue, for example, that one wants to ascribe mental states of a conceptual sort—such as beliefs and desires—to animals that are incapable of learning a language, and that an individual cannot have beliefs and desires unless it possesses the concepts involved in those beliefs and desires. And if that view is right—if an organism can acquire concepts without thereby acquiring a way of expressing those concepts linguistically—then the question of whether an individual possesses the concept of a continuing self may be one that requires quite subtle experimental techniques to answer.

If this view of the matter is roughly correct, there are two worries that one is left with at the level of practical moral decisions, one of which may turn out to be deeply disturbing. The lesser worry is the question just raised: Where is the line to be drawn in the case of infanticide? This is not really a troubling question since there is no serious need to know the exact point at which a human infant acquires a right to life. For in the vast majority of cases in which infanticide is desirable due to serious defects from which the baby suffers, its desirability will be apparent at birth or within a very short time thereafter. Since it seems clear that an infant at this point in its development is not capable of possessing the concept of a continuing subject of experiences and other mental states, and so is incapable of having an interest in its own continued existence, infanticide will be morally permissible in the vast majority of cases in which it is, for one reason or another, desirable. The practical moral problem can thus be satisfactorily handled by choosing some short period of time, such as a week after birth, as the interval during which infanticide will be permitted.

The troubling issue which arises out of the above reflections concerns whether adult animals belonging to species other than Homo sapiens may not also possess a right to life. For once one allows that an individual can possess concepts, and have beliefs and desires, without being able to express those concepts, or those beliefs and desires, linguistically, then it becomes very much an open question whether animals belonging to other species do not possess properties that give them a right to life. Indeed, I am strongly inclined to think that adult members of at least some nonhuman species do have a right to life. My reason is that, first, I believe that some nonhuman animals are capable of envisaging a future for themselves, and of having desires about future states of themselves. Secondly, that anything which exercises these capacities has an interest in its own continued existence. And thirdly, that having an interest in one's own continued existence is not merely a necessary, but also a sufficient, condition for having a right to life.

The suggestion that at least some nonhuman animals have a right to life is not unfamiliar, but it is one that most of us are accustomed to dismissing very casually.

The line of thought advanced here suggests that this attitude may very well turn out to be tragically mistaken. Once one reflects upon the question of the *basic* moral principles involved in the ascription of a right to life to organisms, one may find oneself driven to the conclusion that our everyday treatment of members of other species is morally indefensible, and that we are in fact murdering innocent persons.

Abortion, Infanticide, and Respect for Persons[1]

S. I. Benn

I

Moral problems are commonly presented as arising from conflicts of interest—of the interests of different persons to whom we have obligations, between our own interests and those of others, between those of groups and mankind in general, and so on. And where such interests are acknowledged as legitimate, they are commonly called rights. It is not clear to me, however, that *all* our moral duties need to be specifiable in these terms; there are conservationists and ecologically oriented moralists, for instance, who deplore the rape of the environment not merely for its effects on *human* interests, or for denying the rights of future generations, but on account of values which, though admittedly somewhat difficult to specify, are more likely aesthetic values than either rights or interests. But we don't need to go into that difficult area to find instances of moral arguments that do not rely on the deleterious effects to persons. Someone who allowed an animal to suffer pain he could readily alleviate would commonly be thought morally blameworthy; and to *cause* needless pain, even to the humblest of sentient creatures, would be thought worse still. But to protest at the wanton torture of snails

Note: The articles by Judith Jarvis Thomson and Michael Tooley referred to in the paper were originally published in *Philosophy & Public Affairs,* vol. 1, no. 1 (1971) and vol. 2, no. 1 (1972), respectively. The references in the present paper are, however, to the revised version of Tooley's article, as it appears in the first edition of this book on pp. 51–91.

[1] An early version of this paper was read to a group at Rockefeller University and a later version to my colleagues at the Australian National University. I am indebted to both groups for criticism and suggestions. I am particularly indebted to Geoffrey Mortimore and to Miriam Benn for suggestions that have done much to make the argument clearer, not only to my readers but also to myself.

is not to suppose that snails have rights, as the subjects of interests deserving of our consideration.

I raise these matters because I want to argue that the common presumption, that the problem of abortion *must* be argued in terms of the conflict of rights between the living mother and the unborn fetus, may be a mistake; that there may be morally relevant reasons that do not take this form, that is, that do not need to be specified in terms of the morally defensible interests of the parties in question, and that some of the peculiar difficulties of this subject may evaporate if we are prepared to allow that other kinds of reasons can be very cogent, too.

The trouble with the common presumption is that it makes difficulties for all but the most uncompromising of the anti-abortionists, as well as for the pro-abortionist. The anti-abortionist who wants to make exceptions in favor, for instance, of victims of rape, or of mothers whose lives are endangered by pregnancy, is faced with the difficult task of finding some ground for preferring the rights of the mother to those of the fetus. In the latter case, why *should* it be obvious that the mother's right to life takes precedence? No one would blame *her,* perhaps, if, on grounds of self-preservation, she aborted herself; but we do not generally condone the killing by third parties, by a doctor, for instance, of one innocent person to save the life of another. On what possible grounds could such a choice be made? The case of the victim of rape is no easier; indeed, since the mother's *life* is not in question, the interest of the fetus would seem overriding. One may sympathize with the mother's bad luck; but though we sympathize as readily with a person saddled with the care of an aged parent, we should not condone poisoning the parent to be free of the incubus.

Judith Jarvis Thomson has argued that the fetus's right to life, supposing it to have one, is not, in such a case, to be taken as imposing a corresponding duty on the mother, unless the mother can be said to have accepted it.[2] But surely circumstances can thrust duties upon us, whether we accept them or not. A man who can swim has a moral duty to jump in to rescue one drowning, if he happens to be the only one near; and we should take a poor view of him if he pleaded in excuse: "I was just getting over a cold, and a wetting would have made it worse." If the mother is the only person who *can* sustain life of the fetus (and in the present state of biological technology this is certainly the case), then, if the fetus *has* a right to life, it certainly looks as though that right creates a duty for the mother, as the only *possible* person capable of doing anything about it.

I do not claim that for every ascription of a right there must be a logically correlative ascription of a duty, as "X has a right to $5 from Y" is logically correlative to "Y has a duty to pay X $5"; general assertions of human rights, for instance, like "Every child has a right to be educated" may lay an assignable duty to educate him on no one in particular. The point of ascribing such rights may be to urge upon the community at large, on the government, on the church, perhaps—

---

[2] Judith Jarvis Thomson, "A Defense of Abortion," this volume, pp. 173–187.

on anyone who may have the power—the duty to see that the right is implemented by assigning the correlative duty to someone. But if there were no one who could, by the very nature of the case, collect a duty corresponding however remotely to the right ascribed (and, the mother apart, this seems to be true of a fetus's right to life), the ascription would be quite empty.

Judith Thomson admits, in fact, that there can be reasons against abortions, even in the case of unwanted babies for whose conception the mother cannot be held responsible; but she distinguishes these as considerations of "moral decency" rather than of duty. But I suspect that the distinction is important only on account of the tacit assumption that the only relevant duties must correspond to someone's rights, and that rights can only be acquired by concession and agreement. I hope to show that the distinction need not be insisted upon, since there are other, better ways of stating the issues to be resolved, which recognize that rights are only one among a variety of types of moral consideration.

II

I have been arguing that, the Thomson-style argument apart, allowing the fetus a right to life makes it very difficult to avoid absolute anti-abortionism. *Denying* the fetus a right to life seems, however, to have its problems too. Michael Tooley argues[3]—rightly, in my view—that

> . . . if one says it is wrong to destroy a newborn baby but not a zygote or some intermediate stage in the development of a human being . . . one should be prepared to point to a *morally relevant* difference between a newborn baby and the earlier stage in the development of a human being.

Tooley's paper is designed to show that the morally relevant difference really comes later—but probably not very much later—when the baby attains a certain level of consciousness that, according to Tooley, is necessary to qualify it as a person. *Thereafter,* to kill it would be to infringe its right to life. But Tooley appears to think that to kill fetuses and infants alike before that stage can be quite all right.

Now I am inclined to think that Tooley has hit on a promising strategy, but is mistaken in the inferences he draws from it. He is anxious to justify terminating at the earliest possible stage the lives of deformed and otherwise handicapped infants as well as fetuses.[4] So he distinguishes, first, between the concept of a human being and the concept of a person, arguing that the right to life belongs to the latter, not the former. The argument depends on there being some way of characterizing a person, such that, recognizing the existence of the relevant

---

[3] Michael Tooley, "In Defense of Abortion and Infanticide," first edition, pp. 51–91. [Also this volume, pp. 120–134].

[4] Ibid., p. 91. [Also this volume, p. 133.]

properties, one would be committed to conceding a right to life, where otherwise there would be none. But Tooley does not commit himself to saying what properties would be sufficient; he is content to argue that there are conditions *conceptually necessary* to a right to life that are too stringent to be satisfied by fetuses and infants. The advantage claimed for this approach, and for his account of what it is to be a person, is that it avoids an arbitrary cutoff point, providing instead a minimum condition for being a person such that no one who failed to satisfy it could, logically, have a right to life.

Tooley's account of what it is to have a right is very complicated. For the purposes of my argument, however, I do not think it would weaken Tooley's position to put it thus crudely: An individual has a right to something only if it is the case both that he is capable of desiring it,[5] and that if he did desire it, other individuals would, in virtue of the fact alone, be under a *prima facie* obligation to refrain from denying it to him. But desiring something, he believes, can be described as desiring:

> . . . that a certain proposition be true. Then, since one cannot desire that a proposition be true unless one understands it, and since one cannot understand it without possessing the concepts involved in it, it follows that the desires one can have are limited by the concepts one possesses.

Since desiring something entails having the concept of the thing desired, it is logically impossible to have a right to a thing one cannot conceive and therefore cannot desire. So a newborn kitten may have the right not to be tortured, supposing it to have the concepts of pain and the cessation of pain. But it is not a person, with a right to life, for,

> . . . [an] individual cannot have a right to life unless there is some time at which it exists and at which it is capable either of having a desire to continue to exist as the continuing subject of experiences and other mental states that it is, or of having a desire to become [such a subject].

Neither a newborn kitten, nor a fetus, nor a human infant has the conceptual equipment to entertain this kind of a desire. Therefore they have no right to life, whatever other rights they may have.

Tooley does not confine the condition of having the necessary self-consciousness to subjects with the linguistic capacity to formulate it; he seriously entertains the possibility that this condition for a right to life might be satisfied by some of the higher, though not necessarily very high, animals, which would therefore qualify, on his account, as persons.

---

[5] Editor's note: Tooley has modified his earlier account. Now the concept of an interest plays a role similar to that played formerly by the concept of desire. See this volume, pp. 122–132.

This, then, is the shape of Tooley's argument: whatever the conditions sufficient for a right to life, they must include as necessary conditions ones that a newborn infant, let alone a fetus, cannot satisfy. Abortion and killing defective infants are therefore permissible, because fetus and infant alike are distinguishable in a morally relevant way from the paradigm of personhood, the adult human being.

But is Tooley perhaps opening the door too wide? At what age is a human child equipped with a concept of self, as "a subject of experiences and other mental states," "a continuing entity," believing itself to be such a one, and therefore capable of desiring to go on being so? Tooley offers no opinion. Since he is anxious to show only that there is at least one necessary condition demanding enough to exclude the classes whose right to life he is contesting, he does not have to specify what conditions would be sufficient for a right to life. Consequently he is undisturbed that his characterization of a person may be a bit elusive; it is strict enough to do the job assigned to it. But what if it turned out to be so strict that it excluded well-grown youngsters, too—what would Tooley make of his argument then?

Tooley rightly argues that to warrant a "cutoff point," before which killing a human being is morally permissible, but thereafter not, or to provide a justification for freedom to kill unborn kittens but not human fetuses, one must demonstrate "morally relevant" differences. But Tooley has not shown that his own criteria are morally relevant. He has displayed merely a conceptual connection, such that without a capacity to conceive R there could not be a right to R. But why is this a *morally* relevant difference between subjects? Moreover, his stated premises warrant the conclusion not that abortion and infanticide are permissible, as he seems to suppose, but only that they would not be violations of a right to life. Now Tooley explicitly recognizes that one *could* take the view that "some actions are seriously wrong even though they do not violate anyone's right", but he supposes, without reasons shown, that it involves a "cost" that a moral philosopher would be reluctant to incur.[6] I believe that this represents a fundamental weakness. I shall argue that a moral reason that invokes a right is a special sort of moral reason that can apply only in respect of a particular kind of being—a moral agent or "a person."

Related to Tooley's misunderstanding of the nature of a right is his failure to take seriously the problem of characterizing "a person." While acknowledging that his usage diverges from the more common characterization of a person as one who has rights,[7] he is content to use the term synonymously with "someone having a serious right to life." It is, he says, "a purely moral concept, free of all descriptive content." He is consequently prevented from showing what it is about anyone who *has* a serious right to life, that could count as a moral reason for his having it, distinguishing him from kittens, infants, and fetuses. He can argue only

---

[6] Tooley, op. cit., p. 89. [Cf. this volume, p. 121.]

[7] Ibid., p. 55.

that, if there *were* any such person, he would have to satisfy conditions that these other subjects could not satisfy.

My own strategy depends precisely on my being able to produce a characterization (a) of a right, that will distinguish it from other kinds of moral consideration, and (b) of a person, rounded enough to provide reasons not only necessary but sufficient to qualify such a one, not only as a subject of a right to life, but of any rights at all. I shall argue that the "morally relevant differences" that Tooley properly seeks would exclude not only kittens, infants, and fetuses, but quite well-developed babies, too, from the class of subjects of rights. To preserve something of our moral intuition, then, about the immorality of killing babies, we shall have to take seriously the possibility, which Tooley so lightly dismisses, that some actions are wrong for reasons other than that they violate rights. And so I reopen the questions of abortion and infanticide in a form that permits us to argue about them rationally. I shall not attempt to reach a substantive conclusion.

III

I shall argue the case, first, that certain considerations, relating to the well-being or suffering of a sentient being, while being *reasons* for a person to act in one way rather than another, are not properly speaking *rights* of that sentient being that the person act in that way. One ought to feed one's domestic animals not because they have a right to be fed, but because it is cruel not to feed them, and it is an owner's responsibility to see that they are not left to suffer. We may have duties in respect of such beings, as patients, just as we may have duties in respect of the environment, which may also suffer (though in a somewhat different sense) if we pursue our objectives with a reckless disregard for the damage we do.

To say of someone that he has right to Q is to advance a quite different kind of consideration; paradigmatically, it is to say that by virtue of a set of normative relations that hold between him and some particular respondent or people at large, there are certain demands such that his making them would be a reason for the respondent's acceding to them, and would put the latter in the wrong if, without some overriding reason, he did not accede to them. Equally, the bearer of the right would then have a legitimate grievance, a ground for resentment, for seeking redress or compensation, and so on. There are, in short, a series of normatively significant acts (including speech acts) open to the bearer of a right, which have as their general point enabling him to manipulate his social situation the better to pursue whatever aims or enterprises he may happen to have. It is for this reason that philosophers such as Herbert Hart[8] have considered the liberty *not* to insist on one's right—to waive it—as distinguishing rights from other action

---

[8]Cp. H.L.A. Hart, "Are There Any Natural Rights?", in A. Quinton (ed.), *Political Philosophy,* London, 1967, pp. 57–59.

considerations. Now if this is what is understood by a right it follows that only a moral agent, having the conceptual capabilities of considering whether to insist or not upon his right, of manipulating, too, the "pulls" it gives him on the actions of others, capable, in short of having projects and enterprises of his own, could be said to be a subject of rights.

Like Tooley, then, I am employing a presuppositional argument. I am arguing, however, that to have a right presupposes not simply the capacity to desire the object in question, but to be aware of oneself as the subject of enterprises and projects that could be forwarded by choosing to exercise one's rights. While Tooley confines the significance of something approaching this level of self-consciousness to the right to life alone, I am contending that it is a precondition for any right at all.

This is not, I think, an arbitrary stipulation, but is necessary if the distinction between subjects of rights and other entities is to be based on morally relevant considerations. For the fact that someone happens to have, or is capable of having, desires of any given kind is not *obviously* a reason for anyone else to rec-ognize such a one as having any claim upon him whatsoever. Tooley does not suggest that it is; he takes it to be no more than a necessary condition for there to be such a reason. But he proposes no further condition that *could* count as a morally significant one. The claim I make for my own account is that it not only fits our general conception of what it is to be a person, but that the descriptive content I assign to that notion displays the point of our distinguishing a class of moral considerations that applies to persons but not to other entities.

I characterize a person, therefore, as someone aware of himself, not just as process or happening, but as *agent,* as making decisions that make a difference to the way the world goes, as having projects that constitute certain existing or possible states as "important" and "unimportant," as capable, therefore, of assessing his own performances as successful or unsuccessful. Now, this is how I see myself in the world, and, unless I have a peculiar, solipsistic view of the universe, I recognize others in it that, like me, are persons too. And when, in going about their enterprises, in deciding on the differences they propose to make in the world, they totally disregard my enterprises, as if mine weren't important at all, I *resent* it; for I have a notion of what is my due, as a person. But if I do see myself in this way, my resentment can be rational only if I concede that *any* person ought to have this minimal regard for any other; for what is there peculiar about me, that a person *like* me should respect me, and not I him? Respect for persons amounts then to respect for those who, having the capacity for enter-taining ends and goal-oriented action, and appraising events and states of affairs in the light of such ends, cannot be treated as simply happenings or processes; and "respect" involves conceding a certain minimum of consideration or regard for them, independently of any ends or purposes of my own to which they may relate as means.

Now put like this, the notion of what it is to be a person can plausibly be said to make the kind of difference that Tooley wants it to make, such that killing such a one is an act of quite a different kind from killing a snail. And anyone satisfying these conditions would also satisfy Tooley's somewhat less stringent condition, too. But the characterization of a person is now full enough to display some *point* in the distinction between person and object, such that while objects, as suffering, perhaps pitiable patients, may be subjects of considerations of kindness, or of improvement, only persons can be the subjects of rights.

It may be argued, against my account of what it is to be a person, and therefore the subject of rights, that the corresponding legal concepts are very much broader than those I suggest: in law, infants are persons, and the Supreme Court of the United States appears to have decided that a fetus capable of independent existence has rights. But these concepts, of course, are related to institutional forms; other persons can use the leverage provided by the normative nexus *in the name of* the subject of the right, to manipulate its social situation for its benefit; no capacity for action or decision on the part of the principal is therefore presupposed. So civil responsibility can fall on a legal person as principal, for actions done by an agent whom the principal not merely had not but *could* not have authorized to perform the act. Though the paradigm of a legally responsible agent is still very much like that of a moral agent (so that cases of vicarious criminal liability without authorization or knowledge are exceptional), it has been found convenient to extend these concepts by appropriate institutionalization to cases in which the usual presuppositions are only analogously satisfied.

IV

If my account of the preconditions of a right to life is correct, it seems unlikely that a child would satisfy them until many months after birth. And in that case, the principle that a person has a right to life would not protect infants until well *beyond* the very early weeks that Tooley seems to envisage. That is why I have insisted on the possibility that there might be relevant reasons against infanticide— and perhaps against abortion too—that are not reasons based on the *right* to life of either infant or fetus. What kind of reasons might they be? Mainly consequentialist reasons of a rule-utilitarian kind, I suppose. But precisely because I have ruled out the status of infant and fetus as persons, the *relevant* consequences cannot be advantages for the fetus or the infant, such that to deny them would be to do them an injustice, for these do not, as yet, possess the qualifications for this kind of moral consideration.

I have already suggested, of course, that there may be other morally relevant considerations, such as the evil of pain, that may be a barrier to our treating infants, or other sentient beings, just as we please. But killing as such is peculiar because it is objectionable (when it is) not because it brings about something like pain which is bad, but because it terminates the *existence* of something; and why should that be a bad thing, and for whom? We do not generally treat killing germs that way; and many people do not feel that way about killing rabbits, deer, or fish, just for sport. So why babies?

Well, there are reasons offered against killing just for sport, too; reasons that relate to conservationist ends, but also to a certain alleged coarsening or brutalizing of the persons engaging in it. Now whether or not these are good reasons, they may be of a type that is cogent in respect to babies. In the first place, we have what seems to be an instinctual tenderness and protectiveness toward babies, that one would suppose had some kind of evolutionary warrant for species survival. That might not be an argument for it, of course, in a world threatened with overpopulation; and there have certainly been cultures that managed well enough to suppress it (if ever they had it) to dispose of weaklings and unwanted daughters.

But there is a better reason than species survival for not treating infants as expendable; namely, that some infants do grow up into persons. And if as infants *they* are not treated with at least some minimal degree of tenderness and consideration, they will suffer for it later, as persons.

This is not the argument that infants are *potential* persons, and have rights as such. For if A has rights only because he satisfies some condition P, it doesn't follow that B has the same rights now because he *could* have property P at some time in the future. It only follows that he *will* have rights *when* he has P. He is a potential bearer of rights, as he is a potential bearer of P. A potential president of the United States is not on that account Commander-in-Chief.

The account I suggest of the consideration due to the infant is a different one. It is rather that, because the person that he *will* be (provided he grows up) will be emotionally stunted or impaired if he is deprived of love and tender care as an infant, it is for the sake of those that *will* grow into persons that we take care of all babies now. For not to do so for some—those that we regard as expendable or dispensible—might well lead us into a callous unconcern for others too. But if a case like this can be made for infants, it may apply equally well to fetuses; or at least, to fetuses at a stage of maturity at which we can reasonably associate the way we treat them with the way we treat babies—at a stage, that is, at which we think of them, vividly enough, as a baby in the womb.

I claim for this kind of analysis these advantages over arguments of "a human being's right to life," or of the claims of the fetus or a baby as a person:

1. It preserves (what seems to be essential) the notion that normal adult human beings are not to be treated as expendable, for the sake of some end or advantage which they could not, in the nature of the case, envisage as their own.

2. It relates this consideration to a feature in our experience of ourselves and others, that does seem to provide a reason for distinguishing persons from mere objects or processes in the world.

3. It provides a way of reconciling a number of different intuitive reactions, without arbitrary gaps or cutoff points. Thus, it seems to me absurd to treat a zygote as if it had all the moral dignity of a mature human person. The physical fact of the merger of sperm and ovum is not, to me, an impressive candidate for consideration, as subject of interests. On the other hand, if any distinction we make in our treatment of the fetus at X and $X + N$ months from conception is to be grounded on morally relevant considerations, we need some *form* of argument that has in it greater flexibility than we can get out of "the rights of a person to life." Either one is or is not a person—one entity is not a little more of a person than another (though the actual point at which a *given* being qualifies may be debatable). As between persons, there is a basic equality of consideration.[9]

If one is a person, he can't legitimately be a subject of consequentialist arguments that wholly exclude his interests; he has a right to have his own evaluation of events taken into account. But if he is not, then considerations based on consequential advantages for those who do count may indicate that he be treated differently according to the stage of development he has reached. And the *actual future* persons may suffer if the potential ones now alive are not treated with a certain minimal tenderness. But here there *may* be rational (if somewhat hazy) cutoff points.

I offer this as an instance of a possible form of argument; there may be other, better arguments of the same form. If it has the flexibility I claim for it, it becomes possible to argue whether, in the given circumstances in which we find ourselves, the damage likely to arise from general abortion on demand is likely to be greater or smaller than the damage involved when women have unwanted babies. The mother's right to determine what happens to her own body is still a consideration, but is not left alone in the field, just by denying the fetus a countervailing right to life. Equally, we can argue about whether we do more harm to general attitudes to babies, to human life at all stages, by painlessly destroying deformed infants, or by allowing them to survive. And we can differ *rationally* on these matters, for there can be reasons that everyone can recognize as being reasons, for taking one view rather than another. There may even be reasons of *this* kind (though I doubt it) for being an absolute anti-abortionist.

---

[9] See my "Egalitarianism and the Equal Consideration of Interests" in J. R. Pennock and J. W. Chapman (eds.), *Equality-NOMOS* IX, New York, 1967, pp. 61–78.

Potentiality, Development, and Rights

Joel Feinberg

T he . . . difficulty for the strict potentiality criterion is . . . serious. It is a logical error, some have charged, to deduce *actual* rights from merely *potential* (but not yet actual) qualification for those rights. What follow from potential qualification, it is said, are potential, not actual, rights; what entails actual rights is actual, not potential, qualification. As the Australian philosopher Stanley Benn puts it, "A potential president of the United States is not on that account Commander-in-Chief [of the U.S. Army and Navy]."[1] This simple point can be called "the logical point about potentiality." Taken on its own terms, I don't see how it can be answered as an objection to the strict potentiality criterion. It is still open to an antiabortionist to argue that merely potential commonsense personhood is a ground for *duties* we may have toward the potential person. But he cannot argue that it is the ground for the potential person's *rights* without committing a logical error.

The Modified or Gradualist Potentiality Criterion

"Potential possession of c[2] confers not a right, but only a claim, to life, but that claim keeps growing stronger, requiring ever stronger reasons to override it, until

Excerpted from "Abortion" in *Matters of Life and Death*, ed. by Tom Regan (New York: Random House, 1980), by permission of Random House, Inc.

[1] Stanley I. Benn, "Abortion, Infanticide, and Respect for Persons," [*supra*, p. 135].

[2] Editor's note: The author explained earlier in the essay that he will use the letter c as an abbreviation for the collection of characteristics (consciousness, self-concept, rationality, etc.), whatever they may be, that are necessary and jointly sufficient for "commonsense personhood."

the point when c is actually possessed, by which time it has become a full right to life." This modification of the potentiality criterion has one distinct and important advantage. It coheres with the widely shared feeling that the moral seriousness of abortion increases with the age of the fetus. It is extremely difficult to believe on other than very specific theological grounds that a zygote one day after conception is the sort of being that can have any rights at all, much less the whole armory of "human rights" including "the right to life." But it is equally difficult for a great many people to believe that a full-term fetus one day before birth does not have a right to life. Moreover, it is very difficult to find one point in the continuous development of the fetus before which it is utterly without rights and after which it has exactly the same rights as any adult human being. Some rights in postnatal human life can be acquired instantly or suddenly; the rights of citizenship, for example, come into existence at a precise moment in the naturalization proceedings after an oath has been administered and a judicial pronouncement formally produced and certified. Similarly, the rights of husbands and wives come into existence at just that moment when an authorized person utters the words "I hereby pronounce you husband and wife." But the rights of the fetus cannot possibly jump in this fashion from nonbeing to being at some precise moment in pregnancy. [An] alternative is to think of them as growing steadily and gradually throughout the entire nine-month period until they are virtually "mature" at parturition. There is [on this view] a kind of growth in "moral weight" that proceeds in parallel fashion with the physical growth and development of the fetus.

An "immature right" on this view is not to be thought of simply as no right at all, as if in morals a miss were as good as a mile. A better characterization of the unfinished right would be a "weak right," a claim with some moral force proportional to its degree of development, but not yet as much force as a fully matured right. The key word in this account is 'claim.' Elsewhere I have given an account of the difference between having a right (which I defined as a "valid claim") and having a claim that is not, or not quite, valid. What would the latter be like?

> One might accumulate just enough evidence to argue with relevance and cogency that one has a right . . . although one's case might not be overwhelmingly conclusive. The argument might be strong enough to entitle one to a hearing and fair consideration. When one is in this position, it might be said that one "has a claim" that deserves to be weighed carefully. Nevertheless the balance of reasons may turn out to militate against recognition of the claim, so that the claim is not a valid claim or right. [3]

Now there are various ways in which a claim can fail to be a right. There are many examples, particularly from the law, where *all* the claims to some property,

---

[3] Joel Feinberg, *Social Philosophy* (Englewood Cliffs, N.J.: Prentice-Hall, 1973), p. 66.

including some that are relevantly made and worthy of respect, are rejected, simply because none of them is deemed strong enough to qualify as a right. In such cases, a miss truly is as good as a mile. But in other cases, an acknowledged claim of (say) medium strength will be strong enough to be a right *unless* a stronger claim appears on the scene to override it. For these conflict situations, card games provide a useful analogy. In poker, three-of-a-kind is good enough to win the pot unless one of the other players "makes claim" to the pot with a higher hand, say a flush or a full house. The player who claims the pot with three-of-a-kind "has a claim" to the pot that is overridden by the stronger claim of the player with the full house. The strongest claim presented will, by that fact, constitute a right to take the money. The player who withdrew with a four-flush had "no claim at all," but even that person's hand might have established a right to the pot if no stronger claim were in conflict with it.

The analogy applies to the abortion situation in the following way. The game has at least two players, the mother and the fetus, though more can play, and sometimes the father and/or the doctor are involved too. For the first few weeks of its life, the fetus (zygote, embryo) has hardly any claim to life at all, and virtually any reason of the mother's for aborting it will be strong enough to override a claim made in the fetus's behalf. At any stage in the game, any reason the mother might have for aborting will constitute a claim, but as the fetus matures, its claims grow stronger requiring ever-stronger claims to override them. After three months or so, the fact that an abortion would be "convenient" for the mother will not be a strong enough claim, and the fetus' claim to life will defeat it. In that case, the fetus can be said to have a valid claim or right to life in the same sense that the poker player's full house gives him or her a right to the pot: It is a right in the sense that it is the strongest of the conflicting claims, not in the sense that it is stronger than any conflicting claim that could conceivably come up. By the time the fetus has become a neonate (a newborn child), however, it has a "right to life" of the same kind all people have, and no mere conflicting claim can override it. (Perhaps more accurately, only claims that other human persons make in self-defense to their own lives can ever have an equal strength.)

The modified potentiality criterion has the attractiveness characteristic of compromise theories when fierce ideological quarrels rage between partisans of more extreme views. It shares one fatal flaw, however, with the strict potentiality criterion: Despite its greater flexibility, it cannot evade "the logical point about potentiality." A highly developed fetus is much closer to being a commonsense person with all the developed traits that qualify it for moral personhood than is the mere zygote. But being almost qualified for rights is not the same thing as being partially qualified for rights; nor is it the same thing as being qualified for partial rights, quasi-rights, or weak rights. The advanced fetus is closer to being a person than is the zygote, just as a dog is closer to personhood than a jellyfish, but that is not the same thing as being "more of a person." In 1930, when he was six years old, Jimmy Carter didn't know it, but he was a potential president of the United States. That gave him no claim *then*, not even a very weak claim, to give commands to the U.S. Army and Navy. Franklin D. Roosevelt in 1930 was only two years away from the presidency, so he was a potential president in a much stronger way (the potentiality was much less remote) than was young Jimmy. Nevertheless, he was not actually president, and he had no more of a claim to the prerogatives of the office than did Carter. The analogy to fetuses in different stages of development is of course imperfect. But in both cases it would seem to be invalid to infer the existence of a "weak version of a right" from an "almost qualification" for the full right. In summary, the modified potentiality criterion, insofar as it permits the potential possession of c to be a *sufficient condition* for the actual possession of claims, and in some cases of rights, is seriously flawed in the same manner as the strict potentiality criterion.

The Actual-Possession Criterion

"At any given time t, all and only those creatures who actually possess c are moral persons at t, whatever species or category they may happen to belong to." . . . [T]he actual-possession criterion must face a serious difficulty, namely that it implies that small infants (neonates) are not moral persons. There is very little more reason, after all, to attribute c to neonates than to advanced fetuses still *in utero*. Perhaps during the first few days after birth the infant is conscious and able to feel pain, but it is unlikely that it has a concept of its self or of its future life, that it has plans and goals, that it can think consecutively, and the like. In fact, the whole complex of traits that make up c is not *obviously* present until the second year of childhood. And that would seem to imply, according to the criterion we are considering, that the deliberate destruction of babies in their first year is no violation of their rights. And *that* might seem to entail that there is nothing wrong with infanticide (the deliberate killing of infants). But infanticide *is* wrong. Therefore, critics of the actual-possession criterion have argued that we ought to reject this criterion.

The Killing of Normal Infants

Advocates of the actual-possession criterion have a reply to this objection. Even if infanticide is not the murder of a moral person, they believe, it may yet be wrong and properly forbidden on other grounds. To make this clearer, it is useful to distinguish between (i) the case of killing a normal healthy infant or an infant whose handicaps are not so serious as to make a worthwhile future life impossible, and (ii) the case of killing severely deformed or incurably diseased infants.

Most advocates of the actual-possession criterion take a strong stand against infanticide in the first (the normal) case. It would be seriously wrong for a mother to kill her physically normal infant, they contend, even though such a killing would not violate anyone's right to life. The same reasons that make infanticide in the normal case wrong also justify its prohibition by the criminal law. The moral rule that condemns these killings and the legal rule that renders them punishable are both supported by "utilitarian reasons," that is, considerations of what is called "social utility," "the common good," "the public interest," and the like. Nature has apparently implanted in us an instinctive tenderness toward infants that has proven extremely useful to the species, not only because it leads us to protect our young from death, and thus keep our population up, but also because infants usually grow into adults, and in Benn's words, "if as infants *they* are not treated with some minimal degree of tenderness and consideration, they will suffer for it later, as persons."[4] One might add that when they are adults, others will suffer for it too, at their hands. Spontaneous warmth and sympathy toward babies then clearly has a great deal of social utility, and insofar as infanticide would tend to weaken that socially valuable response, it is, on utilitarian grounds, morally wrong.

There are other examples of wrongful and properly prohibitable acts that violate no one's rights. It would be wrong, for example, to hack up Grandfather's body after he has died a natural death, and dispose of his remains in the trash can on a cold winter's morning. That would be wrong not because it violates *Grandfather's* rights; he is dead and no longer has the same sort of rights as the rest of us, and we can make it part of the example that he was not offended while alive at the thought of such posthumous treatment and indeed even consented to it in advance. Somehow acts of this kind if not forbidden would strike at our respect for living human persons (without which organized society would be impossible) in the most keenly threatening way. (It might also be unhygienic and shocking to trash collectors—less important but equally relevant utilitarian considerations.)

Implications for the Problem of Abortion

The implications of the actual-possession criterion for the question of the status of the fetus as a moral person are straightforward: Since the fetus does not actually possess those characteristics *(c)* that we earlier listed as necessary and sufficient for possessing the right to life, the fetus does not possess that right. Given this criterion, therefore, abortion never involves violating a fetus' right to life, and permitting a fetus to be born is never anything we *owe* it, is never something that is *its* due.

It does not follow, however, that abortion is never wrong. As we saw earlier, despite the fact that infants fail to meet the actual-possession criterion and thus are not moral persons, reasons can be given, of a utilitarian kind, why it is wrong to kill them, at least if they are not radically deformed. It is possible, therefore,

---

[4] Benn, *op. cit.*, [p. 143].

that similar reasons can be given in opposition to aborting fetuses at later stages in their development, if they are likely not to be radically deformed when born.

Utilitarian reasons of the sort we have considered are so very important that they might suffice to rule out harsh or destructive treatment of *any* nonperson whose resemblance or similarity to real persons is very close: not only deceased ex-persons and small babies, but even adult primates and human fetuses in the final trimester of pregnancy. Justice Blackmun may have had such considerations in mind when in his majority opinion in *Roe* v. *Wade* he declared that even though no fetuses are legal persons protected by the law of homicide, nevertheless during the final trimester, "The State in promoting its interest in the potentiality of human life, may if it chooses, regulate, and even proscribe, abortion. . . ."[5] Whatever interest the State has in "the *potentiality* of human life" must be derivative from the plain interest it has in preserving and promoting respect for *actual* human life. It is not potential persons as such who merit our derivative respect but all *near-persons* including higher animals, dead people, infants, and well-developed fetuses, those beings whose similarity to real persons is close enough to render them sacred symbols of the real thing.

In the light of these considerations, it seems that a gradualist approach similar to that discussed earlier is a more plausible solution to the general problem of the moral justifiability of abortion than it is to the narrow problem of the criterion of moral personhood. Even if the fetus as a merely potential person lacks an actual right to life, and even if it would not be homicide therefore to kill it, its potential personhood may yet constitute a *reason* against killing it that requires an even stronger reason on the other side if abortion is to be justified. If that is so, it is not implausible to suppose that the more advanced the potential for personhood, the more stringent the case against killing.

As we have seen, there are reasons relevant to our moral decisions other than considerations of rights, so that sometimes actions can be judged morally wrong even though they violate no one's rights. Killing a fetus, in that case, could be wrong in certain circumstances, even though it violated no rights of the fetus, even though the fetus was not a moral person, even though the act was in no sense a murder. . . .

---

[5] From Justice Blackmun's opinion in *Roe* v. *Wade*, 410 U.S. 113 (1973). [*Infra*, p. 197.]

Abortion and the Concept of a Person

Jane English

T he abortion debate rages on. Yet the two most popular positions seem to be clearly mistaken. Conservatives maintain that a human life begins at conception and that therefore abortion must be wrong because it is murder. But not all killings of humans are murders. Most notably, self defense may justify even the killing of an innocent person.

Liberals, on the other hand, are just as mistaken in their argument that since a fetus does not become a person until birth, a woman may do whatever she pleases in and to her own body. First, you cannot do as you please with your own body if it affects other people adversely.[1] Second, if a fetus is not a person, that does not imply that you can do to it anything you wish. Animals, for example, are not persons, yet to kill or torture them for no reason at all is wrong.

At the center of the storm has been the issue of just when it is between ovulation and adulthood that a person appears on the scene. Conservatives draw the line at conception, liberals at birth. In this paper I first examine our concept of a person and conclude that no single criterion can capture the concept of a person and no sharp line can be drawn. Next I argue that if a fetus is a person, abortion is still justifiable in many cases; and if a fetus is not a person, killing it is still wrong in many cases. To a large extent, these two solutions are in agreement. I conclude that our concept of a person cannot and need not bear the weight that the abortion controversy has thrust upon it.

Reprinted from the *Canadian Journal of Philosophy*, vol. 5, no. 2 (October 1975) by permission of the Canadian Association for Publishing in Philosophy.

[1] We also have paternalistic laws which keep us from harming our own bodies even when no one else is affected. Ironically, anti-abortion laws were originally designed to protect pregnant women from a dangerous but tempting procedure.

I

The several factions in the abortion argument have drawn battle lines around various proposed criteria for determining what is and what is not a person. For example, Mary Anne Warren[2] lists five features (capacities for reasoning, self-awareness, complex communication, etc.) as her criteria for personhood and argues for the permissibility of abortion because a fetus falls outside this concept. Baruch Brody[3] uses brain waves. Michael Tooley[4] picks having-a-concept-of-self as his criterion and concludes that infanticide and abortion are justifiable, while the killing of adult animals is not. On the other side, Paul Ramsey[5] claims a certain gene structure is the defining characteristic. John Noonan[6] prefers conceived-of-humans and presents counterexamples to various other candidate criteria. For instance, he argues against viability as the criterion because the newborn and infirm would then be non-persons, since they cannot live without the aid of others. He rejects any criterion that calls upon the sorts of sentiments a being can evoke in adults on the grounds that this would allow us to exclude other races as non-persons if we could just view them sufficiently unsentimentally.

These approaches are typical: foes of abortion propose sufficient conditions for personhood which fetuses satisfy, while friends of abortion counter with necessary conditions for personhood which fetuses lack. But these both presuppose that the concept of a person can be captured in a strait jacket of necessary and/or sufficient conditions.[7] Rather, 'person' is a cluster of features, of which rationality, having a self concept and being conceived of humans are only part.

What is typical of persons? Within our concept of a person we include, first, certain biological factors: descended from humans, having a certain genetic makeup, having a head, hands, arms, eyes, capable of locomotion, breathing, eating, sleeping. There are psychological factors: sentience, perception, having a concept of self and of one's own interests and desires, the ability to use tools, the ability to use language or symbol systems, the ability to joke, to be angry, to

---

[2] Mary Anne Warren, "On the Moral and Legal Status of Abortion," *Monist* 57 (1973), [*supra*, pp. 102–119].

[3] Baruch Brody, "Fetal Humanity and the Theory of Essentialism," in Robert Baker and Frederick Elliston (eds.), *Philosophy and Sex* (Buffalo, N.Y., 1975).

[4] Michael Tooley, "Abortion and Infanticide," *Philosophy and Public Affairs* 2 (1971). [Revised version *supra*, pp. 120–134.]

[5] Paul Ramsey, "The Morality of Abortion," in James Rachels, ed., *Moral Problems* (New York, 1971).

[6] John Noonan, "Abortion and the Catholic Church: A Summary History," *Natural Law Forum* 12 (1967), pp. 125–131.

[7] Wittgenstein has argued against the possibility of so capturing the concept of a game, *Philosophical Investigations* (New York, 1958), § 66–71.

---

doubt. There are rationality factors: the ability to reason and draw conclusions, the ability to generalize and to learn from past experience, the ability to sacrifice present interests for greater gains in the future. There are social factors: the ability to work in groups and respond to peer pressures, the ability to recognize and consider as valuable the interests of others, seeing oneself as one among "other minds," the ability to sympathize, encourage, love, the ability to evoke from others the responses of sympathy, encouragement, love, the ability to work with others for mutual advantage. Then there are legal factors: being subject to the law and protected by it, having the ability to sue and enter contracts, being counted in the census, having a name and citizenship, the ability to own property, inherit, and so forth.

Now the point is not that this list is incomplete, or that you can find counter-instances to each of its points. People typically exhibit rationality, for instance, but someone who was irrational would not thereby fail to qualify as a person. On the other hand, something could exhibit the majority of these features and still fail to be a person, as an advanced robot might. There is no single core of necessary and sufficient features which we can draw upon with the assurance that they constitute what really makes a person; there are only features that are more or less typical.

This is not to say that no necessary or sufficient conditions can be given. Being alive is a necessary condition for being a person, and being a U.S. Senator is sufficient. But rather than falling inside a sufficient condition or outside a necessary one, a fetus lies in the penumbra region where our concept of a person is not so simple. For this reason I think a conclusive answer to the question whether a fetus is a person is unattainable.

Here we might note a family of simple fallacies that proceed by stating a necessary condition for personhood and showing that a fetus has that characteristic. This is a form of the fallacy of affirming the consequent. For example, some have mistakenly reasoned from the premise that a fetus is human (after all, it is a human fetus rather than, say, a canine fetus), to the conclusion that it is *a* human. Adding an equivocation on 'being', we get the fallacious argument that since a fetus is something both living and human, it is a human being.

Nonetheless, it does seem clear that a fetus has very few of the above family of characteristics, whereas a newborn baby exhibits a much larger proportion of them—and a two-year-old has even more. Note that one traditional anti-abortion argument has centered on pointing out the many ways in which a fetus resembles a baby. They emphasize its development ("It already has ten fingers . . .") without mentioning its dissimilarities to adults (it still has gills and a tail). They also try to evoke the sort of sympathy on our part that we only feel toward other persons ("Never to laugh . . . or feel the sunshine?"). This all seems to be a relevant way to argue, since its purpose is to persuade us that a fetus satisfies so many of the important features on the list that it ought to be treated as a person. Also note that a fetus near the time of birth satisfies many more of these factors than a fetus in the early months of development. This could provide reason for making distinctions among the different stages of pregnancy, as the U.S. Supreme Court has done.[8]

Historically, the time at which a person has been said to come into existence has varied widely. Muslims date personhood from fourteen days after conception. Some medievals followed Aristotle in placing ensoulment at forty days after conception for a male fetus and eighty days for a female fetus.[9] In European common law since the Seventeenth Century, abortion was considered the killing of a person only after quickening, the time when a pregnant woman first feels the fetus move on its own. Nor is this variety of opinions surprising. Biologically, a human being develops gradually. We shouldn't expect there to be any specific time or sharp dividing point when a person appears on the scene.

For these reasons I believe our concept of a person is not sharp or decisive enough to bear the weight of a solution to the abortion controversy. To use it to solve that problem is to clarify *obscurum per obscurius*.

II

Next let us consider what follows if a fetus is a person after all. Judith Jarvis Thomson's landmark article, "A Defense of Abortion,"[10] correctly points out that some additional argumentation is needed at this point in the conservative argument to bridge the gap between the premise that a fetus is an innocent person and the conclusion that killing it is always wrong. To arrive at this conclusion, we would need the additional premise that killing an innocent person is always wrong. But killing an innocent person is sometimes permissible, most notably in self defense. Some examples may help draw out our intuitions or ordinary judgments about self defense.

Suppose a mad scientist, for instance, hypnotized innocent people to jump out of the bushes and attack innocent passers-by with knives. If you are so attacked, we agree you have a right to kill the attacker in self defense, if killing him is the only way to protect your life or to save yourself from serious injury. It does not seem to matter here that the attacker is not malicious but himself an innocent pawn, for your killing of him is not done in a spirit of retribution but only in self defense.

---

[8] Not because the fetus is partly a person and so has some of the rights of persons, but rather because of the rights of person-like non-persons. This I discuss in part III below.

[9] Aristotle himself was concerned, however, with the different question of when the soul takes form. For historical data, see Jimmye Kimmey, "How the Abortion Laws Happened," *Ms.* 1 (April, 1973), pp. 48ff, and John Noonan, *loc. cit.*

[10] J. J. Thomson, "A Defense of Abortion," *Philosophy and Public Affairs* 1 (1971). [*Infra*, pp. 173–187.]

How severe an injury may you inflict in self defense? In part this depends upon the severity of the injury to be avoided: you may not shoot someone merely to avoid having your clothes torn. This might lead one to the mistaken conclusion that the defense may only equal the threatened injury in severity; that to avoid death you may kill, but to avoid a black eye you may only inflict a black eye or the equivalent. Rather, our laws and customs seem to say that you may create an injury somewhat, but not enormously, greater than the injury to be avoided. To fend off an attack whose outcome would be as serious as rape, a severe beating or the loss of a finger, you may shoot; to avoid having your clothes torn, you may blacken an eye.

Aside from this, the injury you may inflict should only be the minimum necessary to deter or incapacitate the attacker. Even if you know he intends to kill you, you are not justified in shooting him if you could equally well save yourself by the simple expedient of running away. Self defense is for the purpose of avoiding harms rather than equalizing harms.

Some cases of pregnancy present a parallel situation. Though the fetus is itself innocent, it may pose a threat to the pregnant woman's well-being, life prospects or health, mental or physical. If the pregnancy presents a slight threat to her interests, it seems self defense cannot justify abortion. But if the threat is on a par with a serious beating or the loss of a finger, she may kill the fetus that poses such a threat, even if it is an innocent person. If a lesser harm to the fetus could have the same defensive effect, killing it would not be justified. It is unfortunate that the only way to free the woman from the pregnancy entails the death of the fetus (except in very late stages of pregnancy). Thus a self defense model supports Thomson's point that the woman has a right only to be freed from the fetus, not a right to demand its death.[11]

The self defense model is most helpful when we take the pregnant woman's point of view. In the pre-Thomson literature, abortion is often framed as a question for a third party: do you, a doctor, have a right to choose between the life of the woman and that of the fetus? Some have claimed that if you were a passer-by who witnessed a struggle between the innocent hypnotized attacker and his equally innocent victim, you would have no reason to kill either in defense of the other. They have concluded that the self defense model implies that a woman may attempt to abort herself, but that a doctor should not assist her. I think the position of the third party is somewhat more complex. We do feel some inclination to intervene on behalf of the victim rather than the attacker, other things equal. But if both parties are innocent, other factors come into consideration. You would rush to the aid of your husband whether he was attacker or attackee. If a hypnotized famous violinist were attacking a skid row bum, we would try to save the individual who is of more value to society. These considerations would tend to support abortion in some cases.

---

[11] *Ibid.*, [p. 187].

But suppose you are a frail senior citizen who wishes to avoid being knifed by one of these innocent hypnotics, so you have hired a bodyguard to accompany you. If you are attacked, it is clear we believe that the bodyguard, acting as your agent, has a right to kill the attacker to save you from a serious beating. Your rights of self defense are transferred to your agent. I suggest that we should similarly view the doctor as the pregnant woman's agent in carrying out a defense she is physically incapable of accomplishing herself.

Thanks to modern technology, the cases are rare in which a pregnancy poses as clear a threat to a woman's bodily health as an attacker brandishing a switchblade. How does self defense fare when more subtle, complex and long-range harms are involved?

To consider a somewhat fanciful example, suppose you are a highly trained surgeon when you are kidnapped by the hypnotic attacker. He says he does not intend to harm you but to take you back to the mad scientist who, it turns out, plans to hypnotize you to have a permanent mental block against all your knowledge of medicine. This would automatically destroy your career which would in turn have a serious adverse impact on your family, your personal relationships and your happiness. It seems to me that if the only way you can avoid this outcome is to shoot the innocent attacker, you are justified in so doing. You are defending yourself from a drastic injury to your life prospects. I think it is no exaggeration to claim that unwanted pregnancies (most obviously among teen-agers) often have such adverse life-long consequences as the surgeon's loss of livelihood.

Several parallels arise between various views on abortion and the self defense model. Let's suppose further that these hypnotized attackers only operate at night, so that it is well known that they can be avoided completely by the considerable inconvenience of never leaving your house after dark. One view is that since you could stay home at night, therefore if you go out and are selected by one of these hypnotized people, you have no right to defend yourself. This parallels the view that abstinence is the only acceptable way to avoid pregnancy. Others might hold that you ought to take along some defense such as Mace which will deter the hypnotized person without killing him, but that if this defense fails, you are obliged to submit to the resulting injury, no matter how severe it is. This parallels the view that contraception is all right but abortion is always wrong, even in cases of contraceptive failure.

A third view is that you may kill the hypnotized person only if he will actually kill you, but not if he will only injure you. This is like the position that abortion is permissible only if it is required to save a woman's life. Finally we have the view that it is all right to kill the attacker, even if only to avoid a very slight inconvenience to yourself and even if you knowingly walked down the very street where all these incidents have been taking place without taking along any Mace or protective escort. If we assume that a fetus is a person, this is the analogue of the view that abortion is always justifiable, "on demand."

The self defense model allows us to see an important difference that exists between abortion and infanticide, even if a fetus is a person from conception. Many have argued that the only way to justify abortion without justifying infanticide would be to find some characteristic of personhood that is acquired at birth. Michael Tooley, for one, claims infanticide is justifiable because the really significant characteristics of person are acquired some time after birth. But all such approaches look to characteristics of the developing human and ignore the relation between the fetus and the woman. What if, after birth, the presence of an infant or the need to support it posed a grave threat to the woman's sanity or life prospects? She could escape this threat by the simple expedient of running away. So a solution that does not entail the death of the infant is available. Before birth, such solutions are not available because of the biological dependence of the fetus on the woman. Birth is the crucial point not because of any characteristics the fetus gains, but because after birth the woman can defend herself by a means less drastic than killing the infant. Hence self defense can be used to justify abortion without necessarily thereby justifying infanticide.

III

On the other hand, supposing a fetus is not after all a person, would abortion always be morally permissible? Some opponents of abortion seem worried that if a fetus is not a full-fledged person, then we are justified in treating it in any way at all. However, this does not follow. Non-persons do get some consideration in our moral code, though of course they do not have the same rights as persons have (and in general they do not have moral responsibilities), and though their interests may be overridden by the interests of persons. Still, we cannot just treat them in any way at all.

Treatment of animals is a case in point. It is wrong to torture dogs for fun or to kill wild birds for no reason at all. It is wrong Period, even though dogs and birds do not have the same rights persons do. However, few people think it is wrong to use dogs as experimental animals, causing them considerable suffering in some cases, provided that the resulting research will probably bring discoveries of great benefit to people. And most of us think it all right to kill birds for food or to protect our crops. People's rights are different from the consideration we give to animals, then, for it is wrong to experiment on people, even if others might later benefit a great deal as a result of their suffering. You might volunteer to be a subject, but this would be supererogatory; you certainly have a right to refuse to be a medical guinea pig.

But how do we decide what you may or may not do to non-persons? This is a difficult problem, one for which I believe no adequate account exists. You do not want to say, for instance, that torturing dogs is all right whenever the sum of its effects on people is good—when it doesn't warp the sensibilities of the torturer so much that he mistreats people. If that were the case, it would be all right to torture dogs if you did it in private, or if the torturer lived on a desert island or died soon afterward, so that his actions had no effect on people. This is an inadequate account, because whatever moral consideration animals get, it has to be indefeasible, too. It will have to be a general proscription of certain actions, not merely a weighing of the impact on people on a case-by-case basis.

Rather, we need to distinguish two levels on which consequences of actions can be taken into account in moral reasoning. The traditional objections to Utilitarianism focus on the fact that it operates solely on the first level, taking all the consequences into account in particular cases only. Thus Utilitarianism is open to "desert island" and "lifeboat" counterexamples because these cases are rigged to make the consequences of actions severely limited.

Rawls' theory could be described as a teleological sort of theory, but with teleology operating on a higher level.[12] In choosing the principles to regulate society from the original position, his hypothetical choosers make their decision on the basis of the total consequences of various systems. Furthermore, they are constrained to choose a general set of rules which people can readily learn and apply. An ethical theory must operate by generating a set of sympathies and attitudes toward others which reinforces the functioning of that set of moral principles. Our prohibition against killing people operates by means of certain moral sentiments including sympathy, compassion and guilt. But if these attitudes are to form a coherent set, they carry us further: we tend to perform supererogatory actions, and we tend to feel similar compassion toward person-like non-persons.

It is crucial that psychological facts play a role here. Our psychological constitution makes it the case that for our ethical theory to work, it must prohibit certain treatment of non-persons which are significantly person-like. If our moral rules allowed people to treat some person-like non-persons in ways we do not want people to be treated, this would undermine the system of sympathies and attitudes that makes the ethical system work. For this reason, we would choose in the original position to make mistreatment of some sorts of animals wrong in general (not just wrong in the cases with public impact), even though animals are not themselves parties in the original position. Thus it makes sense that it is those animals whose appearance and behavior are most like those of people that get the most consideration in our moral scheme.

It is because of "coherence of attitudes," I think, that the similarity of a fetus to a baby is very significant. A fetus one week before birth is so much like a newborn baby in our psychological space that we cannot allow any cavalier treatment of the former while expecting full sympathy and nurturative support for the latter. Thus, I think that anti-abortion forces are indeed giving their strongest arguments when they point to the similarities between a fetus and a baby, and

---

[12] John Rawls, *A Theory of Justice* (Cambridge, Mass., 1971), § 3–4.

158   Jane English

when they try to evoke our emotional attachment to and sympathy for the fetus. An early horror story from New York about nurses who were expected to alternate between caring for six-week premature infants and disposing of viable 24-week aborted fetuses is just that—a horror story. These beings are so much alike that no one can be asked to draw a distinction and treat them so very differently.

Remember, however, that in the early weeks after conception, a fetus is very much unlike a person. It is hard to develop these feelings for a set of genes which doesn't yet have a head, hands, beating heart, response to touch or the ability to move by itself. Thus it seems to me that the alleged "slippery slope" between conception and birth is not so very slippery. In the early stages of pregnancy, abortion can hardly be compared to murder for psychological reasons, but in the latest stages it is psychologically akin to murder.

Another source of similarity is the bodily continuity between fetus and adult. Bodies play a surprisingly central role in our attitudes toward persons. One has only to think of the philosophical literature on how far physical identity suffices for personal identity or Wittgenstein's remark that the best picture of the human soul is the human body. Even after death, when all agree the body is no longer a person, we still observe elaborate customs of respect for the human body; like people who torture dogs, necrophiliacs are not to be trusted with people.[13] So it is appropriate that we show respect to a fetus as the body continuous with the body of a person. This is a degree of resemblance to persons that animals cannot rival.

Michael Tooley also utilizes a parallel with animals. He claims that it is always permissible to drown newborn kittens and draws conclusions about infanticide.[14] But it is only permissible to drown kittens when their survival would cause some hardship. Perhaps it would be a burden to feed and house six more cats or to find other homes for them. The alternative of letting them starve produces even more suffering than the drowning. Since the kittens get their rights second hand, so to speak, *via* the need for coherence in our attitudes, their interests are often overridden by the interests of full-fledged persons. But if their survival would be no inconvenience to people at all, then it is wrong to drown them, *contra* Tooley.

Tooley's conclusions about abortion are wrong for the same reason. Even if a fetus is not a person, abortion is not always permissible, because of the resemblance of a fetus to a person. I agree with Thomson that it would be wrong for a woman who is seven months pregnant to have an abortion just to avoid having to postpone a trip to Europe. In the early months of pregnancy when the fetus hardly resembles a baby at all, then, abortion is permissible whenever it is in the interests of the pregnant woman or her family. The reasons would only need to outweigh the pain and inconvenience of the abortion itself. In the middle months, when the

---

[13] On the other hand, if they can be trusted with people, then our moral customs are mistaken. It all depends on the facts of psychology.

[14] *Op. cit.,* pp. 40, 60–61.

fetus comes to resemble a person, abortion would be justifiable only when the continuation of the pregnancy or the birth of the child would cause harms—physical, psychological, economic or social—to the woman. In the late months of pregnancy, even on our current assumption that a fetus is not a person, abortion seems to be wrong except to save a woman from significant injury or death.

The Supreme Court has recognized similar gradations in the alleged slippery slope stretching between conception and birth. To this point, the present paper has been a discussion of the moral status of abortion only, not its legal status. In view of the great physical, financial and sometimes psychological costs of abortion, perhaps the legal arrangement most compatible with the proposed moral solution would be the absence of restrictions, that is, so-called abortion "on demand."

So I conclude, first, that application of our concept of a person will not suffice to settle the abortion issue. After all, the biological development of a human being is gradual. Second, whether a fetus is a person or not, abortion is justifiable early in pregnancy to avoid modest harms and seldom justifiable late in pregnancy except to avoid significant injury or death.[15]

[15] I am deeply indebted to Larry Crocker and Arthur Kuflik for their constructive comments.

Being a Person—Does It Matter?

Loren E. Lomasky

Within the domain of the physical universe, persons constitute a statistically insignificant part of the whole. But in the moral realm persons bulk overwhelmingly large. It is not necessary to claim that they are its only inhabitants; that, for example, torturing an animal is of moral concern only insofar as it affects the sensibilities of persons. It is reasonable to believe that the simple possession of sentience is itself sufficient to establish the existence of certain minimal moral claims. But sentience is not the entire story.[1] There are numerous moral considerations that apply to persons but either do not apply at all or only with lessened force to nonpersons. One may kill an animal but (logically) cannot murder it. Nor can an animal *be* a murderer. Conventional actions creating obligations such as making a promise can only be performed between persons. Similar cases could be indefinitely multiplied. But what point would there be to doing so? Is it not clear that the mere fact of P's being a person is itself crucial in determining the moral status P enjoys? That is, should we not say that "P is a person" provides a sufficient moral *reason* for treating P in certain ways?

What I shall argue in this paper is that it does *not*; that no debates over normative issues are likely to be advanced by determining whether some affected party is or is not a person. While this claim may seem to be inconsistent with what was said above about the preeminent status of persons, in fact it is not. Persons *are* special, but not because *being a person* is a morally significant property. The nine occupants of a room enjoy a unique judicial status if they happen to be the nine justices of the Supreme Court. But 'occupying room R at

From *Philosophical Topics*, vol. 12, no. 3 (1982). Reprinted by permission of the author and *Philosophical Topics*.

[1] For an account suggesting that it *is* see Peter Singer's "Animal Liberation," *New York Review of Books* (April 5, 1973), pp. 17–21. While Singer argues persuasively that animals are not moral nonentities, his statement of the root of rights and concomitant obligations is simplistic.

time t' is not a significant predicate for any legal institution, although 'being a Supreme Court justice' is. What I shall argue is that 'being a person' is more like the former predicate than the latter one.

Although persons are usually easily distinguishable from nonpersons, it is notoriously difficult to supply necessary and sufficient conditions for being one. That is not to say that philosophers are totally inhibited from attempting to do so. The definitions of 'person' they offer tend to fall within three distinct molds:

(A)   Being a person is nothing other than being a living human being, a member of the species Homo sapiens.

(B)   Being a person is nothing other than possessing rights (or: possessing the particular right to _____).

(C)   Being a person is nothing other than being able to perform feat F (where F typically requires conceptual functioning of a relatively high order).

References to each of the three types of definitions will be cited subsequently. Before doing so, two noncontroversial remarks:

1.   The three definition types are logically distinct from each other. It would surely not be inconsistent to describe an individual as satisfying some one of them without at the same time satisfying either of the other two. (Although, as will be seen, the fact that something satisfies one of (A)–(C) has been taken to be a reason—even a sufficient reason—for holding that it thereby satisfies some one of the other two).

2.   In fact, persons typically *do* satisfy all three purported definitions. To be a human being is, most often, to possess an agglomeration of rights and also to enjoy a particularly elevated level of cognitive capacities.

It is to the borderline cases one must turn to see the definitions diverge in terms of which individuals satisfy them. And, of course, it is on the borderline where thorny and interesting moral problems abound. For example, is an individual who assuredly once was a person and who now has slipped into irreversible coma still a person? Or is someone who has suffered so-called "brain death"[2] a person? And what properly can be done for or to such individuals? If a definition of 'person' holds any promise of being a useful tool in moral debate, it will be with

---

[2] The term "brain death" is misleadingly ambiguous. It can be taken as signifying the permanent cessation of function of an organ of an otherwise living individual. Alternatively, it can be understood to mean the death *of an individual* (necessarily) entailed by the death of his brain. "Brain death" in the first sense no more entails the death of a person whose brain it is than does, say, total kidney failure.

such cases. It is also true though that more than the status as persons of such individuals is at issue, and these additional factors becloud policy decisions. One such factor is the absence of any clear consensus concerning what criteria should be employed in ascertaining when death has resulted. Another is that the irreversibility of coma can rarely, if ever, be adjudged with complete assurance except after the patient has died.

It is at the other end of life that a determination of personhood seems most likely to weigh as a decisive moral reason. It has often been argued—and even more often simply assumed—that the permissibility of abortion must hinge on whether fetuses are persons.[3] Since personhood has so frequently been held to be of prime importance in this context, it is instructive to examine what use has been made of it. It will be seen that all three definition types have been employed; and, for different reasons, each falls short of providing any practical guidance.

Discussions of abortion in which 'person' and 'human being' are taken to be coextensive abound. Roger Wertheimer writes, "I should note that the expressions 'a human life,' 'a human being,' 'a person' are virtually interchangeable in this context."[4] Judith Jarvis Thomson begins her article "A Defense of Abortion" by remarking, "Most opposition to abortion relies on the premise that a fetus is a human being, a person, from the moment of conception."[5] Wertheimer and Thomson agree that, at least at birth, the fetus has become a human being and thus a person. What they find conjectural is how soon before birth, if at all, fetuses become human beings. If a fetus is human from the moment of conception, then every abortion would involve the killing of a person. This, presumably, would count as a significant moral reason for disallowing many or all abortions. (Thomson, while not denying that this would be a reason, argues that it is one which is overridden by other considerations.) Conversely, if no fetus is a human being, that would count as a significant reason for holding many or all abortions to be morally permissible.

This approach to the moral relevance of personhood through an (A) type definition is fundamentally confused. It is reductive in a pernicious way, attempting to ground the ascription of a right to life on straightforwardly biological criteria. Why this should be even *prima facie* credible is mysterious. Suppose that some future space project put us into contact with extra-terrestrial life comparable in intelligence and affective capacities to human beings but biologically distant from us. Would it be convincing to maintain that these beings merit a markedly inferior

---

[3] One notable exception is Judith Jarvis Thomson's "A Defense of Abortion," *Philosophy & Public Affairs*, 1 (1971), [*infra*, pp. 173–187].

[4] "Understanding the Abortion Argument," *Philosophy & Public Affairs*, 1 (1971), [*supra*, p. 44].

[5] Thomson, [*infra*, p. 173]. While Thomson rejects this premise, subsequent comments indicate that she accepts the equation of human being with (human) person.

moral status simply because they are not human? (Or imagine a Wellsian evolution of Homo sapiens into Super Homo sapiens—surely *not* thereby entailing a diminishment of rights.) At most one can claim that being biologically human is a sufficient condition for elevated moral status, not both necessary and sufficient.

But is it even sufficient? True, our intuitions convey a strong presumption against killing (or "letting die," if there is a real difference between that and killing) a human being, based on nothing more than the subject's humanity. But this intuition is not some brute moral fact; it admits of degree and is largely explainable in terms of characteristic human traits. To be brief, human beings paradigmatically are self-aware intentional beings who stand in complex relationships of social interdependency to other human beings. The disvalue of death is thus minimally explicable in virtue of the disruption it causes in the victim's own plans and aspirations as well as those of others. But the further an individual is removed from this paradigm, the more questionable is the applicability of the presumption against killing. That is precisely why fetuses and the irreversibly comatose are borderline cases; one need not deny their biological humanity to recognize that they diverge from the standard case in morally compelling ways. The important question to ask is not whether the fetus (or the irreversibly comatose) is a human life but rather: what *kind* of a life is it; how portentous are the differences that separate it from the paradigm?

In fact, I strongly suspect that this is the question that really interests Wertheimer and others who are ostensibly concerned about the humanity of the fetus. If they really supposed that the permissibility of abortion hinges on whether fetuses are persons and that persons are nothing other than human beings, they would need do little more than consult the biologists. They would be told yes, fetuses are genetically distinct members of the human species, living as opposed to dead or inert. The facts are hardly in dispute; what further data remain to be assembled before ascertaining that the fetus is a person? None at all—if indeed being human is a crucial moral factor rather than a red herring.

Lawrence Becker has attempted to date the attainment of biological personhood at a later stage of fetal development, the point "when the organism (assumed, of course, to be living) has assumed its basic morphology, and when its inventory of histologically differentiated organs is complete."[6] His metamorphic definition can succeed only if it can be established that the conceptus is not already a human being. Accordingly, Becker tries to show that the argument

> This conceptus is a being (i.e., is an entity and is alive);
> It is certainly human (i.e., is of no other species);
> Therefore, it is a human being;

---

[6]"Human Being: The Boundaries of the Concept," *Philosophy & Public Affairs,* 4 (1975), p. 338.

is fallacious for much the same reasons:

> This sperm cell is a being (i.e., an entity and alive);
> It is certainly human (i.e., is of no other species);
> Therefore, it is a human being.

In each case there is an equivocation on 'human,' which appears in both second premises as an adjectival description of certain tissues and in both conclusions as a noun meaning "member of the human species."[7]

Becker's analogy fails because, while a conceptus is *at least* living human tissue, it is also *more* than that. It is a genetically complete (unlike a sperm cell) and distinct individual (unlike a random cell or the agglomeration of tissues in an organ bank) which is in the initial stage of morphogenesis typically undergone by each member of the species Homo sapiens (unlike a cheek scraping which could, in some science fiction scenario, be the basis of a clone). While the fetus is located within its mother's body, it is, of course, not a part of that body. One wants to ask Becker: if it is not a member of the human species, what type of human tissue can it be?

I conclude that since there is no dispute between proponents and opponents of abortion concerning the biological facts about fetuses, it is clear that disputes over whether fetuses are persons are not disputes over whether they are members of species Homo sapiens. Therefore, definition (A) does not pick out a sense of 'person' that is of interest for the abortion debate—nor, so it seems, for any other moral controversy.

Definition (B), which understands persons as repositories of rights (or some specified right) may seem more propitious. It explicitly recognizes that labeling someone a person (or refraining from doing so) is to adopt a moral stance toward that individual. It is not simply to describe in value-neutral terms the way ascribing species membership does.

In a well-known article[8] Michael Tooley carefully distinguishes type (A) definitions from type (B) ones, in the process sharply criticizing those who offer the former. He argues, "In the case of abortion what is primarily at stake is what moral principles one should accept. . . . Settling the issue of the morality of abortion will involve answering the following questions: What properties must something have to be a person, i.e., to have a serious right to life? At what point in the development of a member of the species Homo sapiens does the organism possess the properties that make it a person?"[9] For Tooley, then, personhood

---

[7] Becker, p. 339.

[8] "Abortion and Infanticide," *Philosophy & Public Affairs,* 2 (1972), pp. 37–65. [cf. revised version, *supra,* pp. 120–134.]

[9] Tooley, pp. 42–43.

is of prime moral significance, and he adopts a type (B) definition in equating personhood with having a serious right to life.[10]

Nonetheless, it is clear that, so understood, personhood has no contribution to make to any moral dispute, including the abortion question. The reason is simple: to predicate 'person' of an individual will require first determining whether that individual has a serious right to life, and it is precisely the existence of such a right which is in doubt. Personhood, therefore, is superfluous; if we know whether fetuses have a serious right to life we have no further need of knowing whether they are persons.

By itself a (B) definition is impotent. If, however, it could be supplemented with independent criteria for establishing when a serious right to life obtains, an important result for ethics would have been achieved. One could then construct an argument of the form:

> All (and only) beings possessing property F are persons;
> All (and only) persons have a serious right to life;
> All (and only) beings possessing property F have a serious right to life.

The sticking point is finding a suitable candidate for property F. We have seen that 'being human' is an unsatisfactory choice for F. Perhaps a better one would pick out the ability to perform some kind of activity or attain some state that requires relatively advanced conceptual apparatus. It is, after all, *prima facie* credible to maintain that what distinguishes persons is what they can *do,* specifically what they can do as the result of possessing intellectual prowess beyond that of nonpersons.

In effect this is to move from a (B) to a (C) type definition. Persons are still understood as repositories of some right or rights, but to be such a repository, and thus to be a person, is nothing other than possessing property F. If 'person' is to serve as a morally significant predicate it must either be explicitly defined in terms of property F or else be defined in terms of some property G which obtains only when F obtains. The latter recourse I shall call an indirect (C) type definition.

Tooley, in the article cited above, does offer an indirect (C) type definition. He writes, "an organism possesses a serious right to life only if it possesses the concept of a self as a continuing subject of experiences and other mental states, and believes that it is itself such a continuing entity."[11] Rights, he goes on to

---

[10] Tooley considers but rejects defining 'person' as: having rights. Its drawback is that a being may have some right or other without having a serious right to life. See pp. 40–41.

[11] Tooley, p. 44.

argue, issue from having desires, and only a being that is aware of itself as a continuing subject of experiences and other mental states can desire to live.[12]

There are several vulnerable features accruing to this particular (C) definition. It is notoriously difficult to specify how one can be aware of oneself as *subject* of experiences. Hume, for one, would claim that it is an impossibility. Again, Tooley is on dangerous ground when he claims, roughly, that desires issue in rights. One may respond that they do so only when what is desired is *rightfully* desired; otherwise there is not even a *prima facie* obligation that others refrain from actions which would frustrate the desire. Moreover, you may have a right to X even though you do not desire X (and are in sound mind, awake, etc.), provided that you have not effectively waived your right to X. If either of these claims is correct, Tooley's argument collapses.

I do not pursue these possible criticisms, both because they would take us far afield and also because I am primarily interested in displaying a *general* debilitating consequence of (C) type definitions. When property F involves the possession of some significant conceptual apparatus, it will follow that fetuses are not persons. But it will also follow that infants are not persons and that they, like fetuses, do not possess a serious right to life. Tooley admits as much, claiming: "Human fetuses and infants . . . do not have a right to life," and goes on to urge, "In contrast it may turn out that our treatment of adult members of other species— cats, dogs, polar bears—is morally indefensible. For it is quite possible that such animals do possess properties that endow them with a right to life."[13]

One may approve of Tooley's integrity in accepting the counter-intuitive implications of his program and yet wish that he had given more serious thought to the importance of these implications. What is crucial is that any (C) type definition will have similar consequences vis-a-vis fetuses and infants. Tooley proceeds undaunted, whereas I shall argue that such consequences provide good and

---

[12] Tooley, pp. 44–48. [Editor's note: In this volume, Tooley has modified this account. Cf. pp. 120–134.]

[13] Tooley, p. 37. Mary Anne Warren has also offered a (C) type account ("On the Moral and Legal Status of Abortion," *Monist* 57, 1973 [*supra,* pp. 102–119]) of 'person' in which, unsurprisingly, it turns out that fetuses are nonpersons and thus properly abortable. Unlike Tooley, she seems not to have noticed the consequence that infants are as liable to destruction as newborn kittens. Because Tooley is aware of and attempts to confront the problem, his paper and not Warren's has been chosen as the foil for my argument. It should be noted though that, in a subsequent reprinting of her article, Warren has affixed a "Postscript on Infanticide" in which she argues that infanticide is wrong but not because of any harm done to the infant. Rather, infants are a kind of resource not to be squandered. Potential foster parents abound, and the citizenry is willing to tax itself to support orphanages and the like. So, on her argument, were I to kill my newborn, I would be acting wrongly in much the same way as if I were to discard an appliance I no longer want but someone else does. One may be grateful that Warren has detected *some* flaw with infanticide while remaining extremely dubious that she has hit upon the crucial one.

sufficient reason for rejecting the possibility of formulating a credible (C) type definition. My argument is a simple one, resting on a basic standard of rational acceptability:

1. We have a very strong intuition that infants do enjoy a right to life, i.e., that infanticide is wrong.
2. No (direct or indirect) type (C) definition of 'person' is clearly and intuitively true.
3. Therefore, if a type (C) definition is inconsistent with our intuition that infants do enjoy a right to life, then it is rational to reject that type (C) definition.
4. But all type (C) definitions are inconsistent with the claim that infants do enjoy a right to life.
5. No type (C) definition is rationally acceptable.

The argument turns on a strategy of resolving conflicts among propositions by rejecting that proposition or set of propositions B such that (1) consistency is attained, and (2) there exists no proposition or set of propositions B' such that B' is less warranted than B and that by rejecting B' consistency can be obtained. Surely this strategy does provide a rational basis for resolving inconsistency in that it conserves what is more credible.

As it stands, my argument is incomplete. For while the claim that infants do enjoy a right to life is more strongly warranted than any (C) type definition, there remains a bare possibility that it is less warranted than some other proposition with which it conflicts. I can only respond that I am unaware of any such proposition and that if one does exist, it is surprising that it has not heretofore come to light. Therefore, it is rational to reject Tooley's (C) type definition and conserve the interdiction of infanticide.

Tooley's response is to claim that in fact the prohibition of infanticide is not well-grounded. He writes:

> The typical reaction to infanticide is like the reaction to incest or cannibalism or the reaction of previous generations to masturbation or oral sex. The response, rather than appealing to carefully formulated moral principles, is primarily visceral. When philosophers themselves respond in this way, offering no arguments, and dismissing infanticide out of hand, it is reasonable to suspect that one is dealing with a taboo rather than with a rational prohibition.[14]

The remarks are suggestive. Tooley seems to be giving short shrift to any moral judgment that does not issue from "carefully formulated moral principles." One would like to ask him where these principles come from if not reflection upon strongly held particular moral judgments.[15] Among these, the prohibition of

---

[14] Tooley, pp. 39–40.

[15] The same question could well be put to R. M. Hare. In "Abortion and the Golden Rule," *Philosophy & Public Affairs* 4 (1975), pp. 201–222, Hare repeats his frequently voiced criticism

infanticide is surely one of the firmest. Indeed, in developing his own program Tooley continually relies on moral intuitions of more dubious prescriptive weight. On page 40 he writes, "It seems to me that while it is not seriously wrong to kill a newborn kitten, it is seriously wrong to torture one for an hour." He then proceeds to argue from this that something may have rights without possessing a serious right to life. On page 46 he argues:

> Suppose, for example, that by some technology of the future the brain of an adult human were to be completely reprogrammed, so that the organism wound up with memories (or rather, apparent memories), beliefs, attitudes and personality traits completely different from those associated with it before it was subjected to reprogramming. In such a case one would surely say that an individual had been destroyed, than an adult human's right to life had been violated.

Would one say that? I am unsure; but I am quite confident that such a judgment is intuitively less compelling than that which holds infanticide to be a violation of rights and thus wrong.

I do not cite these examples as instances of illicit moral reasoning. Quite the reverse; one can hardly produce any general moral principles (including Tooley's indirect (C) type definition) except by proceeding from a base of intuitively compelling particular cases. Therefore, when a hypothesized general principle runs afoul of some strongly held prephilosophical belief, one ought to reconsider just how strongly warranted the principle actually is. Unfortunately Tooley does not do so. If he had, he would have found that his (C) type definition of 'person' is no more helpful in providing moral reasons than are (A) and (B) type definitions.

One final comment: Tooley dubs the prohibition of infanticide a "taboo." While the term is clearly intended to be pejorative, I am unsure precisely what else he means to convey by it. That infanticide is generally regarded with extreme disapprobation? Undoubtedly that, but also, I would suppose, that the disapprobation is such that it *cannot* be defended by reference to any good reasons for recognizing in very young children a privileged moral status (as distinguished from that of fetuses or animals).[16]

---

of basing normative arguments on intuitions: "In contrast, a philosopher who wishes to contribute to the solution of this and similar practical problems should be trying to develop, on the basis of a study of the moral concepts and their logical properties, a theory of moral reasoning that will determine which arguments we ought to accept" (p. 202). Hare is quite correct in emphasizing the importance of a theory of moral reasoning, but he neglects the fact that it is notoriously easy for philosophers to spin out such theories; what we need is a *satisfactory theory*. Unlike Hare, I hold out little hope that this can be discovered by purely formal considerations. Well-established (not inviolable) intuitions are the touchstones by means of which theory confronts pretheoretical beliefs and each modifies the other.

[16] Hare, in the article previously referred to, and Roslyn Weiss in "The Perils of Personhood," *Ethics* 89 (1978), pp. 66–75, abandon the attempt to derive pronouncements concerning the morality of abortion and infanticide from considerations of the *rights* of fetuses and the newborn. Each suggests instead that a more perspicuous approach is to consider whether and

In response, it must be admitted that it is very difficult to pinpoint precisely what does count as a reason for ascribing a preferential status to infants. There is little or nothing that an infant can do which a fetus or kitten cannot. But because it is difficult to state such a reason does not show that one does not exist. Let me close by suggesting that the meager results usually attained in this direction stem from a frequent but misguided policy. It is to suppose that an organism has rights only in virtue of its capacities to perform certain actions or attain particular states of consciousness. This is to commit oneself to an atomistic view of the value of individuals. Their relationships to other individuals are taken to be irrelevant to determining their moral status.

I would like to suggest that a more sensitive view would strongly take into account the fact that human beings typically are related to other human beings within a complex web of social relationships. Moral phenomena are simply too diverse to be explained adequately by thinking of individuals as self-contained entities who somehow are said to possess an apparatus of rights in virtue of their intellectual attainments. As argued earlier, this view renders it totally unintelligible how infants can be held to be bearers of a significant right to life. Additionally, it fails to accord with the intuitively plausible belief that those severely retarded, comatose, senile or otherwise mentally handicapped still have a share within the moral community. It does not offer satisfactory grounds for hoping to explain how children unable yet to acknowledge and respect the rights of others can nonetheless merit a moral status that requires others both to avoid harming them and to extend positive benefits. Finally, and most importantly, it fails to respond to the *particularity* of moral situations. One owes more to others than the mere avoidance of trespass across boundaries constituted by natural rights common to all rational (or self-aware or sentient) beings. Nor does the recognition of obligations resulting from consensual actions between individuals suffice to account for the full range of the particularity of moral bonds. Parent and child, friend and friend, citizen and compatriot, are related to each other by ties that do not similarly bind them to all other individuals. Their obligations to each other cannot credibly be explained

---

why any *duties* are owed to these beings. I fear that little aid is to be gained from this direction; whether we owe any duties to fetuses and infants must depend on what kinds of beings they are and thus on what makes it the case that we are obliged to render aid to them or, at least, avoid harming them. Even if such an inquiry avoids any explicit talk of rights, it will have to address just these issues of paramount concern for rights theorists. Weiss suggests (p. 74) that biological humanity may suffice to establish the basis for duties, but she neither provides any reasons for this claim nor states what particular duties we have toward fetuses or infants. Hare argues that, by application of the "Golden Rule," one can demonstrate the wrongness of many (though not all) abortions: "If we are glad that nobody terminated the pregnancy that resulted in *our* birth, then we are enjoined not, *certeris paribus,* to terminate any pregnancy which will result in the birth of a person having a life like ours." (p. 208). As George Sheer cogently argues in "Hare, Abortion and the Golden Rule," *Philosophy & Public Affairs* 6 (1977), pp. 185–190, Hare's appeal to the Golden Rule is question-begging. It must first be established that fetuses are among the class of "others" unto whom I have the duty to act as I am glad others did unto me.

by reference to some explicit or implicit agreement into which they have entered; there is none. (Unfortunately, that has not safeguarded all philosophers from the dubious assumption that particular obligations *must* originate from voluntary agreements. That may account for the persistence of attempts to ground the legitimacy of political units in an actual or hypothetical social contract.) Rather, I urge, it is because human lives as we characteristically live them are [so] *rich* with familial, political and other ties to others that we can make sense of the idea of being morally bound to them.

It would require another—and much longer—paper to spell out the many implications of taking moral attributes to be derived from social relationships. But perhaps some indications of the power of this model can be realized by sketching out in rough detail how it distinguishes between the status of fetuses and that of neonates.

Adopting a moral stance toward some being entails taking it to possess properties that give it unique value. As has been amply illustrated above, there is considerable room for disagreement concerning precisely what those properties are. But fundamental to all such accounts is the recognition of that being as an individual, one whose life and interests are not substitutable for those of any other. Unlike cogs in a machine, human beings are not discardable, replaceable parts of a mechanism. At least they are not when they are viewed as having *moral* worth. Whatever else is involved in recognizing a being as a member of the moral community, it minimally must be identifiable as a distinct individual and thus one capable of entering into particular social relationships. Because I can *identify* distinct individuals, I can be motivated to act by recognition of their interests; because I can *reidentify* these individuals, I can enter into continuing relationships with them. Conversely, where a process of identification and subsequent reidentification is not achievable, one cannot pick out a distinct, temporally continuous being to be assigned unique value.

Fetuses are genetically distinct members of the species Homo sapiens. But throughout their gestation period they differ from other human beings in lacking the publicity and interpersonal contacts that enable identification to take place. For the first several weeks of its life, the fetus' existence may be unknown to all, even the prospective mother. Until several months thereafter, it is quite possible that only the mother will have any knowledge of it. Even when a fairly broad community becomes aware of the fetus' existence, virtually nothing more about it is known. Its sex, dimensions and facial characteristics cannot be specified to any greater extent than is predictable from the laws of embryology plus knowledge of the parents' biological traits. No one has seen, heard or felt the organism. The mother receives some sensations from it, but they are epistemically insufficient to promote even rudimentary identification. They are sensations of *some* fetus but could have been produced by any other one she might have happened to be carrying. If, through some magic, the fetus were suddenly annihilated and replaced by a different one, its demise would be neither known nor lamented by anyone.

Whatever differentiation has taken place during its development is not public, and the organism can be identified only obliquely as the fetus carried by such-and-such a particular woman.

Newborn infants also lack many of the relationships to others that are a regular part of more mature human lives. Nonetheless, birth constitutes a quantum leap forward in the process of establishing social bonds that depend on the ability to be identified and reidentified as a unique individual. Consider a typical infant just a few hours after its birth. Although this is little time in which to enter into contact with other members of one's world, it has already become part of a surprisingly large number of social relationships. It has been handled, fed, and medically cared for by several people. Its weight, height and sex have been determined and made known to concerned parties, including a local newspaper. It has been given a name. Its footprint is on file, and any resemblance to progenitors has been noted. Grandparents, aunts, uncles, siblings and cousins have been notified of their new status, social service agencies stand ready to provide assistance, and an income tax exemption has been established.

Each of these relationships that provide a basis for identification may seem trivial. Some critics will be sure to object that they are wildly out of place in a discussion of what accounts for a being enjoying an elevated moral status, that a mere change of location is an inappropriate reason for beginning to accord rights to some entity. The objector is likely to attempt to clinch his position by noting that the infant is unable to perform any significant activities that it was not also able to perform while in utero.

Neonates *can* do things that fetuses cannot: breathe and nurse, for example. But one would miss seeing the moral significance of birth if one were content to respond to the objector by citing these functions. Rather, what is crucial is not what the newborn baby can *do* but what it now *is:* an identifiable and reidentifiable individual that can thereby elicit responses as a unique object of concern. Throughout its subsequent history it will enter into ever more complex and numerous social relationships. Those relationships, one-sided and simple at first, have commenced with birth. Each of them may, in a sense, be judged trivial, but taken together they provide a basis for the infant's identification as a member of the moral community. Tooley and others may argue that they are insufficient to render it a person but, as I have argued, it is not being a person that matters.

A Defense of Abortion[1]

Judith Jarvis Thomson

Most opposition to abortion relies on the premise that the fetus is a human being, a person, from the moment of conception. The premise is argued for, but, as I think, not well. Take, for example, the most common argument. We are asked to notice that the development of a human being from conception through birth into childhood is continuous; then it is said that to draw a line, to choose a point in this development and say "before this point the thing is not a person, after this point it is a person" is to make an arbitrary choice, a choice for which in the nature of things no good reason can be given. It is concluded that the fetus is, or anyway that we had better say it is, a person from the moment of conception. But this conclusion does not follow. Similar things might be said about the development of an acorn into an oak tree, and it does not follow that acorns are oak trees, or that we had better say they are. Arguments of this form are sometimes called "slippery slope arguments"—the phrase is perhaps self-explanatory—and it is dismaying that opponents of abortion rely on them so heavily and uncritically.

I am inclined to agree, however, that the prospects for "drawing a line" in the development of the fetus look dim. I am inclined to think also that we shall probably have to agree that the fetus has already become a human person well before birth. Indeed, it comes as a surprise when one first learns how early in its life it begins to acquire human characteristics. By the tenth week, for example, it already has a face, arms and legs, fingers and toes; it has internal organs, and brain activity is detectable.[2] On the other hand, I think that the premise is false,

From "A Defense of Abortion" by Judith Jarvis Thomson, *Philosophy & Public Affairs*, vol. 1, no. 1 (copyright © 1971 by Princeton University Press), pp. 47–66. Reprinted by permission of Princeton University Press.

[1] I am very much indebted to James Thomson for discussion, criticism, and many helpful suggestions.

[2] Daniel Callahan, *Abortion: Law, Choice and Morality* (New York, 1970), p. 373. This book gives a fascinating survey of the available information on abortion. The Jewish tradition is

that the fetus is not a person from the moment of conception. A newly fertilized ovum, a newly implanted clump of cells, is no more a person than an acorn is an oak tree. But I shall not discuss any of this. For it seems to me to be of great interest to ask what happens if, for the sake of argument, we allow the premise. How, precisely, are we supposed to get from there to the conclusion that abortion is morally impermissible? Opponents of abortion commonly spend most of their time establishing that the fetus is a person, and hardly any time explaining the step from there to the impermissibility of abortion. Perhaps they think the step too simple and obvious to require much comment. Or perhaps instead they are simply being economical in argument. Many of those who defend abortion rely on the premise that the fetus is not a person, but only a bit of tissue that will become a person at birth; and why pay out more arguments than you have to? Whatever the explanation, I suggest that the step they take is neither easy nor obvious, that it calls for closer examination than it is commonly given, and that when we do give it this closer examination we shall feel inclined to reject it.

I propose, then, that we grant that the fetus is a person from the moment of conception. How does the argument go from here? Something like this, I take it. Every person has a right to life. So the fetus has a right to life. No doubt the mother has a right to decide what shall happen in and to her body; everyone would grant that. But surely a person's right to life is stronger and more stringent than the mother's right to decide what happens in and to her body, and so outweighs it. So the fetus may not be killed; an abortion may not be performed.

It sounds plausible. But now let me ask you to imagine this. You wake up in the morning and find yourself back to back in bed with an unconscious violinist. A famous unconscious violinist. He has been found to have a fatal kidney ailment, and the Society of Music Lovers has canvassed all the available medical records and found that you alone have the right blood type to help. They have therefore kidnapped you, and last night the violinist's circulatory system was plugged into yours, so that your kidneys can be used to extract poisons from his blood as well as your own. The director of the hospital now tells you, "Look, we're sorry the Society of Music Lovers did this to you—we would never have permitted it if we had known. But still, they did it, and the violinist now is plugged into you. To unplug you would be to kill him. But never mind, it's only for nine months. By then he will have recovered from his ailment, and can safely be unplugged from you." Is it morally incumbent on you to accede to this situation? No doubt it would be very nice of you if you did, a great kindness. But do you *have* to accede to it? What if it were not nine months, but nine years? Or longer still? What if the director of the hospital says, "Tough luck, I agree, but you've now got to stay

---

surveyed in David M. Feldman, *Birth Control in Jewish Law* (New York, 1968), Part 5; the Catholic tradition in John T. Noonan, Jr., "An Almost Absolute Value in History," in *The Morality of Abortion,* ed. John T. Noonan, Jr. (Cambridge, Mass., 1970). Noonan's essay is in this volume, pp. 9–14.

in bed, with the violinist plugged into you, for the rest of your life. Because remember this. All persons have a right to life, and violinists are persons. Granted you have a right to decide what happens in and to your body, but a person's right to life outweighs your right to decide what happens in and to your body. So you cannot ever be unplugged from him." I imagine you would regard this as outrageous, which suggests that something really is wrong with that plausible-sounding argument I mentioned a moment ago.

In this case, of course, you were kidnapped; you didn't volunteer for the operation that plugged the violinist into your kidneys. Can those who oppose abortion on the ground I mentioned make an exception for a pregnancy due to rape? Certainly. They can say that persons have a right to life only if they didn't come into existence because of rape; or they can say that all persons have a right to life, but that some have less of a right to life than others, in particular, that those who came into existence because of rape have less. But these statements have a rather unpleasant sound. Surely the question of whether you have a right to life at all, or how much of it you have, shouldn't turn on the question of whether or not you are the product of a rape. And in fact the people who oppose abortion on the ground I mentioned do not make this distinction, and hence do not make an exception in case of rape.

Nor do they make an exception for a case in which the mother has to spend the nine months of her pregnancy in bed. They would agree that would be a great pity, and hard on the mother; but all the same, all persons have a right to life, the fetus is a person, and so on. I suspect, in fact, that they would not make an exception for a case in which, miraculously enough, the pregnancy went on for nine years, or even the rest of the mother's life.

Some won't even make an exception for a case in which continuation of the pregnancy is likely to shorten the mother's life; they regard abortion as impermissible even to save the mother's life. Such cases are nowadays very rare, and many opponents of abortion do not accept this extreme view. All the same, it is a good place to begin: a number of points of interest come out in respect to it.

1. Let us call the view that abortion is impermissible even to save the mother's life "the extreme view." I want to suggest first that it does not issue from the argument I mentioned earlier without the addition of some fairly powerful premises. Suppose a woman has become pregnant, and now learns that she has a cardiac condition such that she will die if she carries the baby to term. What may be done for her? The fetus, being a person, has a right to life, but as the mother is a person too, so has she a right to life. Presumably they have an equal right to life. How is it supposed to come out that an abortion may not be performed? If mother and child have an equal right to life, shouldn't we perhaps flip a coin? Or should we add to the mother's right to life her right to decide what happens in and to her body, which everybody seems to be ready to grant—the sum of her rights now outweighing the fetus' right to life?

The most familiar argument here is the following. We are told that performing the abortion would be directly killing[3] the child, whereas doing nothing would not be killing the mother, but only letting her die. Moreover, in killing the child, one would be killing an innocent person, for the child has committed no crime, and is not aiming at his mother's death. And then there are a variety of ways in which this might be continued. (1) But as directly killing an innocent person is always and absolutely impermissible, an abortion may not be performed. Or, (2) as directly killing an innocent person is murder, and murder is always and absolutely impermissible, an abortion may not be performed.[4] Or, (3) as one's duty to refrain from directly killing an innocent person is more stringent than one's duty to keep a person from dying, an abortion may not be performed. Or, (4) if one's only options are directly killing an innocent person or letting a person die, one must prefer letting the person die, and thus an abortion may not be performed.[5]

Some people seem to have thought that these are not further premises which must be added if the conclusion is to be reached, but that they follow from the very fact that an innocent person has a right to life.[6] But this seems to me to be a mistake, and perhaps the simplest way to show this is to bring out that while we must certainly grant that innocent persons have a right to life, the theses in (1) through (4) are all false. Take (2), for example. If directly killing an innocent person is murder, and thus is impermissible, then the mother's directly killing the innocent person inside her is murder, and thus is impermissible. But it cannot seriously be thought to be murder if the mother performs an abortion on herself

---

[3] The term "direct" in the arguments I refer to is a technical one. Roughly, what is meant by "direct killing" is either killing as an end in itself, or killing as a means of some end, for example, the end of saving someone else's life. See footnote 6 for an example of its use.

[4] Cf. *Encyclical Letter of Pope Pius XI on Christian Marriage,* St. Paul Editions (Boston, n.d.), p. 32: "however much we may pity the mother whose health and even life is gravely imperiled in the performance of the duty allotted to her by nature, nevertheless what could ever be a sufficient reason for excusing in any way the direct murder of the innocent? This is precisely what we are dealing with here." Noonan (*The Morality of Abortion,* p. 43) reads this as follows: "What cause can ever avail to excuse in any way the direct killing of the innocent? For it is a question of that."

[5] The thesis in (4) is in an interesting way weaker than those in (1), (2), and (3): they rule out abortion even in cases in which both mother *and* child will die if the abortion is not performed. By contrast, one who held the view expressed in (4) could consistently say that one needn't prefer letting two persons die to killing one.

[6] Cf. the following passage from Pius XII, *Address to the Italian Catholic Society of Midwives:* "The baby in the maternal breast has the right to life immediately from God.—Hence there is no man, no human authority, no science, no medical, eugenic, social, economic or moral 'indication' which can establish or grant a valid juridical ground for a direct deliberate disposition of an innocent human life, that is a disposition which looks to its destruction either as an end or as a means to another end perhaps in itself not illicit.—The baby, still not born, is a man in the same degree and for the same reason as the mother" (quoted in Noonan, *The Morality of Abortion,* p. 45).

to save her life. It cannot seriously be said that she *must* refrain, that she *must* sit passively by and wait for her death. Let us look again at the case of you and the violinist. There you are, in bed with the violinist, and the director of the hospital says to you, "It's all most distressing, and I deeply sympathize, but you see this is putting an additional strain on your kidneys, and you'll be dead within the month. But you *have* to stay where you are all the same. Because unplugging you would be directly killing an innocent violinist, and that's murder, and that's impermissible." If anything in the world is true, it is that you do not commit murder, you do not do what is impermissible, if you reach around to your back and unplug yourself from that violinist to save your life.

The main focus of attention in writings on abortion has been on what a third party may or may not do in answer to a request from a woman for an abortion. This is in a way understandable. Things being as they are, there isn't much a woman can safely do to abort herself. So the question asked is what a third party may do, and what the mother may do, if it is mentioned at all, is deduced, almost as an afterthought, from what it is concluded that third parties may do. But it seems to me that to treat the matter in this way is to refuse to grant to the mother that very status of person which is so firmly insisted on for the fetus. For we cannot simply read off what a person may do from what a third party may do. Suppose you find yourself trapped in a tiny house with a growing child. I mean a very tiny house, and a rapidly growing child—you are already up against the wall of the house and in a few minutes you'll be crushed to death. The child on the other hand won't be crushed to death; if nothing is done to stop him from growing he'll be hurt, but in the end he'll simply burst open the house and walk out a free man. Now I could well understand it if a bystander were to say, "There's nothing we can do for you. We cannot choose between your life and his, we cannot be the ones to decide who is to live, we cannot intervene." But it cannot be concluded that you too can do nothing, that you cannot attack it to save your life. However innocent the child may be, you do not have to wait passively while it crushes you to death. Perhaps a pregnant woman is vaguely felt to have the status of house, to which we don't allow the right of self-defense. But if the woman houses the child, it should be remembered that she is a person who houses it.

I should perhaps stop to say explicitly that I am not claiming that people have a right to do anything whatever to save their lives. I think, rather, that there are drastic limits to the right of self-defense. If someone threatens you with death unless you torture someone else to death, I think you have not the right, even to save your life, to do so. But the case under consideration here is very different. In our case there are only two people involved, one whose life is threatened, and one who threatens it. Both are innocent: the one who is threatened is not threatened because of any fault, the one who threatens does not threaten because of any fault. For this reason we may feel that we bystanders cannot intervene. But the person threatened can.

A Defense of Abortion

In sum, a woman surely can defend her life against the threat to it posed by the unborn child, even if doing so involves its death. And this shows not merely that the theses in (1) through (4) are false; it shows also that the extreme view of abortion is false, and so we need not canvass any other possible ways of arriving at it from the argument I mentioned at the outset.

2. The extreme view could of course be weakened to say that while abortion is permissible to save the mother's life, it may not be performed by a third party, but only by the mother herself. But this cannot be right either. For what we have to keep in mind is that the mother and the unborn child are not like two tenants in a small house which has, by an unfortunate mistake, been rented to both: the mother *owns* the house. The fact that she does adds to the offensiveness of deducing that the mother can do nothing from the supposition that third parties can do nothing. But it does more than this: it casts a bright light on the supposition that third parties can do nothing. Certainly it lets us see that a third party who says "I cannot choose between you" is fooling himself if he thinks this is impartiality. If Jones has found and fastened on a certain coat, which he needs to keep him from freezing, but which Smith also needs to keep him from freezing, then it is not impartiality that says "I cannot choose between you" when Smith owns the coat. Women have said again and again "This body is *my* body!" and they have reason to feel angry, reason to feel that it has been like shouting into the wind. Smith, after all, is hardly likely to bless us if we say to him, "Of course it's your coat, anybody would grant that it is. But no one may choose between you and Jones who is to have it."

We should really ask what it is that says "no one may choose" in the face of the fact that the body that houses the child is the mother's body. It may be simply a failure to appreciate this fact. But it may be something more interesting, namely the sense that one has a right to refuse to lay hands on people, even where it would be just and fair to do so, even where justice seems to require that somebody do so. Thus justice might call for somebody to get Smith's coat back from Jones, and yet you have a right to refuse to be the one to lay hands on Jones, a right to refuse to do physical violence to him. This, I think, must be granted. But then what should be said is not "no one may choose," but only "*I* cannot choose," and indeed not even this, but "*I* will not *act,*" leaving it open that somebody else can or should, and in particular that anyone in a position of authority, with the job of securing people's rights, both can and should. So this is no difficulty. I have not been arguing that any given third party must accede to the mother's request that he perform an abortion to save her life, but only that he may.

I suppose that in some views of human life the mother's body is only on loan to her, the loan not being one which gives her any prior claim to it. One who held this view might well think it impartiality to say "I cannot choose." But I shall simply ignore this possibility. My own view is that if a human being has any just, prior claim to anything at all, he has a just, prior claim to his own body. And perhaps this needn't be argued for here anyway, since, as I mentioned, the arguments against abortion we are looking at do grant that the woman has a right to decide what happens in and to her body.

But although they do grant it, I have tried to show that they do not take seriously what is done in granting it. I suggest the same thing will reappear even more clearly when we turn away from cases in which the mother's life is at stake, and attend, as I propose we now do, to the vastly more common cases in which a woman wants an abortion for some less weighty reason than preserving her own life.

3. Where the mother's life is not at stake, the argument I mentioned at the outset seems to have a much stronger pull. "Everyone has a right to life, so the unborn person has a right to life." And isn't the child's right to life weightier than anything other than the mother's own right to life, which she might put forward as ground for an abortion?

This argument treats the right to life as if it were unproblematic. It is not, and this seems to me to be precisely the source of the mistake.

For we should now, at long last, ask what it comes to, to have a right to life. In some views having a right to life includes having a right to be given at least the bare minimum one needs for continued life. But suppose that what in fact *is* the bare minimum a man needs for continued life is something he has no right at all to be given? If I am sick unto death, and the only thing that will save my life is the touch of Henry Fonda's cool hand on my fevered brow, then all the same, I have no right to be given the touch of Henry Fonda's cool hand on my fevered brow. It would be frightfully nice of him to fly in from the West Coast to provide it. It would be less nice, though no doubt well meant, if my friends flew out to the West Coast and carried Henry Fonda back with them. But I have no right at all against anybody that he should do this for me. Or again, to return to the story I told earlier, the fact that for continued life that violinist needs the continued use of your kidneys does not establish that he has a right to be given the continued use of your kidneys. He certainly has no right against you that *you* should give him continued use of your kidneys. For nobody has any right to use your kidneys unless you give him such a right; and nobody has the right against you that you shall give him this right—if you do allow him to go on using your kidneys, this is a kindness on your part, and not something he can claim from you as his due. Nor has he any right against anybody else that *they* should give him continued use of your kidneys. Certainly he had no right against the Society of Music Lovers that they should plug him into you in the first place. And if you now start to unplug yourself, having learned that you will otherwise have to spend nine years in bed with him, there is nobody in the world who must try to prevent you, in order to see to it that he is given something he has a right to be given.

Some people are rather stricter about the right to life. In their view, it does not include the right to be given anything, but amounts to, and only to, the right not to be killed by anybody. But here a related difficulty arises. If everybody is to refrain from killing that violinist, then everybody must refrain from doing a great many different sorts of things. Everybody must refrain from slitting his throat, everybody must refrain from shooting him—and everybody must refrain from unplugging you from him. But does he have a right against everybody that they shall refrain from unplugging you from him? To refrain from doing this is to allow him to continue to use your kidneys. It could be argued that he has a right against us that *we* should allow him to continue to use your kidneys. That is, while he had no right against us that we should give him the use of your kidneys, it might be argued that he anyway has a right against us that we shall not now intervene and deprive him of the use of your kidneys. I shall come back to third-party interventions later. But certainly the violinist has no right against you that *you* shall allow him to continue to use your kidneys. As I said, if you do allow him to use them, it is a kindness on your part, and not something you owe him.

The difficulty I point to here is not peculiar to the right to life. It reappears in connection with all the other natural rights; and it is something which an adequate account of rights must deal with. For present purposes it is enough just to draw attention to it. But I would stress that I am not arguing that people do not have a right to life—quite to the contrary, it seems to me that the primary control we must place on the acceptability of an account of rights is that it should turn out in that account to be a truth that all persons have a right to life. I am arguing only that having a right to life does not guarantee having either a right to be given the use of or a right to be allowed continued use of another person's body—even if one needs it for life itself. So the right to life will not serve the opponents of abortion in the very simple and clear way in which they seem to have thought it would.

4. There is another way to bring out the difficulty. In the most ordinary sort of case, to deprive someone of what he has a right to is to treat him unjustly. Suppose a boy and his small brother are jointly given a box of chocolates for Christmas. If the older boy takes the box and refuses to give his brother any of the chocolates, he is unjust to him, for the brother has been given a right to half of them. But suppose that, having learned that otherwise it means nine years in bed with that violinist, you unplug yourself from him. You surely are not being unjust to him, for you gave him no right to use your kidneys, and no one else can have given him any such right. But we have to notice that in unplugging yourself, you are killing him; and violinists, like everybody else, have a right to life, and thus in the view we were considering just now, the right not to be killed. So here you do what he supposedly has a right you shall not do, but you do not act unjustly to him in doing it.

The emendation which may be made at this point is this: the right to life consists not in the right not to be killed, but rather in the right not to be killed unjustly. This runs a risk of circularity, but never mind: it would enable us to square the fact that the violinist has a right to life with the fact that you do not act unjustly toward him in unplugging yourself, thereby killing him. For if you do not kill him unjustly, you do not violate his right to life, and so it is no wonder you do him no injustice.

But if this emendation is accepted, the gap in the argument against abortion stares us plainly in the face: it is by no means enough to show that the fetus is a person, and to remind us that all persons have a right to life—we need to be shown also that killing the fetus violates its right to life, i.e., that abortion is unjust killing. And is it?

I suppose we may take it as a datum that in a case of pregnancy due to rape the mother has not given the unborn person a right to the use of her body for food and shelter. Indeed, in what pregnancy could it be supposed that the mother has given the unborn person such a right? It is not as if there were unborn persons drifting about the world, to whom a woman who wants a child says "I invite you in."

But it might be argued that there are other ways one can have acquired a right to the use of another person's body than by having been invited to use it by that person. Suppose a woman voluntarily indulges in intercourse, knowing of the chance it will issue in pregnancy, and then she does become pregnant; is she not in part responsible for the presence, in fact the very existence, of the unborn person inside her? No doubt she did not invite it in. But doesn't her partial responsibility for its being there itself give it a right to the use of her body?[7] If so, then her aborting it would be more like the boy's taking away the chocolates, and less like your unplugging yourself from the violinist—doing so would be depriving it of what it does have a right to, and thus would be doing it an injustice.

And then, too, it might be asked whether or not she can kill it even to save her own life: If she voluntarily called it into existence, how can she now kill it, even in self-defense?

The first thing to be said about this is that it is something new. Opponents of abortion have been so concerned to make out the independence of the fetus, in order to establish that it has a right to life, just as its mother does, that they have tended to overlook the possible support they might gain from making out that the fetus is *dependent* on the mother, in order to establish that she has a special kind of responsibility for it, a responsibility that gives it rights against her which are not possessed by any independent person—such as an ailing violinist who is a stranger to her.

On the other hand, this argument would give the unborn person a right to its mother's body only if her pregnancy resulted from a voluntary act, undertaken in full knowledge of the chance a pregnancy might result from it. It would leave out entirely the unborn person whose existence is due to rape. Pending the availability of some further argument, then, we would be left with the conclusion that unborn persons whose existence is due to rape have no right to the use of their mothers' bodies, and thus that aborting them is not depriving them of anything they have a right to and hence is not unjust killing.

---

[7] The need for a discussion of this argument was brought home to me by members of the Society for Ethical and Legal Philosophy, to whom this paper was originally presented.

And we should also notice that it is not at all plain that this argument really does go even as far as it purports to. For there are cases and cases, and the details make a difference. If the room is stuffy, and I therefore open a window to air it, and a burglar climbs in, it would be absurd to say, "Ah, now he can stay, she's given him a right to the use of her house—for she is partially responsible for his presence there, having voluntarily done what enabled him to get in, in full knowledge that there are such things as burglars, and that burglars burgle." It would be still more absurd to say this if I had had bars installed outside my windows, precisely to prevent burglars from getting in, and a burglar got in only because of a defect in the bars. It remains equally absurd if we imagine it is not a burglar who climbs in, but an innocent person who blunders or falls in. Again, suppose it were like this: people-seeds drift about in the air like pollen, and if you open your windows, one may drift in and take root in your carpets or upholstery. You don't want children, so you fix up your windows with fine mesh screens, the very best you can buy. As can happen, however, and on very, very rare occasions does happen, one of the screens is defective; and a seed drifts in and takes root. Does the person-plant who now develops have a right to the use of your house? Surely not—despite the fact that you voluntarily opened your windows, you knowingly kept carpets and upholstered furniture, and you knew that screens were sometimes defective. Someone may argue that you are responsible for its rooting, that it does have a right to your house, because after all you *could* have lived out your life with bare floors and furniture, or with sealed windows and doors. But this won't do—for by the same token anyone can avoid a pregnancy due to rape by having a hysterectomy, or anyway by never leaving home without a (reliable!) army.

It seems to me that the argument we are looking at can establish at most that there are *some* cases in which the unborn person has a right to the use of its mother's body, and therefore *some* cases in which abortion is unjust killing. There is room for much discussion and argument as to precisely which, if any. But I think we should sidestep this issue and leave it open, for at any rate the argument certainly does not establish that all abortion is unjust killing.

5. There is room for yet another argument here, however. We surely must all grant that there may be cases in which it would be morally indecent to detach a person from your body at the cost of his life. Suppose you learn that what the violinist needs is not nine years of your life, but only one hour: all you need do to save his life is to spend one hour in that bed with him. Suppose also that letting him use your kidneys for that one hour would not affect your health in the slightest. Admittedly you were kidnapped. Admittedly you did not give anyone permission to plug him into you. Nevertheless it seems to me plain you *ought* to allow him to use your kidneys for that hour—it would be indecent to refuse.

Again, suppose pregnancy lasted only an hour, and constituted no threat to life or health. And suppose that a woman becomes pregnant as a result of rape. Admittedly she did not voluntarily do anything to bring about the existence of a child. Admittedly she did nothing at all which would give the unborn person a right to the use of her body. All the same it might well be said, as in the newly emended violinist story, that she *ought* to allow it to remain for that hour—that it would be indecent of her to refuse.

Now some people are inclined to use the term "right" in such a way that it follows from the fact that you ought to allow a person to use your body for the hour he needs, that he has a right to use your body for the hour he needs, even though he has not been given that right by any person or act. They may say that it follows also that if you refuse, you act unjustly toward him. This use of the term is perhaps so common that it cannot be called wrong; nevertheless it seems to me to be an unfortunate loosening of what we would do better to keep a tight rein on. Suppose that box of chocolates I mentioned earlier has not been given to both boys jointly, but was given only to the older boy. There he sits, stolidly eating his way through the box, his small brother watching enviously. Here we are likely to say "You ought not to be so mean. You ought to give your brother some of those chocolates." My own view is that it just does not follow from the truth of this that the brother has any right to any of the chocolates. If the boy refuses to give his brother any, he is greedy, stingy, callous—but not unjust. I suppose that the people I have in mind will say it does follow that the brother has a right to some of the chocolates, and thus that the boy does act unjustly if he refuses to give his brother any. But the effect of saying this is to obscure what we should keep distinct, namely the difference between the boy's refusal in this case and the boy's refusal in the earlier case, in which the box was given to both boys jointly, and in which the small brother thus had what was from any point of view clear title to half.

A further objection to so using the term "right" that from the fact that A ought to do a thing for B, it follows that B has a right against A that A do it for him, is that it is going to make the question of whether or not a man has a right to a thing turn on how easy it is to provide him with it; and this seems not merely unfortunate, but morally unacceptable. Take the case of Henry Fonda again. I said earlier that I had no right to the touch of his cool hand on my fevered brow, even though I needed it to save my life. I said it would be frightfully nice of him to fly in from the West Coast to provide me with it, but that I had no right against him that he should do so. But suppose he isn't on the West Coast. Suppose he has only to walk across the room, place a hand briefly on my brow—and lo, my life is saved. Then surely he ought to do it, it would be indecent to refuse. Is it to be said "Ah, well, it follows that in this case she has a right to the touch of his hand on her brow, and so it would be an injustice in him to refuse"? So that I have a right to it when it is easy for him to provide it, though no right when it's hard? It's rather a shocking idea that anyone's rights should fade away and disappear as it gets harder and harder to accord them to him.

So my own view is that even though you ought to let the violinist use your kidneys for the one hour he needs, we should not conclude that he has a right to do so—we should say that if you refuse, you are, like the boy who owns all the chocolates and will give none away, self-centered and callous, indecent in fact, but not unjust. And similarly, that even supposing a case in which a woman pregnant due to rape ought to allow the unborn person to use her body for the hour he needs, we should not conclude that he has a right to do so; we should conclude that she is self-centered, callous, indecent, but not unjust, if she refuses. The complaints are no less grave; they are just different. However, there is no need to insist on this point. If anyone does wish to deduce "he has a right" from "you ought," then all the same he must surely grant that there are cases in which it is not morally required of you that you allow that violinist to use your kidneys, and in which he does not have a right to use them, and in which you do not do him an injustice if you refuse. And so also for mother and unborn child. Except in such cases as the unborn person has a right to demand it—and we were leaving open the possibility that there may be such cases—nobody is morally *required* to make large sacrifices, of health, of all other interests and concerns, of all other duties and commitments, for nine years, or even for nine months, in order to keep another person alive.

6. We have in fact to distinguish between two kinds of Samaritan: the Good Samaritan and what we might call the Minimally Decent Samaritan. The story of the Good Samaritan, you will remember, goes like this:

> A certain man went down from Jerusalem to Jericho, and fell among thieves, which stripped him of his raiment, and wounded him, and departed, leaving him half dead.
> And by chance there came down a certain priest that way; and when he saw him, he passed by on the other side.
> And likewise a Levite, when he was at the place, came and looked on him, and passed by on the other side.
> But a certain Samaritan, as he journeyed, came where he was; and when he saw him he had compassion on him.
> And went to him, and bound up his wounds, pouring in oil and wine, and set him on his own beast, and brought him to an inn, and took care of him.
> And on the morrow, when he departed, he took out two pence, and gave them to the host, and said unto him, "Take care of him; and whatsoever thou spendest more, when I come again, I will repay thee."
>
> *(Luke 10:30–35)*

The Good Samaritan went out of his way, at some cost to himself, to help one in need of it. We are not told what the options were, that is, whether or not the priest and the Levite could have helped by doing less than the Good Samaritan did, but assuming they could have, then the fact they did nothing at all shows they were not even Minimally Decent Samaritans, not because they were not Samaritans, but because they were not even minimally decent.

These things are a matter of degree, of course, but there is a difference, and it comes out perhaps most clearly in the story of Kitty Genovese, who, as you will remember, was murdered while thirty-eight people watched or listened, and did nothing at all to help her. A Good Samaritan would have rushed out to give direct assistance against the murderer. Or perhaps we had better allow that it would have been a Splendid Samaritan who did this, on the ground that it would have involved a risk of death for himself. But the thirty-eight not only did not do this, they did not even trouble to pick up a phone to call the police. Minimally Decent Samaritanism would call for doing at least that, and their not having done it was monstrous.

After telling the story of the Good Samaritan, Jesus said "Go, and do thou likewise." Perhaps he meant that we are morally required to act as the Good Samaritan did. Perhaps he was urging people to do more than is morally required of them. At all events it seems plain that it was not morally required of any of the thirty-eight that he rush out to give direct assistance at the risk of his own life, and that it is not morally required of anyone that he give long stretches of his life—nine years or nine months—to sustaining the life of a person who has no special right (we were leaving open the possibility of this) to demand it.

Indeed, with one rather striking class of exceptions, no one in any country in the world is *legally* required to do anywhere near as much as this for anyone else. The class of exceptions is obvious. My main concern here is not the state of the law in respect to abortion, but it is worth drawing attention to the fact that in no state in this country is any man compelled by law to be even a Minimally Decent Samaritan to any person; there is no law under which charges could be brought against the thirty-eight who stood by while Kitty Genovese died. By contrast, in most states in this country women are compelled by law to be not merely Minimally Decent Samaritans, but Good Samaritans to unborn persons inside them. This doesn't by itself settle anything one way or the other, because it may well be argued that there should be laws in this country—as there are in many European countries—compelling at least Minimally Decent Samaritanism.[8] But it does show that there is a gross injustice in the existing state of the law. And it shows also that the groups currently working against liberalization of abortion laws, in fact working toward having it declared unconstitutional for a state to permit abortion, had better start working for the adoption of Good Samaritan laws generally, or earn the charge that they are acting in bad faith.

I should think, myself, that Minimally Decent Samaritan laws would be one thing, Good Samaritan laws quite another, and in fact highly improper. But we are not here concerned with the law. What we should ask is not whether anybody should be compelled by law to be a Good Samaritan, but whether we must accede to a situation in which somebody is being compelled—by nature, perhaps—to be a Good Samaritan. We have, in other words, to look now at third-party interventions. I have been arguing that no person is morally required to make large sacrifices to sustain the life of another who has no right to demand them, and this even where the sacrifices do not include life itself; we are not morally required to be Good Samaritans or anyway Very Good Samaritans to one another. But what if a man cannot extricate himself from such a situation? What if he

---

[8] For a discussion of the difficulties involved, and a survey of the European experience with such laws, see *The Good Samaritan and the Law,* ed. James M. Ratcliffe (New York, 1966).

A Defense of Abortion

appeals to us to extricate him? It seems to me plain that there are cases in which we can, cases in which a Good Samaritan would extricate him. There you are, you were kidnapped, and nine years in bed with that violinist lie ahead of you. You have your own life to lead. You are sorry, but you simply cannot see giving up so much of your life to the sustaining of his. You cannot extricate yourself, and ask us to do so. I should have thought that—in light of his having no right to the use of your body—it was obvious that we do not have to accede to your being forced to give up so much. We can do what you ask. There is no injustice to the violinist in our doing so.

7. Following the lead of the opponents of abortion, I have throughout been speaking of the fetus merely as a person, and what I have been asking is whether or not the argument we began with, which proceeds only from the fetus' being a person, really does establish its conclusion. I have argued that it does not.

But of course there are arguments and arguments, and it may be said that I have simply fastened on the wrong one. It may be said that what is important is not merely the fact that the fetus is a person, but that it is a person for whom the woman has a special kind of responsibility issuing from the fact that she is its mother. And it might be argued that all my analogies are therefore irrelevant— for you do not have that special kind of responsibility for that violinist, Henry Fonda does not have that special kind of responsibility for me. And our attention might be drawn to the fact that men and women both *are* compelled by law to provide support for their children.

I have in effect dealt (briefly) with this argument in section 4 above; but a (still briefer) recapitulation now may be in order. Surely we do not have any such "special responsibility" for a person unless we have assumed it, explicitly or implicitly. If a set of parents do not try to prevent pregnancy, do not obtain an abortion, and then at the time of birth of the child do not put it out for adoption, but rather take it home with them, then they have assumed responsibility for it, they have given it rights, and they cannot *now* withdraw support from it at the cost of its life because they now find it difficult to go on providing for it. But if they have taken all reasonable precautions against having a child, they do not simply by virtue of their biological relationship to the child who comes into existence have a special responsibility for it. They may wish to assume responsibility for it, or they may not wish to. And I am suggesting that if assuming responsibility for it would require large sacrifices, then they may refuse. A Good Samaritan would not refuse—or anyway, a Splendid Samaritan, if the sacrifices that had to be made were enormous. But then so would a Good Samaritan assume responsibility for that violinist; so would Henry Fonda, if he is a Good Samaritan, fly in from the West Coast and assume responsibility for me.

8. My argument will be found unsatisfactory on two counts by many of those who want to regard abortion as morally permissible. First, while I do argue that abortion is not impermissible, I do not argue that it is always permissible. There may well be cases in which carrying the child to term requires only Minimally Decent Samaritanism of the mother, and this is a standard we must not fall below.

I am inclined to think it a merit of my account precisely that it does *not* give a general yes or a general no. It allows for and supports our sense that, for example, a sick and desperately frightened fourteen-year-old schoolgirl, pregnant due to rape, may *of course* choose abortion, and that any law which rules this out is an insane law. And it also allows for and supports our sense that in other cases resort to abortion is even positively indecent. It would be indecent in the woman to request an abortion, and indecent in a doctor to perform it, if she is in her seventh month, and wants the abortion just to avoid the nuisance of postponing a trip abroad. The very fact that the arguments I have been drawing attention to treat all cases of abortion, or even all cases of abortion in which the mother's life is not at stake, as morally on a par ought to have made them suspect at the outset.

Secondly, while I am arguing for the permissibility of abortion in some cases, I am not arguing for the right to secure the death of the unborn child. It is easy to confuse these two things in that up to a certain point in the life of the fetus it is not able to survive outside the mother's body; hence removing it from her body guarantees its death. But they are importantly different. I have argued that you are not morally required to spend nine months in bed, sustaining the life of that violinist; but to say this is by no means to say that if, when you unplug yourself, there is a miracle and he survives, you then have a right to turn round and slit his throat. You may detach yourself even if this costs him his life; you have no right to be guaranteed his death, by some other means, if unplugging yourself does not kill him. There are some people who will feel dissatisfied by this feature of my argument. A woman may be utterly devastated by the thought of a child, a bit of herself, put out for adoption and never seen or heard of again. She may therefore want not merely that the child be detached from her, but more, that it die. Some opponents of abortion are inclined to regard this as beneath contempt—thereby showing insensitivity to what is surely a powerful source of despair. All the same, I agree that the desire for the child's death is not one which anybody may gratify, should it turn out to be possible to detach the child alive.

At this place, however, it should be remembered that we have only been pretending throughout that the fetus is a human being from the moment of conception. A very early abortion is surely not the killing of a person, and so is not dealt with by anything I have said here.

A Defense of Abortion

Ethical Problems of Abortion

Sissela Bok

. . . In discussing the ethical dilemmas of abortion, I shall begin with the basic conflict—that between a pregnant woman and the unborn life she harbors.

I. Mother and Fetus

Up to very recently, parents had only limited access to birth prevention. Contraception was outlawed or treated with silence. Sterilization was most often unavailable and abortion was left to those desperate enough to seek criminal abortions. Women may well be forgiven now, therefore, if they mistrust the barrage of arguments concerning abortion, and may well suspect that these are rearguard actions in an effort to tie them still longer to the bearing of unwanted children.

Some advocates for abortion hold that women should have the right to do what they want with their own bodies, and that removing the fetus is comparable to cutting one's hair or removing a disfiguring growth. This view simply ignores the fact that abortion involves more than just one life. The same criticism holds for the vaguer notions which defend abortion on the grounds that a woman should have the right to control her fate, or the right to have an abortion as she has the right to marry. But no one has the clear-cut right to control her fate where others share it, and marriage requires consent by two persons, whereas the consent of the fetus is precisely what cannot be obtained. How, then, can we weigh the rights and the interests of mother and fetus, where they conflict?

The central question is whether the life of the fetus should receive the same protection as other lives—often discussed in terms of whether killing the fetus is to be thought of as killing a human being. But before asking that question, I would

Excerpted from *The Hastings Center Studies*, vol. 2, no. 1 (January 1974) by permission of the author and the Hastings Center.

like to ask whether abortion can always be thought of as *killing* in the first place. For abortion can be looked upon, also, as the withdrawal of bodily life support on the part of the mother.

A. Cessation of Bodily Life Support

Would anyone, before or after birth, child or adult, have the right to continue to be dependent upon the bodily processes of another against that person's will? It can happen that a person will require a sacrifice on the part of another in order not to die; does he therefore have the *right* to this sacrifice?

Judith Thomson has argued most cogently that the mother who finds herself pregnant, as a result of rape or in spite of every precaution, does not have the obligation to continue the pregnancy:

> I am arguing only that having a right to life does not guarantee having either a right to be given the use of or a right to be allowed the continued use of another person's body—even if one needs it for life itself. [1]

Abortion, according to such a view, can be thought of as the cessation of continued support. It is true that the embryo cannot survive alone, and that it dies. But this is not unjust killing, any more than when Siamese twins are separated surgically and one of them dies as a result. Judith Thomson argues that at least in those cases where the mother is involuntarily pregnant, she can cease her support of the life of the fetus without infringing its right to live. Here, viability—the capability of living independently from the body of the mother—becomes important. Before that point, the unborn life will end when the mother ceases her support. No one else can take over the protection of the unborn life. After the point where viability begins, much depends on what is done by others, and on how much assistance is provided.

It may be, however, that in considering the ethical implications of the right to cease bodily support of the fetus we must distinguish between causing death indirectly through ceasing such support and actively killing the fetus outright. The techniques used in abortion differ significantly in this respect. [2] A method which prevents implantation of the fertilized egg or which brings about menstruation is much more clearly cessation of life support than one which sucks or scrapes out the embryo. Least like cessation of support is abortion by saline solution, which

---

[1] Judith Thomson, "A Defense of Abortion," *Philosophy and Public Policy* 1 (1971), [*supra*, pp. 173–187].

[2] See Selig Neubardt and Harold Schulman, *Techniques of Abortion* (Boston: Little, Brown and Company, 1972).

kills and begins to decompose the fetus, thus setting in motion its expulsion by the mother's body. This method is the one most commonly used in the second trimester of pregnancy. The alternative method possible at that time is a hysterotomy, or "small Cesarean," where the fetus is removed intact, and where death very clearly does result from the interruption of bodily support.

If we learn how to provide life support for the fetus outside the natural mother's body, it may happen that parents who wish to adopt a baby may come into a new kind of conflict with those who wish to have an abortion. They may argue that *all* that the aborting mother has a right to is to cease supporting a fetus with her own body. They may insist, if the pregnancy is already in the second trimester, that she has no right to choose a technique which also kills the baby. It would be wrong for the natural parents to insist at that point that the severance must be performed in such a way that others cannot take over the care and support for the fetus. But a conflict could arise if the mother were asked to postpone the abortion in order to improve the chances of survival and well-being of the fetus to be adopted by others.

Are there times where, quite apart from the technique used to abort, a woman has a *special* responsibility to continue bodily support of a fetus? Surely the many pregnancies which are entered upon voluntarily are of such a nature. One might even say that, if anyone ever did have special obligations to continue life support of another, it would be the woman who had *voluntarily undertaken* to become pregnant. For she has then brought about the situation where the fetus has come to require her support, and there is no one else who can take over her responsibility until after the baby is viable.

To use the analogy of a drowning person, one can think of three scenarios influencing the responsibility of a bystander to leap to the rescue. First, someone may be drowning and the bystander arrives at the scene, hesitating between rescue and permitting the person to drown. Secondly, someone may be drowning as a result of the honestly mistaken assurance by the bystander that swimming would be safe. Thirdly, the bystander may have pushed the drowning person out of a boat. In each case the duties of the bystander are different, but surely they are at their most stringent when he has intentionally caused the drowning person to find himself in the water.

These three scenarios bear some resemblance, from the point of view of the mother's responsibility to the fetus, to: first, finding out that she is pregnant against her wishes; second, mistakenly trusting that she was protected against pregnancy; and third, intentionally becoming pregnant.

Every pregnancy which has been intentionally begun creates special responsibilities for the mother.[3] But there is one situation in which these dilemmas are presented in a particularly difficult form. It is where two parents deliberately enter

---

[3] But lines are hard to draw here. There are many intermediate cases between the pregnancy intentionally begun and, for instance, that resulting from carelessness with contraceptives.

upon a pregnancy, only to find that the baby they are expecting has a genetic disease or has suffered from damage in fetal life, so that it will be permanently malformed or retarded. Here, the parents have consciously brought about the life which now requires support from the body of the mother. Can they now turn about and say that this particular fetus is such that they do not wish to continue their support? This is especially difficult when the fetus is already developed up to the 18th or 20th week. Can they acknowledge that they meant to begin a human life, but not *this* human life? Or, to take a more callous example, suppose, as sometimes happens, that the parents learn that the baby is of a sex they do not wish?[4]

In such cases the justification which derives from wishing to cease life support for a life which had not been intended is absent, since this life *had* been intended. At the same time, an assumption of responsibility which comes with consciously beginning a pregnancy is much weaker than the corresponding assumption between two adults, or the social assumption of responsibility for a child upon birth.

To sum up at this point, ceasing bodily life support *of a fetus or of anyone else* cannot be looked at as a breach of duty except where such a duty has been assumed in the first place. Such a duty is closer to existing when the pregnancy has been voluntarily begun. And it does not exist at all in cases of rape. Certain *methods* of abortion, furthermore, are more difficult to think of as cessation of support than others. Finally, pregnancy is perhaps unique in that cessation of support means death for the fetus up to a certain point of its development, so that nearness *to* this point in pregnancy argues against abortion. . . .

---

[4] See Morton A. Stenchever, "An Abuse of Prenatal Diagnosis," *Journal of the American Medical Association* 221 (July 24, 1972), 408.

The 1973 Supreme Court Decisions on State Abortion Laws: Excerpts from Opinion in Roe v. Wade

In decisions handed down on January 22, 1973, the U.S. Supreme Court declared unconstitutional the Texas and Georgia abortion laws. The Texas case, *Roe* v. *Wade,* concerned a statute which restricted legal abortions to those deemed necessary to save the woman's life. The Georgia case, *Doe* v. *Bolton,* dealt with a state law permitting abortions only when required by the woman's health, or to prevent birth of a deformed child, or when pregnancy resulted from rape. The court's invalidation of these laws implied that similarly restrictive laws in most other states are also unconstitutional. The following abridgment of the opinions in the Texas case is taken from the Newsletter of the Association for the Study of Abortion.

Following are excerpts from the majority opinion in the Texas case, written by Justice Harry A. Blackmun (concurred in by six other justices), and from the dissent written by Justice Byron R. White (concurred in by Justice William H. Rehnquist):

Majority Opinion

. . . A recent review of the common law precedents argues . . . that even post-quickening abortion was never established as a common law crime. This is of some importance because while most American courts ruled, in holding or dictum, that abortion of an unquickened fetus was not criminal under their received common law, others followed Coke in stating that abortion of a quick fetus was a "misprison," a term they translated to mean "misdemeanor." That their reliance on Coke on this aspect of the law was uncritical and, apparently in all the reported cases, dictum (due probably to the paucity of common law prosecutions for post-quickening abortion), makes it now appear doubtful that abortion was ever firmly established as a common law crime even with respect to the destruction of a quick fetus. . . .

It is thus apparent that at common law, at the time of the adoption of our Constitution, and throughout the major portion of the 19th century, abortion was viewed with less disfavor than under most American statutes currently in effect. Phrasing it another way, a woman enjoyed a substantially broader right to terminate a pregnancy than she does in most States today. At least with respect to the early stage of pregnancy, and very possibly without such a limitation, the opportunity to make this choice was present in this country well into the 19th century. Even later, the law continued for some time to treat less punitively an abortion procured in early pregnancy . . . .

Three reasons have been advanced to explain historically the enactment of criminal abortion laws in the 19th century and to justify their continued existence.

It has been argued occasionally that these laws were the product of a Victorian social concern to discourage illicit sexual conduct. Texas, however, does not advance this justification in the present case, and it appears that no court or commentator has taken the argument seriously. . . .

A second reason is concerned with abortion as a medical procedure. When most criminal abortion laws were first enacted, the procedure was a hazardous one for the woman. This was particularly true prior to the development of antisepsis. Antiseptic techniques, of course, were based on discoveries by Lister, Pasteur, and others first announced in 1867, but were not generally accepted and employed until about the turn of the century. Abortion mortality was high. Even after 1900, and perhaps until as late as the development of antibiotics in the 1940's, standard modern techniques such as dilation and curettage were not nearly so safe as they are today. Thus it has been argued that a State's real concern in enacting a criminal abortion law was to protect the pregnant woman, that is, to restrain her from submitting to a procedure that placed her life in serious jeopardy.

Modern medical techniques have altered this situation. Appellants and various *amici* refer to medical data indicating that abortion in early pregnancy, that is, prior to the end of first trimester, although not without its risk, is now relatively safe. Mortality rates for women undergoing early abortions, where the procedure is legal, appear to be as low as or lower than the rates for normal childbirth. Consequently, any interest of the State in protecting the woman from an inherently hazardous procedure, except when it would be equally dangerous for her to forgo it, has largely disappeared. Of course, important state interests in the area of health and medical standards do remain. The State has a legitimate interest in seeing to it that abortion, like any other medical procedure, is performed under circumstances that insure maximum safety for the patient. This interest obviously extends at least to the performing physician and his staff, to the facilities involved, to the availability of after-care, and to adequate provision for any complication or emergency that might arise. The prevalence of high mortality rates at illegal "abortion mills" strengthens, rather than weakens, the State's interest in regulating the conditions under which abortions are performed. Moreover, the risk to the woman increases as her pregnancy continues. Thus the State retains a definite interest in protecting the woman's own health and safety when an abortion is performed at a late stage of pregnancy.

The third reason is the State's interest—some phrase it in terms of duty—in protecting prenatal life. Some of the argument for this justification rests on the theory that a new human life is present from the moment of conception. . . .

Parties challenging state abortion laws have sharply disputed in some courts the contention that a purpose of these laws, when enacted, was to protect prenatal life. Pointing to the absence of legislative history to support the contention, they claim that most state laws were designed solely to protect the woman. Because medical advances have lessened this concern, at least with respect to abortion in early pregnancy, they argue that with respect to such abortions the laws can no longer be justified by any state interest. There is some scholarly support for this view of original purpose. The few state courts called upon to interpret their laws in the late 19th and early 20th centuries did focus on the State's interest in protecting the woman's health rather than in preserving embryo and fetus. . . .

The Constitution does not explicitly mention any right of privacy. In a line of decisions, however, going back perhaps as far as *Union Pacific R. Co.* v. *Botsford,* 141 U.S. 250, 251 (1891), the Court has recognized that a right of personal privacy, or a guarantee of certain areas or zones of privacy, does exist under the Constitution. In varying contexts the Court or individual Justices have indeed found at least the roots of that right in the First Amendment, . . . in the Fourth and Fifth Amendments . . . in the penumbras of the Bill of Rights . . . in the Ninth Amendment . . . or in the concept of liberty guaranteed by the first section of the Fourteenth Amendment. . . . These decisions make it clear that only personal rights that can be deemed "fundamental" or "implicit in the concept of ordered liberty," . . . are included in this guarantee of personal privacy. They also make it clear that the right has some extension to activities relating to marriage, . . . procreation, . . . contraception, . . . family relationships, . . . and child rearing and education. . . .

This right of privacy, whether it be founded in the Fourteenth Amendment's concept of personal liberty and restrictions upon state action, as we feel it is, or, as the District Court determined, in the Ninth Amendment's reservation of rights to the people, is broad enough to encompass a woman's decision whether or not to terminate her pregnancy. . . .

. . . Appellants and some *amici* argue that the woman's right is absolute and that she is entitled to terminate her pregnancy at whatever time, in whatever way, and for whatever reason she alone chooses. With this we do not agree. Appellants' arguments that Texas either has no valid interest at all in regulating the abortion decision, or no interest strong enough to support any limitation upon the woman's sole determination, is unpersuasive. The Court's decisions recognizing a right of privacy also acknowledge that some state regulation in areas protected by that right is appropriate. As noted above, a state may properly assert important interests in safe-guarding health, in maintaining medical standards, and in protecting potential life. At some point in pregnancy, these respective interests become sufficiently compelling to sustain regulation of the factors that govern the abortion decision. The privacy right involved, therefore, cannot be said to be absolute. . . .

We therefore conclude that the right of personal privacy includes the abortion decision, but that this right is not unqualified and must be considered against important state interests in regulation.

We note that those federal and state courts that have recently considered abortion law challenges have reached the same conclusion. . . .

Although the results are divided, most of these courts have agreed that the right of privacy, however based, is broad enough to cover the abortion decision; that the right, nonetheless, is not absolute and is subject to some limitations; and that at some point the state interests as to protection of health, medical standards, and prenatal life, become dominant. We agree with this approach.

The appellee and certain *amici* argue that the fetus is a "person" within the language and meaning of the Fourteenth Amendment. In support of this they outline at length and in detail the well-known facts of fetal development. If this suggestion of personhood is established, the appellant's case, of course, collapses, for the fetus' right to life is then guaranteed specifically by the Amendment. The appellant conceded as much on reargument. On the other hand, the appellee conceded on reargument that no case could be cited that holds that a fetus is a person within the meaning of the Fourteenth Amendment.

All this, together with our observation, *supra,* that throughout the major portion of the 19th century prevailing legal abortion practices were far freer than they are today, persuades us that the word "person," as used in the Fourteenth Amendment, does not include the unborn. . . . Indeed, our decision in *United States* v. *Vuitch,* 402 U.S. 62 (1971), inferentially is to the same effect, for we there would not have indulged in statutory interpretation favorable to abortion in specified circumstances if the necessary consequence was the termination of life entitled to Fourteenth Amendment protection.

. . . As we have intimated above, it is reasonable and appropriate for a State to decide that at some point in time another interest, that of health of the mother or that of potential human life, becomes significantly involved. The woman's privacy is no longer sole and any right of privacy she possesses must be measured accordingly.

. . . We need not resolve the difficult question of when life begins. When those trained in the respective disciplines of medicine, philosophy, and theology are unable to arrive at any consensus, the judiciary, at this point in the development of man's knowledge, is not in a position to speculate as to the answer.

It should be sufficient to note briefly the wide divergence of thinking on this most sensitive and difficult question. There has always been strong support for the view that life does not begin until live birth. This was the belief of the Stoics. It appears to be the predominant, though not the unanimous, attitude of the Jewish faith. It may be taken to represent also the position of a large segment of the Protestant community, insofar as that can be ascertained; organized groups that have taken a formal position on the abortion issue have generally regarded abortion as a matter for the conscience of the individual and her family. As we have noted, the common law found greater significance in quickening. Physicians and their scientific colleagues have regarded that event with less interest and have tended to focus either upon conception or upon live birth or upon the interim point at which the fetus becomes "viable," that is, potentially able to live outside the mother's womb, albeit with artificial aid. Viability is usually placed at about seven months (28 weeks) but may occur earlier, even at 24 weeks. . . .

In areas other than criminal abortion the law has been reluctant to endorse any theory that life, as we recognize it, begins before live birth or to accord legal rights to the unborn except in narrowly defined situations and except when the rights are contingent upon live birth. . . . In short, the unborn have never been recognized in the law as persons in the whole sense.

In view of all this, we do not agree that, by adopting one theory of life, Texas may override the rights of the pregnant woman that are at stake. We repeat, however, that the State does have an important and legitimate interest in preserving and protecting the health of the pregnant woman, whether she be a resident of the State or a nonresident who seeks medical consultation and treatment there, and that it has still *another* important and legitimate interest in protecting the potentiality of human life. These interests are separate and distinct. Each grows in substantiality as the woman approaches term and, at a point during pregnancy, each becomes "compelling."

With respect to the State's important and legitimate interest in the health of the mother, the "compelling" point, in the light of present medical knowledge, is at approximately the end of the first trimester. This is so because of the now established medical fact . . . that until the end of the first trimester mortality in abortion is less than mortality in normal childbirth. It follows that, from and after this point, a State may regulate the abortion procedure to the extent that the regulation reasonably relates to the preservation and protection of maternal health. Examples of permissible state regulation in this area are requirements as to the qualifications of the person who is to perform the abortion; as to the licensure of that person; as to the facility in which the procedure is to be performed, that is, whether it must be a hospital or may be a clinic or some other place of less-than-hospital status; as to the licensing of the facility; and the like.

This means, on the other hand, that, for the period of pregnancy prior to this "compelling" point, the attending physician, in consultation with his patient, is free to determine, without regulation by the State, that in his medical judgment the patient's pregnancy should be terminated. If that decision is reached, the judgment may be effectuated by an abortion free of interference by the State.

With respect to the State's important and legitimate interest in potential life, the "compelling" point is at viability. . . . State regulation protective of fetal life after viability thus has both logical and biological justifications. If the State is interested in protecting fetal life after viability, it may go so far as to proscribe abortion during that period except when it is necessary to preserve the life or health of the mother. . . .

To summarize and repeat:

1. A state criminal abortion statute of the current Texas type, that excepts from criminality only a *life saving* procedure on behalf of the mother, without regard to pregnancy stage and without recognition of the other interests involved, is violative of the Due Process Clause of the Fourteenth Amendment.

(a) For the stage prior to approximately the end of the first trimester, the abortion decision and its effectuation must be left to the medical judgment of the pregnant woman's attending physician.

(b) For the stage subsequent to approximately the end of the first trimester, the State, in promoting its interest in the health of the mother, may, if it chooses, regulate the abortion procedure in ways that are reasonably related to maternal health.

(c) For the stage subsequent to viability the State, in promoting its interest in the potentiality of human life, may, if it chooses, regulate, and even proscribe, abortion except where it is necessary, in appropriate medical judgment, for the preservation of the life or health of the mother.

2. The State may define the term "physician," as it has been employed in the preceding numbered paragraphs of this Part XI of this opinion, to mean only a physician currently licensed by the State, and may proscribe any abortion by a person who is not a physician as so defined.

. . . The decision leaves the State free to place increasing restrictions on abortion as the period of pregnancy lengthens, so long as those restrictions are tailored to the recognized state interests. The decision vindicates the right of the physician to administer medical treatment according to his professional judgment up to the points where important state interests provide compelling justifications for intervention. Up to those points the abortion decision in all its aspects is inherently, and primarily, a medical decision, and basic responsibility for it must rest with the physician. If an individual practitioner abuses the privilege of exercising proper medical judgment, the usual remedies, judicial and intraprofessional, are available. . . .

Dissent

At the heart of the controversy in these cases are those recurring pregnancies that pose no danger whatsoever to the life or health of the mother but are nevertheless unwanted for any one or more of a variety of reasons—convenience, family planning, economics, dislike of children, the embarrassment of illegitimacy, etc. The common claim before us is that for any one of such reasons, or for no reason at all, and without asserting or claiming any threat to life or health, any woman is entitled to an abortion at her request if she is able to find a medical advisor willing to undertake the procedure.

The Court for the most part sustains this position: During the period prior to the time the fetus becomes viable, the Constitution of the United States values the convenience, whim or caprice of the putative mother more than the life or potential life of the fetus; the Constitution, therefore, guarantees the right to an abortion as against any state law or policy seeking to protect the fetus from an abortion not prompted by more compelling reasons of the mother.

With all due respect, I dissent. I find nothing in the language or history of the Constitution to support the Court's judgment. . . . As an exercise of raw judicial power, the Court perhaps has authority to do what it does today; but in my view its judgment is an improvident and extravagant exercise of the power of judicial review which the Constitution extends to this Court.

The Court apparently values the convenience of the pregnant mother more than the continued existence and development of the life or potential life which she carries. . . .

It is my view, therefore, that the Texas statute is not constitutionally infirm because it denies abortions to those who seek to serve only their convenience rather than to protect their life or health. . . .

Bibliography

Books

Brody, Baruch, *Abortion and the Sanctity of Human Life: A Philosophical View.* Cambridge, Mass · The M.I.T. Press, 1975.

Callahan, Daniel, *Abortion: Law, Choice and Morality.* London: Collier-Macmillan, Ltd., 1970.

Devine, Philip E., *The Ethics of Homicide.* Ithaca and London: Cornell University Press, 1978. Chapters II–IV.

Glover, Jonathan, *Causing Death and Saving Lives.* Harmondsworth, Middlesex: Penguin Books, 1977. Chapters 9–12.

Granfield, David, *The Abortion Decision.* Garden City, N.Y.: Doubleday Image Books, 1971.

Grisez, Germaine G., *Abortion: The Myths, the Realities, and the Arguments.* New York: Corpus Books, 1970.

Kluge, Eike-Henner W., *The Practice of Death.* New Haven and London: Yale University Press, 1975. Chapters 1, 4.

Kohl, Marvin, *The Morality of Killing.* Atlantic Highlands, N.J.: Humanities Press, 1974. Chapters 3–5.

Lader, Lawrence, *Abortion.* Indianapolis, Ind.: Bobbs-Merrill, 1966.

Noonan, John T., Jr., *How to Argue About Abortion.* New York, 1974.

———, *A Private Choice: Abortion in America in the Seventies.* New York: The Free Press, 1979.

Ramsey, Paul, *The Ethics of Fetal Research.* New Haven: Yale University Press, 1975.

Singer, Peter, *Practical Ethics.* Cambridge and New York: Cambridge University Press, 1979. Chapters 5, 6.

Sumner, L. W., *Abortion and Moral Theory.* Princeton: Princeton University Press, 1981.

Tooley, Michael, *Abortion and Infanticide.* Oxford University Press, 1983, forthcoming.

Anthologies of Articles

Cohen, Marshall; Nagel, Thomas; and Scanlon, Thomas, eds., *Rights and Wrongs of Abortion.* Princeton: Princeton University Press, 1974.

Guttmacher, Alan F., ed., *The Case for Legalized Abortion.* Berkeley, Calif.: Diablo Press, 1967.

Hall, Robert E., ed., *Abortion in a Changing World.* New York and London: Columbia University Press, 1970. Two volumes.

Noonan, John T., Jr., ed., *The Morality of Abortion: Legal and Historical Perspectives.* Cambridge, Mass.: Harvard University Press, 1970.

Perkins, Robert, ed., *Abortion.* Cambridge, Mass.: Schenkman Publishing Co., 1974.

Smith, D. T., ed., *Abortion and the Law.* Cleveland: The Press of Case Western Reserve University, 1967.

Other Articles

Becker, Lawrence C., "Human Being: The Boundaries of the Concept," in *Philosophy & Public Affairs,* Vol. 4, 1975.

Brandt, Richard B., "The Morality of Abortion," in *The Monist,* Vol. 36, 1972.

Brody, Baruch A., "Abortion and the Law," in *Journal of Philosophy,* Vol. 68, 1971.

———, "Abortion and the Sanctity of Human Life," in *American Philosophical Quarterly,* Vol. 10, 1973.

Englehardt, H. Tristram, Jr., "The Ontology of Abortion," in *Ethics,* Vol. 8, 1974.

———, "Bioethics and the Process of Embodiment," in *Perspectives in Biology and Medicine,* Vol. 18, 1975.

Feinberg, Joel, "Abortion," in *Matters of Life and Death,* ed. by Tom Regan. New York: Random House, 1978.

Finnis, John, "The Rights and Wrongs of Abortion: A Reply to Judith Thomson," in *Philosophy & Public Affairs,* Vol. 2, 1973.

Foot, Phillippa, "The Problem of Abortion and the Doctrine of Double Effect," in *The Oxford Review,* Vol. 5, 1967.

Hare, Richard M. "Abortion and the Golden Rule," in *Philosophy & Public Affairs,* Vol. 4, 1975.

Herbenick, Raymond M., "Remarks on Abortion, Abandonment, and Adoption Opportunities," in *Philosophy & Public Affairs,* Vol. 5, 1975.

Ramsey, Paul, "The Morality of Abortion," in *Life or Death: Ethics and Options,* ed. by Daniel H. Labby. Seattle: University of Washington Press, 1968.

———, "Abortion: A Review Article," in *The Thomist,* Vol. 37, 1973.

———, "Protecting the Unborn," in *Commonweal,* Vol. C, No. 13, 1974.

Sher, George, "Hare, Abortion, and the Golden Rule," in *Philosophy & Public Affairs,* Vol. 6, 1977.

———, "Subsidized Abortion: Moral Rights and Moral Compromise," in *Philosophy & Public Affairs,* Vol. 10, 1981.

Thomson, Judith J., "Rights and Deaths," in *Philosophy & Public Affairs,* Vol. 2, 1972.